In Advance of Fate:

Portrait of an Abolitionist

In Advance of Fate:

Portrait of an Abolitionist

CHARLES E. HELLER

In Advance of Fate:
Portrait of an Abolitionist

Copyright © 2014
by Charles E. Heller

cover design by
Josh Levitas

Published by

~Star Cloud Press~
6137 East Mescal Street
Scottsdale, Arizona 85254-5418

ISBN:

978-1-932842-69-2 — $ 19.95

StarCloudPress.com

Reprinted by permission of the Greenwood Press
of Westport, Connecticut.
Originally published under the title
Portrait of An Abolitionist: A Biography of
George Luther Stearns, 1809-1867

Printed in the United States of America

For her love and support
I dedicate this book to my wife, Michelle.

Contents

Preface

History is what is remembered and recorded. More times than modern scholars would like to admit, facts, ideas, and people from the past have been lost from view. Sometimes the disappearance is of no consequence; at other times the gap is significant and hinders a meaningful appreciation of the past until the missing information is discovered. Such was the case of the contribution African-Americans made to achieve a Union victory ending the American Civil War. Today, most Americans are aware of the fact, long hidden, that black soldiers were instrumental in winning the war. The success of the Hollywood production *Glory* gave public recognition to this fact by honoring the first northern African-American regiment, the Fifty-fourth Massachusetts Infantry. Yet this story was not complete. The movie failed to recognize the one individual who more than any other figure was responsible for the Fifty-fourth's recruitment. He was Medford, Massachusetts, businessman George Luther Stearns.

George L. Stearns stands out among the spectrum of abolitionists, enough so that one could say he is in a category by himself. A very wealthy and successful merchant, he had earned a fortune that had given him all that a humble beginning seemed to preclude. Yet he sought more from life than material rewards. In any event Stearns, the shy, conservative, hardworking merchant, made a clear decision to challenge the establishment, and defy the laws of the land to end the institution of slavery. In joining the Liberty party, and then harboring a fugitive slave, he moved toward greater and greater risks. Eventually he became director of the Massachusetts Kansas Aid Society. Through this organization, in 1857, Stearns met John Brown. As their relationship matured each man came to use the other for his own ends. Stearns became the single most important financial backer of Brown as one of the "Secret Six." He personally owned the two hundred Sharps rifles this violent revolutionary brought to Harpers Ferry.

Brown's passing did not deter Stearns, and once the Civil War began he used money openly to work for emancipation first and then civil rights. It was Massachusetts Governor John Andrew who turned to Stearns, the one man he trusted with the task, to recruit the Fifty-fourth Massachusetts Infantry. Accomplishing this and also raising a sister regiment, the Fiftyfifth, Stearns was recognized for his work by Secretary of War Edwin M. Stanton and given a commission as major, Assistant Adjutant General for the Recruitment of Colored Troops. Not only did this man recruit over thirteen thousand other African-Americans, he established schools for family members and found work for the soldiers' wives.

While accomplishing all this he also widened his already long list of famous and influential acquaintances. Personal friends included the Emersons and the Alcotts. He knew a vast array of abolitionists from William Lloyd Garrison to Wendell Phillips and Lydia Maria Child, who was his wife's aunt. Politicians such as John Andrew, Charles Sumner, and Andrew Johnson were acquaintances of this shy businessman. African-Americans such as Frederick Douglass were part of his circle of acquaintances.

When emancipation was certain he turned his organizational talents to civil rights including suffrage, leading the way by creating organizations which would lobby for the Thirteenth, Fourteenth, and Fifteenth Amendments to the Constitution. On the way to his objectives he bought one newspaper, the Boston *Commonwealth*, and founded another, *The Right Way*, and was the prime mover in establishing a literary magazine, *The Nation*. His efforts on behalf of African-Americans were endless and included a company that purchased cotton plantations which he hoped would show Southerners how much more profitable free labor was than slavery. His untimely death in 1867 was probably hastened by his exertions for the cause of freedom.

Despite all Stearns's contributions on behalf of African-Americans and winning the war for the Union he is relatively unknown. Historians, like those in any other profession, are limited in their intellectual inquiry by the availability of material. There is no vast single collection of Stearns letters. The largest available group is at the Kansas State Historical Society. His letters are found in other collections of some of best known figures of the Civil War era. These include the papers of Andrew Johnson, Charles Sumner, Frederick Douglass, John Brown, and a host of other widely known men and women. These collections are the holdings of institutions throughout the country from local libraries in Boston, New York, and Concord to those at such universities as Massachusetts/Amherst, Harvard, Cornell, Atlanta, and Yale, and historical societies from Kansas to Massachusetts. There are also one-of-a-kind holdings including the National Park Service collection at the Washington home of Frederick Douglass. After a search, a story unto itself, I was fortunate to correspond briefly with George Lindsey Stearns, the grandson of George L. Stearns. From him I gained valuable insights into the Stearns family and the family estate in Medford, The Evergreens.

It took much detective work to locate material. *The Official Records of the War of the Rebellion* became a valuable source. The National Archives collection of documents for the Bureau of Colored Troops provided additional information. The *Congressional Record* yielded much information on the Harpers Ferry Raid and the role of Stearns. Period newspapers, including Stearns's Boston *Commonwealth* and *The Right Way*, and papers from New York, Philadelphia, Boston, Nashville, and elsewhere were also good sources for material. The many printed collections of letters such as those of Ralph Waldo Emerson and Bronson Alcott all yielded bits and pieces of the story.

Secondary sources were also invaluable; they and included two books by Stearns's older son, Frank Preston Stearns, *The Life and Times of George L. Stearns* and *Cambridge Sketches*. Also helpful for Stearns's early life were the Medford Historical Register and Charles Brooks and James Usher's *The History of the Town of Medford Massachusetts 1630-1885*. Allan Nevins's classic multi-volume work *The War for the Union* was one of the best sources for detailed background material and provided leads to other sources.

I would like to acknowledge two contemporary historians without whom this work would never have been accomplished. The first is my friend and mentor, Stephen B. Oates, who taught me what good historical writing was all about and whose faith kept me going until the manuscript was completed. The other was James McPherson, whose work *The Struggle for Equality* yielded the most useful contemporary information available on Stearns with valuable leads that I vigorously pursued. Professor McPherson took the time to write a very discouraged author words that nagged at me and kept the work going.

I extend my grateful appreciation to the many archivists, librarians and historians with whom I corresponded and those I met in person. Were it not for their assistance my research would have come to naught. There are also other individuals who gave me encouragement and assistance. My former advisor, Dr. Stephen B. Oates, who taught me how to write for publication; Major General William A. Stofft, now retired, who gave me the confidence to complete the manuscript and my publisher, Dr. Steven Swerdfeger, who saw the merit of an "unknown and unacknowledged" hero's efforts in the struggle for emancipation and civil right for African-Americans. Most of all I thank my wife, partner, and friend, Michelle. If it were not for her prodding and encouragement I would have not sought out my publisher. I am also in debt to her for this because we believe George L. Stearns deserves long overdue recognition.

1

The Making of a Man

Unless a boy is thoroughly a boy, he never will make a genuine man.
                                                            –George L. Stearns

Across from the wide steps leading to the gold-domed Massachusetts State House is a striking bronze relief set in a stone terrace. Created by Augustus St. Gaudens, the work honors Colonel Robert Gould Shaw, a Boston Brahmin, and his "bell-cheeked Negro Infantry" of the Fifty-fourth Massachusetts Infantry Regiment. Mustered into federal service in 1863, this first northern African-American regiment lost its young colonel that same year during the storming of Fort Wagner guarding the sea approach to Charleston, South Carolina.[1]

In May 1897, after thirty years in the planning and execution, the monument to Shaw and his regiment was unveiled at the Boston Music Hall. Massachusetts Governor Roger Wolcott, Boston Mayor Josiah Quincy, and Professor William James of Harvard University, Shaw's alma mater, took part in the ceremony. All spoke in glowing terms of the brave "lean as a compass needle" colonel and the Fifty-fourth's black "American Volunteers." Tuskegee Institute president Booker T. Washington also addressed the crowd and pointedly gave credit to the white man responsible for recruiting the Fifty-fourth,

"George Luther Stearns, who with hidden generosity and a great sweet heart generosity and a great sweet heart helped to turn the darkest hour into day, and in doing so freely gave service, fortune, and life itself to the cause. . . ." Many in the crowd did not recognize the name of the man who recruited this "brave black regiment" of Shaw's "American volunteers."[2]

In the hall sat Joshua B. Smith, a Fifty-fourth Massachusetts veteran and a well-known Boston caterer. He was one of many responsible for the erection of the monument to Shaw and the black regiment. Smith and the African-American community never forgot Stearns and his many contributions to their race beyond recruiting this regiment. Motivated by Washington's remarks, he began a campaign for a memorial to George Luther Stearns, the man responsible not only for the recruitment of the Fifty-fourth, and more than thirteen other "men of color" regiments, but also his support of John Brown, Kansas free state emigration, and African-American emancipation and civil rights. Finally, in 1901, the Massachusetts legislature placed a tablet in the outer lobby of the State House,

> in honor of the late Major George Luther Stearns, for the purpose of commemorating the path taken by him in securing the enlistment of colored troops, and the other valuable services rendered by him to the United States and to this Commonwealth in the War of the Rebellion.[3]

This "Merchant of Boston," as the memorial describes him, came from an old New England family whose ancestors arrived in the Massachusetts Bay Colony shortly after the first settlers. Isaac Sterne and his wife, Mary, were residents of Stoke, Suffolk County, England, when they took passage on the tiny barque *Arabella* with John Winthrop, the new governor. On June 12, 1630, the couple disembarked at Salem. Isaac found no suitable farmland and, after some searching, eventually purchased acreage at a place called Watertown, not far from Boston on the graceful Charles River. He and his young bride soon became prominent figures in the pioneer community. Leadership, seemingly a family trait, came easily to the young settler. His neighbors consistently elected him selectman. In addition to farming and politics, Isaac showed a marked talent for carpentry. As a result, he became the foreman of the workers who constructed the first bridge to span the Charles River. An industrious and frugal person, Isaac prospered, and when he died, he left property amounting to the considerable sum of almost $3,000.[4]

The coastal area soon filled with other settlers and good farmland became scarce. When the children of Isaac and Mary Sterne came of age, they had no choice but to move to new locations in the Bay colony in search of a livelihood. The family members, while never wealthy, were always comfortable, not just monetarily, but also within the communities in which they settled. One son, David, became a Calvinist minister in Lunenburg. For reasons forgotten over time, David petitioned for a change in the spelling of the family name. His brothers, including Thomas, a farmer who resided in Littleton, agreed to the modification to Stearns. When the differences between the colonists and the Crown became revolution, one of Thomas's sons, Josiah, served along with twenty other Stearns men in the fight for independence. Josiah led a company of militia from the town of Lunenburg. After the war, Josiah, with a taste and knack for leadership, entered politics and won several elections to the Massachusetts General Court. The capstone of his political career came with election to Samuel Adams's Governor's Council for three consecutive years. When Josiah died in April 1822, his children and grandchildren selected a single sentence for the memorial stone: "He discharged the obligations of a citizen and magistrate with integrity, prudence, and fidelity." These words would also apply to Josiah's eldest son, Luther.[5]

Luther Stearns was born in Lunenburg on February 17, 1770. The excitement of the days before the American Revolution and the lean war years formed a backdrop for his early life. Regardless of the hardships caused by the war's impact, including the absence of his father, Luther received more than a rudimentary education. In 1787 he entered Dartmouth College, New Hampshire. After a number of years of study there, Luther decided to complete his education at Harvard College in Cambridge, Massachusetts. After graduation from Harvard with honors in 1791, the young man remained uncertain about choosing a profession and remained in Cambridge for many years as a Latin tutor. Eventually, Luther decided to pursue a career in medicine and took additional courses at Harvard. In the days before state medical licensing, all a would-be doctor needed was an apprenticeship under a practicing physician. On the recommendation of several family members, he became an assistant to Dr. John Brooks of Medford. The town, a short distance northwest of the college, was known primarily for its crackers and rum. Dr. Brooks, a general in the War for Independence, gained an excellent reputation both as a physician and as a concerned citizen. His contemporaries considered him "in the first class of practitioners," a physician who "watched the operation of Nature and never interfered unless it was obvious he could aid and support her."[6]

Dr. Brooks trained Luther for several years. Finally, he believed the young man ready to establish a practice. Fortunately, at this time Brooks decided to go into politics, and Luther began to treat many of the former's patients. While practicing medicine in Medford, Luther became acquainted with the prestigious Hall family and with one member in particular, Mary Hall. Her father, Colonel Willis Hall, as townspeople recalled, "a large, courtly man and possessed of an imperious will," was one of the town's leading citizens. Colonel Hall served his community as town moderator, clerk, selectman, and assessor. Because of his status, he was also able to defy the community by remaining friends with Colonel Isaac Royall, a Tory, who eventually fled to England after the British evacuated Boston. Hall's friends claimed that before Royall left, the Tory almost convinced him to support the Crown. Hall resisted his friend's pleas and eventually managed to save part of Royall's landholdings from confiscation. Royall never returned, and the land changed hands many times, eventually becoming the property of Luther's son.[7]

Luther Stearns was almost twice the age of sixteen-year-old Mary Hall. The age difference was not unusual, however, and when he proposed marriage she agreed. The wedding took place on December 29, 1799. Shortly thereafter the couple bought a modest-looking frame home on Emerson Street near the site chosen for the new Middlesex Canal. Mary's family provided many of the furnishings. As her father's favorite, she received a number of family heirlooms, including a silver tea set, which was placed in a conspicuous location within the small but comfortable home.[8]

Domestic matters in order, Luther immersed himself in work. He specialized in obstetrics and soon earned a reputation as a skilled and sympathetic physician, as a resident remembered, whose "sensitive temperament made surgical operations terrible to him, unrelieved, as they then were by modem anesthetics." Luther had little family time, for his profession demanded long hours away from home. Many nights he woke from a sound sleep to a frantic knock on the door by someone seeking assistance. The fees never justified the long, uncertain hours, yet he was happy and the family comfortable.[9]

Following adjustment to married life, Luther and Mary assumed roles they were to keep until death separated them. Mary often displayed an iron will and a temper. She was also opinionated and intolerant. At times she drove Luther to take on more responsibilities and tasks than he wanted. Yet, Mary did have a compassionate side, for both Stearns and his young wife paid special attention to the less fortunate citizens of Medford. For many years they prepared packages of useful articles and every Christmas Eve drove through town delivering them to poor families. In contrast to his young wife, the doctor, a neighbor said, was a "very pleasant man, not much given to jesting but of a remarkably smooth, even temperament." The doctor possessed an easygoing personality, enjoying life and people. As water seeks its own level, unlike Mary, Luther moved through life avoiding confrontation and obstacles, content and happy.[10]

This temperament, a genuine concern for his fellow citizens, plus Mary's urging led Luther to involvement in town government. It certainly helped to have a father-in-law like Willis Hall and the extensive Hall family supporting his political efforts. At a town meeting in 1803, neighbors elected him town clerk. In 1810 he assumed the responsibilities of a selectman and was elected again for the years 1812-17 and 1819. He also acted as moderator for the town meetings from 1816 to 1817. One unusual responsibility Luther shared with another selectman concerned the award ing of fishing rights for shad and alewives on the Mystic River between Medford and Charlestown.[11]

Luther took on other civic duties. He became the fire ward of the local district, a serious responsibility in an era of wood dwellings and open cooking fires. One hotly debated issue that arose at a committee meeting in November 1818 concerned Medford's use of its own fire fighting equipment to aid surrounding communities. On Luther's recommendation, the meeting decided that if a call came for assistance, fire engines and "engine men" would gather at a central location with the selectmen and fire wards. As the situation dictated, the group would "forthwith . . . determine . . . the proper measures to be adopted." At the same meeting, a general discussion began as to what further measures the town could take to prepare for fire. The answer was to increase the number of ladders to be hung at strategic locations throughout Medford. After the meeting Stearns and the other members of the committee met at a local tavern for a "collation and chowder." These refreshments were paid for by a twelve-and-a-half cent fine Luther levied on members unfortunate enough to miss the roll call at the meeting's commencement. In addition to the fine, a late-arriving member also became the target of jests explaining his tardiness.[12]

In 1803 Luther and other citizens of Medford saw an opportunity to benefit the town and their personal finances. At this time twelve hundred people lived in the growing community. For years people talked about a shorter land route to Boston. On April 11, 1803, a group of prominent citizens met at the home of Hezekiah Blanchard, Jr., to discuss construction of a turnpike, originating near Stearns's home and ending at the Charlestown neck. Luther joined with General Brooks and others, including his wife's relatives, to form the Turnpike Corporation. The clerk position in the corporation fell to Luther, who acted in this capacity until his death. The corporation agreed to offer one hundred shares. Luther, a member of the subscription committee, purchased four. The Massachusetts Court of General Sessions granted permission for the establishment of a turnpike three rods wide (fifteen and a half yards on solid ground and twice that on marshy soil), provided it be completed within three years. If any of the articles of incorporation were violated, the organization would be fined $13.33.[13]

Looking back, one local resident observed, "Of course no turnpike was a gilt-edged security, but the Medford must have been one of the best." "Shunpikers," persons who avoided the toll booth, however, soon cut into profits. To protest revenue losses, the corporation petitioned the General Court. The court ordered persons who were caught bypassing the toll booth to "forfeit and pay three times as much as the legal toll." But profits from the turnpike never fully met the expectations of the investors. The quarter ending January 1, 1812, showed a balance of almost seven hundred dollars; three hundred dollars went toward maintenance, and the balance amounted to a dividend of four dollars per share.[14]

Luther appeared solidly entrenched in the Medford community by the time the turnpike was finished. Soon after, on St. Valentine's Day 1806, the couple's first child, named for her grandmother, Elizabeth Hall, arrived. Three years later, on January 8, 1809, Mary again gave birth, this time to a boy, who was a "fair, rosy child, with beautiful brown and sunny hair." The pleased parents named their son George Luther. The family home now seemed a small container for the growing family. As a consequence Luther found it necessary to move the family to larger quarters in West Medford.[15]

The home in West Medford was the one George remembered best. It was a large ten-room "mansion house" in Federal period architecture. The parlor served as the family room, where a large, bright Oriental rug covered the dark, wide planked floor. A smaller rug lay in front of the large hearth, flanked by highly polished brass andirons and an expensive "fireset." Facing the hearth was a cane "Canton made" sofa. Nearby on a small table lay a wooden backgammon board. The most expensive item in this room was a mirror valued at $25. In addition to the parlor, on the first floor were four rooms, two on the north side and two on the south. Directly behind these rooms on each side were rooms forming a U-shape to the house. Luther's office and examining room were in the north chamber. George occupied the room off his father's office and to the rear of the dwelling. It was a sparsely furnished space with a small "looking glass," a table with three chairs, and a narrow bedstead. On the opposite side of the house was the master bedroom crammed with furniture, including a "musician's stool" and an "old and broken" secretary. It was a comfortable house by any standard and large enough for any number of additional children. Indeed, after the move on March 20, 1812, the third child was born to the couple, Henry Laurens.[16]

Stearns's practice continued to grow, and he eventually obtained a medical degree from the Harvard Medical School in 1811. Still, Luther believed his income would not be sufficient to support the family. As a consequence he embarked on a second career while continuing to practice medicine. With the experience gained as a tutor at Harvard, Luther opened a boys' "classical" preparatory school in the Stearns home. From the arrangements in the ten-room "mansion," it appears that not more than ten children were enrolled at any given time. At least five of the students boarded with the Stearns family in a rear upstairs room; the balance stayed with family or friends. According to accounts, the children were from the "first families of New England," with an occasional "sprinkling of French and Spanish blood from the West Indies." Luther's talents as a teacher and warm, outgoing personality ensured the success of the preparatory school and many boys he trained entered college.[17]

Unfortunately, his own sons would be denied the tutoring and the financial support that would have allowed them to obtain a college education. Returning from a house call, Luther, ashen faced and bent over with severe pain, asked Mary to call Dr. Daniel Swain. The diagnosis was "lungfever" or pneumonia. The next day, April 28, 1820, Luther Stearns died. The boarding school, medical practice, and many other activities had taken a toll on his strength. All that was needed was a chill, brought on by the unpredictable New England spring weather, to hasten his early death.

Stearns's wife, remembered by neighbors in her later years as "a very determined woman, high-spirited, and rather imperious," at first displayed no emotion at Luther's passing away. There were few who ever saw Mary shed a tear on any occasion. But there is a limit to emotional endurance, and after stoically completing funeral ceremonies, she reached a breaking point. For one week after the funeral the poor woman remained in bed. Mary's emotional control, townspeople remarked, was a personality trait inherited from her father. Then, too, it also reflected the impact of the strict Calvinist doctrine that surrounded her early life and reinforced such cold behavior.[18]

Mary's early Calvinist indoctrination led her to believe that evil existed everywhere and that daily life was a battleground on which people struggled against temptation. Because of this, she stressed morals and manners constantly; young people must learn to tell the truth and to be diligent students. Her formula for preparing children to conquer evil included the following regimen: prescribed hours of sleep, a set time to get up in the morning, a rapid toilet in the morning, and silence at the dining table.

George and the other Stearns children learned early not to make a sound in the house and never interrupt adults. Mary would prefer to see her children "dead rather than they should grow up in idle, vicious courses," and all of the children from an early age were given chores around the house. Now, as man of the house, George toiled around the homestead. One chore was milking a very large red cow, who was also a family pet. His father's carriage and horses had to be sold eventually, but until they were, George also cared for them. Mary and the children attended the First Parish Church in Medford. The minister, David Osgood, although a Calvinist, softened the demanding doctrine and led his congregation toward a gradual acceptance of Unitarianism. Mary, though, found it difficult to change her many Calvinist beliefs, especially those regarding child rearing.[19]

Mary did take comfort in Reverend Osgood's preaching. George also was much taken with David Osgood, who exhibited a manner "ardent, but not glowing; free but always reverent; and . . . excelled in illustrating and enforcing moral truths." One parishioner explained, "Dr. Osgood never called himself Unitarian, but there can be no doubts that for the latter part of his life he was much more in accord with Dr. Channing than with John Calvin." Channing and others rejected the notion of predestination and preached "religion as a life rather than a mode of belief." In keeping with this new spirit, Osgood believed "each of us ought to think and judge for himself, using the reason God has given us." When the minister died in 1823, his liberal leanings were implanted in many parishioners, including George. They, like Osgood, believed that if it were the Maker's intent that a large portion of humankind was damned forever, they "could not conceive what worse business God could have been engaged in."[20]

After Reverend Osgood died, his parishioners accepted Andrew Bigelow as their new spiritual leader. Bigelow also preached views that were more Unitarian than Calvinistic. At one point, however, seventeen members of the congregation refused to follow the continuing drift toward the new humanist doctrine and separated. In 1823 Bigelow and his followers, including the Stearns family, formed the Medford Unitarian Church. Following numerous Massachusetts Supreme Court decisions concerning the division of church property, the original, or First Parish, retained it all. For the newly formed church, the court decisions meant that all affiliation with the town ceased, including financial support and the use of the old church for town meetings.

Yet the church survived and George remained a loyal parishioner seeking and obtaining comfort from the successive church ministers, for the young man harbored a strong sense of loss after his father died. Lutlier, with his gentle, warm personality, seemed more a friend to his children than just a father. Mary did not relate to a child's world. She "lamented the indulgent and neglectful manner" in which her neighbors brought up their children. Madam Stearns also showed an obvious preference for her younger son, Henry, "who was the more handsome and attractive of the two boys." However, as do so many children in like circumstances, George endured and lived through his early boyhood much like other Medford youths.[21]

George found Medford winters a special time. The Middlesex Canal, an early "triumph of engineering," provided an excellent ice skating surface because of its shallow four-foot depth and lack of current. The canal's existence was due in part to George's grandfather, Willis Hall, who joined with other citizens to incorporate as the "Proprietors of the Middlesex Canal." In 1802, the first water entered the system of locks and aqueducts. The canal stretched from the Merrimack to the Charles River. Its smooth surface sometimes froze as early as Thanksgiving. One Christmas Day, George strapped on a new pair of skates and followed some older friends on their way to Lowell, twenty miles away. Tired by the trip, he spent the night at the home of a friend of his father. On his return the following day, his mother told him to clean up for supper. Looking at the wash stand, he cried out, "the bowl isn't large enough." Delirious with exhaustion, he recovered after sleeping until the next day.[22]

Other winter activities were less demanding, but potentially more dangerous. The Thatcher Magoun estate, whose owner was the wealthiest shipbuilder in town, had an excellent slope from the entrance down to the Mystic River. Sleds launched at the crest of the hill picked up tremendous speed as they hurdled over ice-packed surfaces. Sometimes two or three would careen out of control halfway down the hill and crash against the posts and trees that surrounded the Unitarian parsonage. Of course, winter also brought "glorious shindies," snowball fights, between the Medford "maggots" and the Charlestown "pigs." The rivalry of the two gangs was so intense that even adults joined in the frays.[23]

Summer also provided much entertainment for a young boy in Medford. George, remembered by townspeople as an "active, bright-faced boy, full of life," made the most of his limited free time. At fourteen he took pride in swimming more than a mile on the Mystic, "with its sinuous and graceful course and its bright water." But George, a shy youth, stayed away from the most crowded bathing spot on the river at Blanchard's Wharf across from the Lawrence distillery. At high tide, boys leaped into the water from log rafts anchored to the pilings. Also a swift runner, George occasionally took part in such games as football, tag, and prisoners' base.[24]

While enjoying an active out-of-doors life, George also attended his father's school. After her husband's death, Mary hired John Angier, who, like Luther, was a Harvard graduate, as the school's headmaster. Under Angier's guidance, though, George showed little inclination for scholarship for he had a temperament that was too active to concentrate on studies. But he did have a keen mind for mathematics and enjoyed completing complicated problems. After finishing the math primer, he worked backward through it. Although his father excelled in classics, George did not care for Latin though he managed to learn enough to read Caesar and Virgil. The family library consisted of medical works, Luther's college texts, and a twenty-volume history of the world, which had once belonged to Willis Hall. There was little else to read, for Mary shunned contemporary literature. According to her, novels were a waste of time, especially for women, who should be knitting and sewing. Poetry, she claimed, "weakened" the mind and the body, an observation she made after listening to accounts of Lord Byron's *Childe Harold*. Mary saw a danger to youthful minds in the "peculiar, fascinating quality of Byron's verse." She need not have worried about George, who would spend rainy Sundays locked away reading world history books. As for penmanship, George had the misfortune of having large and bony hands, which made writing difficult.[25]

Writing was not George's only difficulty in school. His shyness sometimes made him the target of school bullies. One rainy afternoon George put his head out a window to check on the weather. A classmate pulled the peg holding the sash. The window crashed down, breaking the skin on the back of his neck. Catching his breath, George turned and gave the tormentor a sound beating. When aroused, "George Stearns was the toughest little fighter we had at school," a classmate remarked. "He never knew he was whipped."[26]

On October 30, 1828, George's sister lost her fight with consumption. To some, George appeared as depressed by her death as his father's. He always blamed Elizabeth's passing on the way young ladies restricted their diets. Even in the demanding New England climate, a lady-in order to be a lady-had to refrain from eating meat and butter. To make matters worse, clothing styles dictated the use of thin fabrics that were really not suitable for keeping out the winter cold. This combination and a frail constitution, he believed, caused the loss of his sister.

George's family faced other tragedies. For two years after Luther's death, Mary kept the preparatory school going with John Angier as headmaster. Angier, however, believed he could do better on his own and left, taking all the students with him. George, in addition to assuming many more household chores, now had to work outside his home. At first he took odd jobs, such as tending locks on the Middlesex Canal. Yet, despite his limited free time, he continued to enjoy the activities of boyhood. Remembering his youth, Stearns would tell his sons, "Unless a boy is thoroughly a boy, he will never make a genuine man." Eventually, Mary arranged to have George take a position as a dry goods store clerk, working for one of her brothers in Brattleboro, Vermont.[27]

On the evening of April 16, 1824, Stearns walked from his mother's home to a tavern in West Cambridge. Huddled in a small room with a dawning realization he would be leaving family and friends for a long time, he passed the night lonely and fearful of the unknown. The following morning Stearns boarded the Fitchburg, Massachusetts, stagecoach. After many bone-jolting miles, he reached Brattleboro, a sleepy little village situated on a steep hillside overlooking the Connecticut River in the southeastern comer of Vermont. In the years before railroads, towns like Brattleboro functioned as trade centers. Each center contained a variety of stores that catered to the needs of the inhabitants as well as the people who lived in a wide radius surrounding the town.

The isolation of the area heightened Stearns's loneliness. Although the town had frequent social events, the new clerk could not take part because of his age. So, not quite a man and no longer a boy, Stearns found little to occupy his free time, although he did learn to ride horseback and row a boat. Exceedingly shy, Stearns did not make any lasting friends during three and a half years in Brattleboro.

The following summer he received a letter that brought welcome news. Through relatives, his mother managed to secure a position for George in a ship chandlery on Boston's India Wharf. In August he returned to Medford to take on the new job. Stearns had matured physically during those three years in Vermont. His face lost its boyish oval, and its bone structure seemed more pronounced. The active life in Vermont filled his medium frame with muscle. However, one physical trait that had caused him trouble in school was now proving a liability in his career as a clerk. His large, bony hands still made it difficult to hold a pen and as a consequence his penmanship remained poor. Stearns also had a more serious problem to overcome than penmanship. His shyness was now even more pronounced, especially compared with the rough and tumble types he worked with along the Boston waterfront. George's nervousness at times prevented understanding what people said to him. After a few weeks on the job, Stearns's employer bluntly told him that he was not working up to expectation and that it would be best to seek other employment. Stearns's dismay showed on his features. The chandler, a sympathetic person, after observing the youth's crestfallen expression, offered him a second chance. To retain his position, George practiced penmanship religiously. After a month, there was a noted improvement in the young man's handwriting and his attempts to be more assertive. The store owner told George not to worry, for now he would not part with him. The daily five-mile walk from the Stearnses' home in Medford to India Wharf became too much, so George rented an attic room in a dismal boardinghouse for young clerks in Boston. Stearns turned most of the wages over to his mother. In the evenings he continued to practice penmanship.

To relieve the stiffness in his fingers, he placed his hands in hot water. For amusement, the young clerk read and sometimes played cards with other occupants of the dwelling. After closing the store each Saturday evening, he walked home to Medford over the turnpike his father had helped finance. On Sunday, without fail, he accompanied his mother and younger brother to the Medford Unitarian Church. Then, long before the sun rose on Monday mornings, he began the long walk back to Boston and India Wharf.

The workday was demanding. At first his duties included not only keeping ledgers, but also performing physical labor. Handling the heavy stock items on a daily basis helped him maintain a muscular frame. Stearns continued to do well at the ship chandlery, although he described the workday as a "dull, hard, monotonous grind." During the course of several years, he moved from clerk to salesman to bookkeeper, absorbing a great deal of knowledge concerning the business world.[28]

Salary increases allowed him to move to better accommodations, and he now had spending money for entertainment, which meant attending the theater in Boston. He preferred only the best plays, finding low comedy in poor taste. George made certain the reviews were favorable before attending a performance. Mary Stearns's "Boston connections" began to invite the twenty-three-year-old bachelor to social functions. But the young clerk had little in common with the more privileged youth in Boston. When in attendance at parties Stearns usually sat uncomfortably alone while contemporaries socialized. Others attending the various affairs dressed in the latest fashion, yet Stearns's wardrobe remained conservative. Still exceedingly shy, he saw himself as a "most unprepossessing youth," and never mastered the art of idle conversation. Although women could have found him handsome, with his rugged features, hazel eyes, and clear, bright complexion, Stearns seemed ill at ease when young ladies approached. He could not even unbend enough to talk to men, unless he considered the subject serious. George would listen attentively to those who were willing to break through the wall shyness created.[29]

Stearns's willingness to listen, concern for others, and hard work gained respect from even slight acquaintances. Once, two clerks sharing an adjoining room returned in the early morning hours. Their conversation woke Stearns who listened in amazement as they spoke of him in complimentary terms. They spent their salaries on clothes and entertainment yet admired Stearns for his frugal habits and self-control. Finally, one said that if any one of the residents of the boardinghouse became a success, it would be the man in the next room, George Stearns. George Stearns never lacked ambition and slowly raised his expectations.

His nervous energy and sensitivity to criticism led him to cast about for an opportunity to become self-employed. Since his birth in 1809, the shipbuilding industry in Medford had increased dramatically. Stearns grew up with the steady rhythm of hammers and the clean, sweet smell of cut wood coming from the town's numerous shipyards. George contemplated constructing a mill to distill linseed into oil, an item indispensable in curing and maintaining lumber for ships. At the time such a mill would have few competitors, and if the shipbuilding boom continued, a modest initial investment had the possibility of offering a good return.

Geographically and historically, Medford was certainly a good prospect for a boom in shipbuilding and its companion industries. The narrow Mystic River's depth, sufficient to float ships up to twenty-five tons, surprised the first settlers. Beginning as early as 1631, ships coming up the Mystic docked at Medford, because it allowed easy access to the raw material from the hinterland. If a seagoing vessel had too large a draft, lighters would carry material from the Medford docks to Boston harbor. In 1681, Governor John Winthrop commissioned one of the first sea going ships built in the Commonwealth of Massachusetts, the *Blessing of the Bay*. However, it took the vision and enterprise of one man, Thatcher Magoun, to establish the shipbuilding industry firmly in the town.[30]

Thatcher Magoun learned ship carpentry in Salem, Massachusetts. One clear day in 1802, Magoun climbed to a hill overlooking the serpentine Mystic River and saw it running its course through Medford. He noted the advantages of a location for a large shipyard. After making inquiries of local sea captains and checking on the availability of raw materials, Magoun established the river's first major shipyard for oceangoing vessels. In the next fifty years, nine other yards were built in Medford. In the 1830s, the China trade made Medford clippers famous. Medford shipping, New England seamen claimed, "skim[med] the cream off the China trade." The demand for ships brought an increase in ship carpenters, most of them from Salem, and their arrival was referred to locally as Medford's "second settlement."[31]

Building and launching ships provided not only income but entertainment for the Stearns family and their Medford neighbors. The activity of the shipyards fascinated George as a child. He and almost everyone in town shared an interest in the construction of the vessels. The carpenters built the ships on the inclined plane of the sloping river bank. A rock maple keel supported the ribs, each usually six separate pieces of oak bolted together and shaped by hand. When the hull reached the final stage of completion, workmen laid launching ways into the river. Eager adults and excited children attended each launch. The Stearns family would even interrupt special family dinners to watch. Tallow and castile soap prepared the way for a smooth launch (launchings in the summer had to be at midnight to prevent the sun from melting the lubricants). Wooden wedges driven home by workmen separated the hull and the underlying timbers.

Finally, crews split the blocks under the keel, and slowly at first, then gathering momentum, the completed hull slid into the waiting river.32 Stearns, his shipping knowledge broadened by work in the chandlery, realized that expanding trade would bring about further increases in shipbuilding.

He became determined to build a linseed oil mill and accumulated some capital, but not the thousands necessary to start construction. The young entrepreneur approached several of his mother's wealthy relatives. Although all expressed interest and offered encouragement, they were reluctant to provide funds. He refused to give up and finally turned to a neighbor, Samuel Train, for assistance. Samuel Train, a successful merchant, began his career as an importer of hides from 1800 to 1810. After a few years, his brother joined him, and together they purchased several large cargo ships. Their small fleet carried on extensive trade with South American and Cuban ports. Train, a deacon and a Congregational church pillar, had the reputation of being a "gentleman, one of the old school." Stearns was comfortable approaching the deacon for capital. Train appreciated the company of young men like Stearns, "who enjoyed his quaint and bright chats on different subjects." Stearns saw that the deacon loved to stretch the truth, believing no one would listen unless he told a story in a "most extravagant style."[33]

Stearns admired this outgoing and successful. businessman. Train, in turn, saw in Stearns the virtues that were the foundation for his own success, determination and willingness to work. Perhaps the shrewd and practical deacon also noticed the attention George was paying to his daughter, Mary. Train agreed to lend Stearns $10,000, if he could come up with a matching sum. On learning Train's decision, the Halls supplied $5,000 to Stearns. Still short of funds, George prevailed upon his mother, and in a gesture of confidence in her enterprising elder son, she mortgaged the home in West Medford. With funds now available, Stearns began the mill's construction. The brick structure was about fifty yards south of the Mystic Bridge on Back Street. In 1835 Stearns watched as the first smoke rose from the fifty-foot brick chimney.[34]

Stearns soon became a recognized member of the town's business community. As had his father, he assumed civic responsibilities. Stearns's first reform stirrings also prompted him to join the "Medford Association for Discountenancing Intemperance and Its Kindred Vices." This proved to be an early indication of Stearns's willingness to embark on unpopular causes. Soon after it formed, the organization's members decided to acquire a building for a temperance hall. In May 1835, according to the town's records, "a company of thirty-five [men] and one lady" purchased one hundred and eighty shares at a par value of $100 each to use as capital for the purchase of a hall. The association eventually purchased a tavern, which they enlarged to accommodate meetings and alcohol-free social gatherings-a noble experiment, perhaps, but doomed to failure in a town noted for its distillation of rum. Membership in the association required courage, for many influential men owned distilleries and exercised a great deal of political and economic influence in town. The venture failed, and when the stockholders sold the hall after ten years, the new owners changed it back to a tavern.[35]

As 1835 drew to a close and people in New England began to prepare for the coming winter, Stearns proposed to Mary Train. The engagement notice appeared on December 20, 1835. A courtship relatives described as long and happy preceded a relatively brief engagement, and the couple exchanged vows before the Reverend Levi Pratt of the Second Congregational Church on January 31, 1836. Six years younger than Stearns, this "cheerful vivacious young lady," as the family remembered her, was a "suitable contrast to her sober, phlegmatic husband."[36]

Mary saw little of her energetic husband, who worked long hours supervising the mill's operation. Stearns's younger brother Henry joined the business as an equal partner in the division of the profits. However, Henry contributed little or nothing to the business for he had become an alcoholic. George's gesture was either an act of charity or one intended to please their mother.

The Stearns brothers apparently were concerned more with profits than with public safety. A number of people in town complained that, using the shortest distance possible out of the mill, they constructed an exhaust steam pipe that discharged at ground level. The steam from the huge vats used to boil linseed passed through this pipe, out of the mill on the building's north side, and into a public school yard. One child who played in the yard later remembered that the hot steam escaped regularly into a flock of forty to fifty students. Although the scalding mist severely injured at least one child, the Stearns brothers left the mill's steam pipe in place. Year by year profits from the mill continued.[37]

During the mill's first five years of operation, the demand for linseed oil continued to increase, as sixty major vessels, totaling 24,195 tons and valued at $1,112,170, one sixth of the total shipping built in Massachusetts, slid down the ways into the Mystic River. Stearns found a ready market for the amber finishing oil. In the mill's best year it produced 13,500 gallons of oil from 7,300 bushels of seed. The Panic of 1837 had little effect on Stearns's operation, and in slightly less than five years, his creditors were repaid. This success gave him the confidence and capital needed for another business.[38]

Before he could launch a new commercial venture, a family crisis took George away from his business. Described by friends as always "frail and delicate," Mary had what doctors called "weakness of the heart," the result of childhood rheumatic fever. In the spring of 1840 the family physician recommended a stay at the hot sulfur springs in Virginia. Escorted by George, as well as by her father and sister, Mary made the pilgrimage to Virginia. She did not improve and in August, the family returned to Medford. Early in October, Mary Train Stearns died. George accepted her death stoically, but her passing took an emotional toll. In later years, he refused to discuss this period of his life because of the pain it brought.[39]

Stearns immersed himself in work. In 1841, he attended a convention of linseed oil manufacturers in New York City. Not satisfied with the current profit margins, the delegates chose a committee consisting of Stearns and several others to petition Congress "to shape the tariff of 1842" in such a way as to exclude foreign linseed oil imports. The men convinced congressmen that this would help save the industry from competition. Shortly after the passage of the act, profits increased. But the manufacturers' prosperity lasted only a short time, because so many "new men" entered into the industry that in a few years the processing of linseed no longer produced a lucrative return. By this time, however, Stearns had moved into a new commercial field.[40]

In 1842, Albert Fearing, a partner in the ship chandlery where Stearns once worked, approached his former employee with a business proposition. Fearing not only carried a reputation as a successful merchant, but also became noted for many acts of charity. He even found time to serve as president of the American Colonization Society, an organization dedicated to returning freed slaves to Africa. At the time Fearing approached Stearns, he was in the Massachusetts Senate as a conservative Whig. This new responsibility detracted from business interests, and the senator looked for a partner to help establish another ship chandlery. He chose Stearns because of the young man's success and because he remembered his reliability and hard work in the chandlery on India Wharf.[41]

Fearing not only wanted Stearns to manage the new chandlery, but also needed additional capital. Stearns did have some funds available, but not enough. He again turned to Deacon Train for a loan to launch the business venture. Train responded without hesitation, "George, my daughter is gone from us but I shall always consider you as my son; you shall have the money." This time George did not have to ask his mother's relatives for money. The linseed oil profits and a loan from Train were enough. As a result, in 1843, after considerable time and energy had gone into renovating a warehouse and stocking it with seafaring equipment, the ship chandlery of Albert Fearing and Company began operation at Number One, City Wharf, a prime location in Boston. Riding on the crest of prosperity in the heyday of the age of sail, Stearns had no difficulty in repaying the kindly deacon.[42]

NOTES

1. Robert Lowell, "For the Union Dead," *For the Union Dead* (New York: Farrar, Straus and Giroux, 1966), pp. 70-72.
2. Ibid.; Letters Robert Gould Shaw (Cambridge: University Press, 1964), p. 275; Boston City Council, *Exercises at the Dedication of the Monument to Colonel Robert Gould Shaw and the Fifty-fourth Regiment of Massachusetts Infantry* (Boston: Municipal Printing Office, 1897), pp. 57-58.
3. Boston, Exercises, p. 65; Tablet in the entrance lobby of the Massachusetts State House, Boston, Massachusetts.
4. Tablet, Massachusetts State House. Unless otherwise cited, except for direct quotes, all information pertaining to George and the Stearns family is from Frank Preston Stearns, *The Life and Public Services of George Luther Stearns* (Philadelphia: J. B. Lippincott, 1907; reprint, New York: Kraus Reprint, 1969) (hereafter cited as Stearns, *Life*).
5. Stearns, *Life*, p. 16.
6. Charles Brooks and James M. Usher, *History of Medford, Middlesex County: From Its First Settlement in 1630 to 1855: Revised, Enlarged, and Brought Down to 1885* (Boston: Rand, Avery, 1886), p. 137.
7. David Brainard Hall, *Halls of New England, Genealogical and Biographical* (Albany, NY: J. Munsell's, 1883), p. 334.
8. Stearns, *Life*, p. 17.
9. Brooks and Usher, *Medford*, p. 460.
10. Stearns, *Life*, p. 18.
11. "Medford a Century Ago–1819," *Medford Historical Register* 22 (December 1919) :71 (hereafter cited as *MHR*).
12. Samuel G. Jepson, "Incidents and Reminiscences of the Fire Department of Medford," *MHR* 4 (January 1901):7-8.
13. M.W.M., "Medford Turnpike Corporation," MHR 23 (March 1920):1-13.
14. Ibid., p. 7.
15. Brooks and Usher, *Medford*, p. 461.
16. Luther Stearns, Last Will and Testament, Probate April1820, file 21287, Middlesex County Court House, Cambridge, Massachusetts; Brooks and Usher, *Medford*, p. 299.
17. Stearns, *Life*, pp. 18-19.
18. Ibid., Life, pp. 18, 20.
19. Ibid., Life, p. 20.

20. Brooks and Usher, *Medford*, p. 238; Thomas S. Harlow, "Some Notes of the History of Medford, 1801 to 1851," *MHR* 2, July 1898: 86; Brooks and Usher, *Medford*, p. 242.
21. Stearns, *Life*, p. 19.
22. Lorin L. Dame, "The Middlesex Canal," *MHR* 1, April1898: 45; Stearns, *Life*, p. 25.
23. Thomas M. Stetson, "An Old Medford School Boy's Reminiscences," *MHR* 17 (October 1914):79; Stearns, Life, p. 85 .
24. Stearns, *Life*, p. 24; Stetson, "Reminiscences," p. 79; Stearns, *Life*, p. 76.
25. Stearns, p. 21.
26. Ibid., p. 23.
27. Ibid., p. 24.
28. Ibid., p. 30.
29. Ibid., p. 32.
30. Brooks and Usher, *Medford*, pp. 19, 20; James A. Hervey, "Shipbuilding in Medford," *MHR* 1 (July 1898):69.
31. Hall Gleason, "Medford's Part in American Shipbuilding," *MHR* 38, March 1934: 12; Hervey, "Shipbuilding in Medford," p. 76. 32. Charles Cummings, "Medford in 1847," MHR6 (April1903): 43-44.
33. H. D. Hall, "Deacon Samuel Train," *MHR* 2 (October 1899):167, 169; Stearns, *Life*, p. 34.
34. Stearns, *Life*, p. 35; Brooks and Usher, Medford, p. 413; "The Towers of Medford," *MHR* 24 (March 1921):10.
35. "The Taverns of Medford," *MHR* 8 (April1905):28-29.
36. Stearns, *Life*, p. 36.
37. Stetson, "Reminiscences," p. 75 .
38. Brooks and Usher, Medford, p. 427; Cummings, "Medford in 1847," p. 45.
39. Stearns, *Life*, pp. 37-38.
40. Brooks and Usher, *Medford*, p. 413.
41. James Grant Wilson and John Fiske, eds., *Appleton's Cyclopaedia of American Biography*, 6 vols. (New York: D. Appleton, 1887-1889), Ill:423-424.
42. Stearns, *Life*, p. 40.

2

The Successful Merchant in Society

In the strong sense and practical character of one who is a businessman without being a worldly man.

— Reverend Caleb Stetson

As Stearns matured it was natural for him to want more from life than the pleasure and material rewards of business success. He continued to have strong religious feelings. Over the years, this honest and concerned businessman became increasingly involved in Medford church activities. One person, the Reverend Caleb Stetson, influenced him perhaps more than anyone else in his life, including the Reverend Osgood. Stetson, a Harvard graduate, received his ordination on February 28, 1827, the same year Stearns returned from Brattleboro, Vermont. Stetson, as Osgood had, made an impression on the fatherless boy, for the minister had a reputation, a parishioner remarked, as "a man whose heart was warm toward every good cause, whose hand was outstretched toward every needy brother." Residents of the town saw him as a "delightful" person, an outgoing conversationalist with a quick smile and a ready wit. Parishioners described Stetson as a member of "a class of reformers who were not so distinguished as the extremist, but who did perhaps as much good."[1]

Other than his mother's strict discipline, Stearns never was exposed to the harsh Calvinist religion, growing up with the preaching of the Reverend Osgood. The acceptance of Stetson's Unitarian and reform creed came as a natural progression in Stearns's maturing. The doctrine fit his striving for success, for it preached that the individual had to claim responsibility for his own life and destiny. To Stearns, being a good Christian meant practicing honesty and forthrightness in dealings with others. Those people in society who were well off should take responsibility for those less fortunate. Stearns believed that practicing a religion entailed an obligation to make the world a better place in which to live. In the 1840s, Stearns assumed a leadership role in religious matters. Stetson introduced the young merchant to the Reverend R. C. Waterston, another minister involved in numerous reform movements. As a result of this contact, Stearns became active in the Bethel Sunday School in Boston, which was founded and administered by Waterston. Several years later, Stearns became superintendent of an Interdenominational Sunday School for Medford's Protestant sects. These churches pooled their resources and conducted religious training for all children in the community.

During 1842 Stearns supervised twenty-one teachers who gave instruction to 124 "scholars," as he called them. The businessman put a great deal of time and energy into his religious calling. He made certain that his teachers took personal interest in and made a strong impression on each of their young charges. Stearns expressed uncertainty as to "what course of instruction would best promote the object we have in view." Discussing the matter with Reverend Waterston and others, he decided, "after much thought and conversation," that teachers should spend less time on theology and the Scriptures. Stearns concluded that adults could not expect children to "understand and feel what we have only imperfectly mastered." He declared that the teachers must "depend more on themselves," by enforcing those aspects of "divine truth" the adults had themselves discovered, and then "speak from the soul to the soul" to "enforce . . . precepts by example." Stearns told Waterston that if these guidelines were followed, "Christ [would] strengthen and aid us in this glorious work."[2]

Although concerned about moral truths, Stearns found little agreement with the early antislavery agitation of reformers such as Boston *Liberator* publisher William Lloyd Garrison and abolitionist Wendell Phillips. A conservative, Stearns was repelled by the unorthodox manner in which the abolitionists conducted their protests. Also, he failed to see any practical way to abolish slavery in America and believed abolitionists were deluding themselves in thinking their approach would eliminate the evil. In 1835, when Garrison's attacks on Southerners caused Boston merchants to drag him through the streets, practical-minded Stearns dismissed the violence as a consequence of the antagonistic literature the abolitionist insisted on publishing and distributing. Yet, he expressed sympathy for the plight of the slave and often said that "those who labored and were heavy laden" should receive a share of the wealth generated by their efforts) These ideas and his rejection of Garrisonians led him to seek an alternative in the antislavery Liberty party. The party evolved when a group of New York abolitionists became disenchanted by the selection of General William Henry Harrison, a proslavery man, as the Whig presidential candidate. This splinter group's platform seemed modest in Stearns's eyes. It called for the abolition of slavery in Washington and in all federal territories. The platform also sought to end interstate slave trade. It challenged, however, the traditional two-party structure of American politics and therefore was shunned by many men who abhorred slavery. But convinced that he should set a moral example for the community and that through constitutional means slavery would be abolished, Stearns stood out as the only man in Medford to cast a ballot for the antislavery Liberty party in the presidential election of 1840. For Stearns this ballot was a significant step on the road to reformer for, prior to the election, the young businessman had not exhibited any great interest in national politics.[4]

Stearns saw the Liberty party defeated in 1840 and his new political affiliation challenged by family and friends. His outspoken support of an antislavery and antiextension party horrified his mother. She could not accept the fact that her eldest son would consort with abolitionists of any shade, all of whom she called "vulgar fanatics." George's brother, Henry, echoed her objections. Stearns's family now constantly attacked him for his growing concern about slavery. One evening an elderly relative, Turell Tufts, engaged in a rather heated argument with Stearns. The old man admired George and had even written him into his will. His young relative's new political views were too much. After many harsh words, Tufts stormed out of the Stearns house, and the next day cut the errant young man out of his will.[5]

Besides his new involvement in political abolitionism, Stearns sought to overcome his natural shyness and began to engage in the social life of Medford and Boston. In the course of one season, Stearns met and became enchanted with, as he remembered, a "bright but plain" young woman from an aristocratic family in Boston. This young lady returned the interest shown her. But George, who acknowledged that he was an "unprepossessing youth," did not realize she cared for him. It did not matter, however, for the woman's invalid mother did not approve of the match and finally forced her daughter to cease her interest in Stearns.[6]

Stearns also spent time in the company of Thomas Starr King, whose background was somewhat similar to George's. While youngsters, both men lost fathers to whom they were very attached. Both youths were put to work as clerks in dry goods stores to supplement family incomes. Stearns knew King when the latter held the position of headmaster of Medford's West Grammar School. He maintained the friendship when King became a clerk in the Charlestown Navy Yard. King had a quick mind and could express ideas that Stearns could think but not verbalize immediately in conversation. When King entered the ministry, he pleased George with sermons admonishing reformers to have "more confidence in truth and less in human passion." From the pulpit of the Hollis Street Church in Boston, King claimed that abolitionists would have better results if they spoke "carelessly and with personal unconcern" and not with the passion of abolitionists like Garrison.[7]

In the fall of 1842, George Stearns's busy life almost came to an end. In the late afternoon, as he returned from Boston, his horse, Fanny Esler, named for a popular dancer, stumbled and fell near the abandoned ruins of the Charlestown nunnery. Stearns, a fairly good horseman, failed to jump clear, and the horse landed on top of the rider's right leg. Half-conscious and unable to move, George lay on the damp ground until a passerby found him. The man raced to Medford and returned with a wagon. On the painful, bone-jolting ride home, Stearns later remembered "counting the stones" over which the iron-rimmed wheels passed. When the wagon reached Medford, George's mother had him carried into the house and then sent for two local physicians. After examining Stearns's leg, they decided it must be amputated. Mother and son flatly rejected the suggestion. Mary had the presence of mind to send for a renowned Boston doctor, Amasa Walker, who had a reputation for saving damaged limbs. Walker arrived the next day and agreed with the Stearnses. He set the leg in splints and ordered Stearns to bed until the limb mended.[8]

After a number of weeks, Stearns beg an to move slowly and painfully about on crutches. He did no work and spent a good deal of time visiting friends in town. While resting on a couch at Caleb Stetson's home, he looked up to see a vaguely familiar young woman. Her piercing eyes looked at him from an oval face framed with dark, straight hair. The woman, Mary Elizabeth Preston, reminded Stearns that they had met the past summer at church services. At the time Reverend Stetson had called her attention to both George and his brother, explaining that he thought them the "finest" men in his parish and "pillars" of the church. After church that summer Sunday, Stetson introduced the brothers to Mary.[9]

Mary was a native of Maine, but she made frequent visits to her mother's hometown of Medford. Her maternal great-grandfather had settled in Medford at the outset of the American Revolution as a refugee from the British bombardment of Charlestown, Massachusetts. His son, Convers Francis, became a doctor of divinity and professor of pulpit eloquence at Harvard College. Francis married and became the father of two daughters. One of the daughters, Lydia Maria, eventually married David Lee Child. The other, Mary, married an ambitious young lawyer, Warren Preston, who took her to Bangor, Maine, which was then a part of Massachusetts. In 1837 they settled in Norridgewock, the court seat for the Kennebec region of Maine. Many members of Massachusetts families of cultivated background, professionals and college graduates, settled in this provincial town and made it a cultural center in the wilderness of Maine's forests. Here the Prestons had a son and four daughters, one of whom they named Mary Elizabeth.[10]

Mary Elizabeth's father, Warren Preston, had deep roots in the American past. His grandfather, Amarial Preston, served with the colonial militia and took part in the storming of Crown Point and the capture of Quebec in the French and Indian War. Later his experience made him a valuable asset during the War for Independence as an officer of the Massachusetts Continental Line, taking part in every major campaign from Valley Forge to Yorktown.

Amarial's grandson, Warren, graduated from Brown University in 1804 and then studied law with a noted Maine judge. The aggressive young man soon established his own practice. Preston's reputation grew, and he received an appointment as a commissioner on a board to oversee the separation of the District of Maine from the Commonwealth of Massachusetts. In 1819, soon after the final settlement, Preston served on the first governor of Maine's staff. As a reward for his services, the governor appointed him judge of probate for Somerset County in Norridgewock. According to relatives, Preston had a reputation as a person of "great refinement of feeling, cultivation and liberality; very devoted to every good cause; and a pronounced abolitionist." Preston's children saw their father often because their home was situated close to the courthouse. All of them, but especially Mary, were close to him. When Mary reached her teens, she began to visit Medford to see her aunt, Lydia Maria Child, a noted feminist author and abolitionist. Through her aunt she met Stetson and, like Stearns, formed a close friendship with the kindly minister.[11]

While on this most recent visit to Medford, she called on the Stetsons and walked in on Stearns. Mary sat beside the young merchant and soon they were alone. To entertain George, the young woman began to describe Maine. She spoke of the clear blue rivers on which loggers floated lumber rafts and of the great Atlantic salmon, whose silver scales glistened as they leaped over the falls trying to reach the spawning pools far up the river. Fascinated by her animated conversation, Stearns sought a subject she would find interesting and brought up the dialogue he was having with Stetson on religious matters. He asked about the church she attended and her views on religion. Much to his delight, he found they mutually shared ideas on subjects that most concerned him. The serious-minded Stearns became favorably impressed with the young woman. The two saw much of each other on this and subsequent visits. Mary confessed to relatives that her relationship with Stearns gave her a deep feeling of happiness. Stearns thought the same, but as with his earlier experiences with women, he could not believe his affections were reciprocated.

The following May, Stearns set out on a business trip to New Brunswick, Maine. Business was not the only subject on his mind for he decided to take a chance on the return trip and ask Mary to marry. He spent what he described as a wretched time the night before arriving at Norridgewock. All his doubts surfaced. Would Mary accept him? After all, Mary was twelve years younger than he. The following morning George arrived at the Preston home, and when the two were alone, the shy businessman proposed. Much to his relief, she agreed.

Their mutual friend, Caleb Stetson, thought the two would make an excellent match. He wrote to Mary, expressing certainty that George would make her happy "both in what he differs from you in and what he resembles you [and] . . . in the strong sense and practical character of one who is a businessman without being a worldly man." Mary already knew this from the tone of George's letters to her. He wrote on May 17, 1843, "The past week has been an exhausting one; my business did not suit me, and I became anxious, nervous-yes, these things take too deep hold, and I must hide the spirit of worldliness, that true life may come. I have resolved it." He also spoke

27

to her of their "future existence, bright and beautiful." He enjoyed every moment of their courtship and wrote that their relationship "spoke peace to his soul."[12]

On October 12, 1843, in Bangor, Maine, George and Mary were married by the Reverend Frederick H. Hedge. The couple left immediately for Medford. To make the journey as pleasant and smooth as possible, the methodical Stearns had worked out all the details before he left for Maine. Arriving in Medford by train, he took a friend's carriage and drove Mary to his mother's home, where the couple would live. He then drove the vehicle back and returned by foot to his waiting bride.

The young bride had a difficult time adjusting to her new life. Even though Mary knew many people and had relatives in Medford, she became homesick. Her mother-in-law had little sympathy for the young woman. In fact, the large, broad-shouldered Mary ruled her home much like a "drill sergeant," as members of the family called her when she was not around. Not only did her family sometimes cringe under her oppressive rule, but many people in town feared this opinionated, headstrong woman. No wonder, aside from the press of business, Stearns spent so much of his time in Boston. He left promptly at eight in the morning and returned each evening after six.

Stearns's long absence each day put a strain on his relationship with Mary. The young bride dreaded each day alone with her overbearing mother-in-law. Without George to intervene, the inevitable clashes occurred, making Mary's life miserable. She never ceased complaining about the time Stearns spent away. She wanted him to follow the same routine her father had and stay with her after breakfast "to read and talk." Mary's unhappiness increased when, several months after her marriage, she became ill. Madam Stearns, however, soon diagnosed Mary's problem, and the news changed the tense situation into a happy one, for Mary would soon bear a child. Although George looked forward to the coming birth, he realized he would soon have to find a new home for his family.[13]

On November 29, 1844, Mary gave birth to a son, whom the couple named Henry Laurens, Harry to the family, for George's brother. Tensions again rose in the household. Madam Stearns's strict ideas about raising children clashed with Mary's, for the latter remembered her happy childhood days and easygoing parents. Furthermore, Mary was pregnant again. Before the arrival of their second child, Frank Preston, born on January 4, 1846, Stearns decided for his own sake and the sake of his family to find a home of their own.

At this time Stearns's income was more than $15,000 a year. He often dreamed of owning the mansion his grandfather had saved for his Tory friend during the American Revolution. A merchant in town, William Rea, now owned the property and had recently put the estate up for sale. Over the years, the house and grounds had fallen into disrepair, enough to bring the price within Stearns's reach. On March 13, 1845, Stearns obtained the deed for twenty-six acres of land on which stood the brick mansion and a number of outbuildings.[14]

The mansion occupied the crest of Walnut Hill. The red brick structure, near the center of the property, faced southeast toward Charlestown. Standing on the columned front porch, Stearns could see the Bunker Hill Monument and the masts of ships in the Charles River. To his left he looked down upon the town center and the graceful Mystic River. A long drive lined with sugar maple trees led from what is now Stearns Avenue around to the left side of the three-story building. Jutting from the mansard roof were three dormers, and at each end of the mansion two large chimneys stood, each with many flues. As he went inside his home, Stearns faced a sweeping grand staircase and black walnut wainscoting on the downstairs walls. A substantial kitchen abutted the house at the right rear. A gravel drive of red granite curved around to the barns and stable in the back. Nearby, to the west along the side of the Boston and Lowell railroad tracks, stood a cottage for the grounds keeper.[15]

Stearns took pride in the estate and soon after occupying the mansion started work renovating and improving the building and grounds. He first planted an orchard, unfortunately too close to the edge of the property. The local children often stole the ripe fruit before the Stearns family harvested it. The Stearnses enjoyed the greenhouse George built. They ate green peas in early April, quite an achievement in snowbound Massachusetts, where farmers have always waited until that month or later to plant.[16]

Stearns called his elegant mansion "The Evergreens" (see illustration). Now, with a home of their own, the couple moved into the Medford social circle. As Stearns's wealth grew, his contacts in the Boston community increased. The couple's parties at The Evergreens attracted many interesting and famous people, from nationally known politicians to members of the Concord literati. Mary enjoyed entertaining prominent people, and she made a point of cultivating the friendships of those people whose opinions carried weight in the community or within their own circle of acquaintances. The large gatherings continued until the birth of the couple's third son, Carl, on June 26,

29

The Evergreens

1854. Until that time, on a regular basis, depending on the season, coaches or sleighs would glide up to the front door of the mansion from whose windows light blazed. There the Stearnses would meet the occupants. Mary would be attired in the latest fashion, and George, in a finely tailored, conservative suit, would stand by her side.[17]

Despite the growing demands on his time, Stearns continued to be active in the Unitarian Church. As a result, he found himself involved in an increasingly tense situation revolving around the ministry of his friend, Caleb Stetson.

Over the years Stearns watched his minister become entangled in two reform movements. In May 1845, Stetson joined other Unitarian clergymen at the Bullfinch Street Vestry in Boston to discuss, he recalled, "their duty in relation to slavery," that "unchristian and inhuman" institution. The same year, caught in the fever of reform, Stetson and his wife, to the consternation of Medford rum distillers, helped found the Female Union Temperance Society. The organization's charter pledged that its members would "abstain wholly from intoxicating drinks, to discountenance the use of them in the community and to purchase nothing whatever at stores or shops where they are known to be sold." Stetson's stand on both slavery and spirits offended, as any controversial position would, a number of parishioners. However, his increasing, uncompromising militancy on the subjects and the manner in which he addressed reform issues in his sermons caused some opposition among the parishioners. Many members of the church believed that he had gone too far and that his verbal attacks were directed at them. All "preferred that they should be let alone." Several parishioners, including Stearns, warned Stetson of the growing unrest created by his preaching reform in such a manner. A stubborn man, Stetson continued, as a member of the congregation said, to "preach upon them, [and] he prayed about them," until most of his parishioners decided that they "did not find his ministrations altogether edifying." As a result, a number of influential and wealthy church members decided to oust Stetson and find a minister not interested in worldly reform. Stearns, although, as a relative recalled, "never a believer in total abstinence" and a man who "always enjoyed his bottle of Haute Sauterne," believed he must support his embattled friend.[18]

While George was in the middle of this controversy, his brother, Henry, returned from a European tour "in a rather demoralized condition" and took sides against George with those wishing to depose Stetson. Henry's alcoholism was so pronounced that it seemed he would, said a friend of Mary's, always be a "chronic patient under the malady." At a parish meeting Henry aligned himself with the owners of Medford's three largest distilleries. Their agenda called for Stetson's resignation because he had become so caught up in reform that he no longer satisfied their own spiritual needs. Old Madam Stearns disregarded the pain from a broken leg and rallied many of the parish women in support of their minister. By a narrow margin; Stetson survived a vote calling for his resignation.[19]

The distillers and their wealthy allies refused to accept this defeat. Failing in their attempt to remove Stetson, they left the church and eventually established the Medford Episcopal Society. "The silks and velvets have-gone, Mrs. Mary," Lucy Osgood told George's wife, and "now you must don your finest apparel for the benefit of the faithful and my father's church." To keep the church solvent, Stearns purchased all the departed members' pews. But his efforts could not stem the continuing opposition to Stetson's manner of preaching. A residue of dislike and bitterness lingered among the remaining parishioners, for they blamed Stetson for the congregation's division.

Stearns saw only one solution to the problem. He persuaded Stetson to step down. On March 24, 1848, Stetson resigned and left Medford, believing Stearns had betrayed him. Lucy Osgood tried to defend Stearns's actions to the embittered minister. She wrote to Stetson, explaining that "George Stearns and Mary never harbored towards you an unkind or unfriendly thought," and further suggested that Stearns believed "he was conscientiously acting . . . for your benefit." Stetson, still suffering from the aftermath of a stroke he had suffered earlier, eventually made peace with Stearns and settled on a farm in Lexington, Massachusetts, occasionally preaching in local churches.[20]

Samuel Johnson, a recent graduate of the Harvard Divinity School, had taken Stetson's place during his illness and now filled in while the congregation decided on a replacement. Johnson's spirituality impressed the Stearns family. Other members of the congregation, however, were not happy with the young minister. Thomas Harlow thought Johnson's sermons were nothing but "dry pickings." Oblivious to the growing opposition, Stearns remained enthusiastic about Johnson and nominated him as pastor. In April 1849 the congregation voted on whether to hire him. The thirty-nine nays to thirty-four yeas finally put the question to rest. Someone suggested that they wait for the next "harvest" of Harvard Divinity graduates with the anticipation that the class would probably have some suitable candidates. Characteristically, the stubborn Stearns ignored the problems caused by the opposition and continued to seek Johnson's acceptance by the congregation. Stearns wrote to the minister, suggesting that if he wanted to "give comfort to the small but chosen flock," he could "wait until the tide turns again." But Johnson possessed more sense than his benefactor and declined to pursue the position. The clergyman did come away from the incident impressed with Stearns. Johnson remained a friend of the Medford businessman and years later remembered "the modesty of the man, his unready speech, his ready credence to first impressions of men, his frank disclosure of motive and plan, his absence of policy, his press of business and benevolent interest."[21]

After their reconciliation, Stetson continued to take an interest in Stearns and church activities in Medford. Thomas Harlow, a mutual acquaintance, said to Stetson, "We are more divided than ever . . . . I have no idea that two thirds of the parish could give a call to anyone." Still, the community continued to look for a suitable minister. After a number of names were proposed and rejected, Stearns suggested sixty-eight-year-old Reverend John Pierpont, a veteran of the pulpit. Pierpont, a long-time abolitionist, possessed a great deal more tact when preaching sermons than Stetson. In order to obtain the necessary votes, Stearns allowed a condition in the invitation to Pierpont. The church would ask the minister to settle initially for one year, and either party could break the contract with six months' notification. On June 25, 1849, after counting the votes, Stearns announced that Pierpont's invitation had passed by only one vote: yeas, twenty-five; nays, twenty-four. Two weeks later, a few members who were tired of the continual bickering joined those who opposed Pierpont's selection. They amended the minister's contract, stating that in light of the past conflict within the congregation, "it is regarded as inexpedient and hazardous to our best interests as a Christian church, for our pastor to preach any political abolition sermons." Stearns stalked out of the meeting, furious at the attempt to limit "the topics upon which the pastor is to be at liberty to treat in the pulpit." Never a good orator, Stearns decided to meet individually with the opposition leaders. The issue, he told them, did not revolve around abolition, but rather the right of a person to speak his conscience. On July 23, ashamed of their actions in denying freedom of speech to the pastor, the conservatives joined Stearns and unanimously rescinded the new contract.[22]

This victory turned out to be a hollow one for Stearns. Pierpont, in attempting to please everyone, satisfied no one. Stearns endured what many parishioners called Pierpont's "tame and monotonous" preaching for four years.

He complained to a friend that the congregation filled a "gagged pulpit" and wrote that as a parishioner, he would relinquish his say and object no longer, for he could "not hear Him." The word of God, he exclaimed, "shall not come to me through a keyhole." In 1854, in despair of a true church, Stearns told a friend, "I established in my home my altar of sacrifice." An acquaintance remarked that his defection mattered little, for "the churches could add nothing to such a man; the best they could do is to put others on the tracks that lead where he is found."[23]

Even though Stearns's search for a moral life had led him to the Liberty party in 1840, as a businessman, he was attracted to the Whig party's economic platform of internal improvement, a strong national bank, and a protective tariff. When Salmon P. Chase, a congressman and Whig from Ohio, defected to the new party, Stearns was impressed. Chase's appeal seemed to Stearns more rational than the Garrisonians' rejection of the Constitution as a document that supported the institution of slavery. Chase believed that the "slave power" must be defeated by the ballot and not by rejection or nullification of the Constitution. The Ohio congressman's economic arguments against slavery echoed Stearns's own ideas. He believed that slavery's demise would stimulate the growth of the entire nation. Writing to a Southerner, Stearns explained that more capital would flow to the South only if free labor existed. "Fair wages, good treatment and prompt pay," he declared, along with the "ballot box" and "good free schools," would provide "the security for capital investment" in the South as it did in the North.[24]

The Mexican War increased the animosity between northern and southern politicians. In August 1846, President James K. Polk, a Democrat, asked Congress for $2 million to purchase Mexican territory. David Wilmot, a northern Democrat, attempted to amend the proposed legislation to forbid the extension of slavery into any land purchased from Mexico. The Wilmot Proviso, as it became known, created a furor in Congress and added to the widening division within the Whig party. Earlier, in 1844, two political issues had created another breach, this time within the Whig Party in Massachusetts. That year the issue of the annexation of Texas brought forth a group of young men, Henry Wilson, Charles Francis Adams, Charles Allen, and Charles Sumner, who were impatient with the party leadership and vocal in their demands for a party platform denouncing slavery. Dissatisfied with their obscure position, these young men may have also wanted to expand their own political horizons by ousting the current party leaders. An event far from the shores of the Bay State brought this simmering revolt into the open. The Massachusetts legislature dispatched a prominent lawyer, Samuel Hoar, to Charleston, South Carolina, to persuade authorities to cease jailing free black Massachusetts sailors when their vessels docked. Charlestonians thought that this routine jailing was necessary in order to prevent northern blacks from inciting a slave rebellion. The violent reaction of the South Carolina citizenry astounded Hoar. Mobs of prominent citizens threatened the lawyer, and the South Carolina legislature voted his expulsion from the state. When word reached Boston of this perceived insult to the Commonwealth of Massachusetts, Stearns and others became more vocal in their demands that their political leadership take a stand against the root cause of this intolerable southern behavior. Hoar's son, Ebenezer Rockwell Hoar, a Whig congressman, urged Massachusetts men to support the "conscience" of the state, rather than the "cotton" interest. The "cotton" interest referred to the Whigs who were merchants and manufacturers with commercial and social contacts with slaveholding Southerners.[25]

As a manufacturer and a latent Whig, Stearns took a keen interest in the party squabbling. An admirer of Daniel Webster, senator from Massachusetts and Whig party leader in New England, Stearns placed an engraving of the senator over his fireplace. Stearns did not think the issue serious enough to demand a change in party leadership and remained on good terms with those in power. In October 1846, Rufus Choate, the Massachusetts Whig senator, came to Medford to speak, spending the night at The Evergreens. For several years it seemed to Stearns and to many others that the division amounted to nothing more than a family disagreement, because the "cotton" and "conscience" factions continued to stand together on many issues.

In 1848, Massachusetts Conscience Whigs met in Boston to decide strategy for the upcoming national Whig convention. Those present decided that if a proslavery candidate received the nomination, they would leave the party. On June 7, 1848, Whigs gathered in Philadelphia to determine a slate of candidates and to hammer out a party platform for the presidential campaign. A Southerner, Zachary Taylor, received the nomination, whereupon a Conscience Whig gained the floor and announced, "The Whig party is here and this day dissolved . . . ."[26]

Conscience Whigs returned to Massachusetts "willing to sacrifice their fortunes, court political suicide, and face social ostracism." They convened in Worcester, a city with strong antislavery sentiments. Stearns decided to take advantage of the half fare offered by the railroad and attend the meeting. He arrived in time to hear John Palfrey declare that "the insolent Slave Power has trampled Whig principles under foot." Palfrey's message and the appeals of other speakers moved Stearns, who found himself caught in the almost religious fervor in the crowd of five thousand. Stearns had no political ambitions and admitted to friends that he did not associate to any great extent with politicians, "but rather with those who represent the advanced moral sense of the country and earnestly labor for the good of our people, without hope of, or even desire for, office or other immediate reward." After the Worcester Convention Stearns would enter the antislavery debate, using his wealth to speak for him.[27]

Although many of those attending the Worcester Convention were abolitionists, there were others-the anti-extensionists-who merely did not wish to see slavery spread beyond its existing borders. Some of these people challenged slavery on moral grounds; others used racial, economic, and political reasons to argue against slavery. To those in sympathy with its purpose, the tone set by the convention appeared to be both antiextension and antislavery. The opposition press, however, lumped all the participants together and called the convention, "a gathering in which it is true, were some able men who have formally acted with the Whigs, but it was nothing but an abolitionist meeting drawing to itself malcontents of all classes." This statement annoyed Stearns. He certainly did not consider himself a malcontent, but rather a concerned citizen who saw southern slavery as a danger to democracy and free labor. Stearns came away from the convention thrilled with the wording of the final resolution, which read, "Massachusetts wears no chains, and spurns all bribes: Massachusetts goes now and will ever go for free soil and free men, for free lips, and a free press, for a free land and a free world."[28]

The convention gave birth to the Free Soil party, which nominated former President Martin Van Buren, a Democrat, for president and Charles Francis Adams, a Whig, as his running mate. Stearns did not appreciate the selection of the former president, for many spoke of him as a "northern man with southern principles." Stearns believed, as Charles Sumner did, that "men were less important than principles anyway." As a consequence, Stearns contributed liberally to the party's war chest and also canvassed his business associates for funds. His efforts were in vain, for in the 1848 national elections, the infant third party was defeated.[29]

Stearns took the defeat in stride. He surmised that the party might have only a slim chance of success, but at least it showed that an increasing number of his fellow citizens recognized the threat of slavery. The campaign fund-raising occupied only a fraction of his time. He continued to devote most of his energy to the operation of the ship chandlery and the linseed oil mill. The earlier enactment of the 1842 tariff had stimulated domestic oil production, and falling prices had caused profits from the Stearnses' mill to decline steadily. In 1847 the Stearns brothers suspended operations and then resumed production the following year. Their efforts to turn a greater profit caused increasing resentment among neighboring townspeople. First, the use of the live steam pipe running into the schoolyard created a furious debate at several town meetings, and then came complaints about air pollution. In order to save money, Stearns decided to use the cheaper bituminous, or soft, coal rather than the cleaner-burning anthracite. As a consequence, Medford town selectmen received a petition from 0 . Blake and others asking the board to take "proper measures to abate a nuisance at the Oil Mill of Mess. Stearns by the use of bituminous coals at said mill." On January 30, 1849, at eleven o'clock at night, before the board could take any action, the mill caught fire, probably from coal sparks, and burned to the ground, leaving only a tall, gaunt brick chimney standing amid the charred ruins. Boston newspapers reported an estimated loss of $12,000. Stearns held only $8,000 insurance with the Aetna and Protection Offices, Hartford, Connecticut. But over the years, the mill more than paid for itself. Stearns was even able to sell the fifty-foot-high detached chimney to James O. Curtis. Curtis awed the town by moving it in its upright position to his shipyard across the Branch canal. Stearns regretted the loss, but he had previously decided to take on a new manufacturing venture).[30]

At some time during late 1850 or early 1851, Stearns met George H. Lorin, owner of a lead pipe manufacturing mill producing lead paint and fabricated lead shot for the government. Unknown to the trusting Stearns, Lorin had stolen a recently patented lead pipe casting process that turned out superior pipe at less cost than his competitors. Lorin naturally hoped that no one would discover that he was using a process patented by the Tatham brothers, who operated mills on South Fifth Street in Philadelphia and on Beekman Street in New York. Word did reach the Tathams, however, and they threatened to sue. Lorin knew Stearns, by reputation, to be a sympathetic person and went to him for advice. After investigating the pipe, Stearns found it even better than his and the Boston Lead Company's product, for it could be bent at a greater angle than the pipe they both produced. Stearns suggested to his partner, Albert Fearing, that they help Lorin by taking over what George suspected would be a profitable business. But first Stearns needed to obtain the patent rights from the Tatham brothers)!

For many years, lead pipe had to be manufactured by hand. Workers first cut the lead into plates about six inches thick, flattened the plates between steel rollers, rolled the sheets into cylinders, and then soldered the seam to make a pipe. In 1779 an Englishman named Bramah revolutionized the industry with a new process for forming lead pipe by hydraulic pressure. The Tathams bought the patent for this process in 1840. After experimenting for almost ten years, the brothers improved the method so much, "in the genuine Yankee Way," as Stearns remarked, that they applied for and received their own patent on September 3, 1849.[32]

Their process required pouring molten lead into a heated cylindrical cavity in a cast-iron block and then using two to three hundred tons of hydraulic pressure to force the white hot substance out through an annular space that varied in size according to the diameter of the pipe required. Forming the base of the pipe was a steel rod attached to a piston that passed through the cavity containing the lead and out a hole at the top of the chamber. The steel rod rose in slow motion, forcing the molten lead out the chamber through the circular opening created by the die and the core. The formed pipe slowly cooled as it left the top of the machine and coiled around a large drum. The process was continuous: the piston rose into the chamber containing melted lead and then descended with the die in the piston as the core thrust up through it from the bottom of the chamber.[33]

Lead pipe was much in demand as a household product because it could be bent to any angle required. When water inside a lead pipe froze, a common occurrence in poorly heated nineteenth-century homes, the damage could be repaired without difficulty. Using lead pipe for domestic purposes did have one significant drawback. Many informed people, including Stearns, knew that as water collected in the pipe lead entered it. The only solution was to run the water for several minutes prior to its use for drinking or cooking. Constant controversy raged over the use of lead pipes. Dr. Dana of Lowell, Massachusetts, came out against the use of the pipe for domestic purposes. The Boston *Daily Evening Transcript* sarcastically responded to his plea by asking, "Will the learned Doctor let us know what he proposed as a substitute? Glass is too dear and liable to be broken." A board of consulting physicians also reported on the dangers, suggested impractical alternatives, and admitted "the imperfection of accurate knowledge on this subject." The threat of lead poisoning remained, but so did the demand for pipes in the ever growing cities of the Northeast.[34]

Arriving in New York City, Stearns made his way to the Tatham brothers' counting house at 22 Beekman Street, on the Lower East Side of Manhattan. There he met with William and Benjamin Tatham. William, the younger brother, supervised the mills, while Benjamin, who Stearns thought was "a very shrewd Quaker," managed the accounts. Both men appreciated George Stearns's honesty. Benjamin invited the Boston merchant to stay at his home at 36 Stuyvesant Street. The following day the brothers worked out a reasonable agreement with Stearns.[35]

Excited and determined to do well in this new business venture, Stearns returned to Boston. He asked Fearing to keep Lorin on as an agent because no one else had the expertise to run the mill in Charlestown. Lorin left Boston soon afterward. Fearing approved Stearns's alternate proposal that he, Stearns, supervise the mill operation and said, "I think, Stearns, you will have to take this new business; if you cannot make a success of it, nobody can."[36]

For a while, Stearns was unable to achieve a good quality product. He had to rework much of the pipe produced because of imperfections, most likely variations in the thickness of the wall. Stearns's greatest problems were finding skilled workers, training foremen, and organizing an effective production team. Stearns remarked that the process of teaching people to produce pipe to exacting standards was similar to "training men to watchmaking," for the timing was crucial. Because he kept hiring and firing foremen, Stearns himself had to oversee production much of the time. He practically lived at the mill, sometimes going home at twelve or one o'clock in the morning. These long hours eventually strained his marriage. Mary stayed up at night, waiting for him to return. She cried constantly and told him that she and the children would "rather live in a cottage" than have him "continue in this mode of life."[37]

Stearns, too, was discouraged. He had taken a chance and dissolved his partnership with Fearing, receiving the mill as his share of the capital. Now his funds were dangerously low. Fortunately, he found a foreman, an Englishman by the name of York, to relieve him of the need to supervise the process directly. Hiring York left Stearns free to exercise his "decided talent for mechanics" and to arrange the equipment in his small one-and-a-half-story building in a "most compact and economical manner." Contemporaries claimed that the "perfection of the work and integrity of his methods soon placed him at the head of that business in New England." His market extended from western Massachusetts to northern New England, but received most orders from the Boston area.[38]

Stearns enjoyed a great sense of satisfaction at this point in his life. He gained repute in Massachusetts business circles, and his new income allowed for a comfortable life-style. His childhood experience and temperament made him an outsider, a person who was most comfortable going it alone. He relished independence. Perhaps unconsciously, in order to hide his shyness and inability to relax completely with others, he took on very formal manners. His slowness of speech compensated for a slight stutter, which disappeared when he became angry. Before his income had increased, he and his family were the poor relations. Now he no longer required capital from affluent relatives. With wealth and status in the business world, he explained to his son, equality was a "Jeffersonian fiction" that existed only on the frontier. Stearns believed that the tradesmen he dealt with preferred his formal and "dignified manners."[39]

In 1852, after incorporating the lead business, he opened a counting house at 23 Water Street in Boston. This move left the mill operation entirely in York's hands. Stearns now made numerous business trips to New York to consult with the Tathams and to act as his own agent in the purchase of lead ingots. He kept busy investing money in other businesses, such as the Boston and Lowell Railroad, whose tracks bordered his property in Medford. Regardless of Stearns's investment portfolio, he always kept one half his profits in gold.[40]

Mary Stearns enjoyed the luxuries her husband's profits brought her, but she disliked being thought of as a lead pipe manufacturer's wife. She believed it was not "a fine-sounding profession" and said as much to her aunt, Lydia Maria Child. She and "Aunt Maria" maintained a close relationship. When Mary was a child Maria had lived with the Prestons. Now apart, the two women corresponded frequently, although Mary was more diligent in writing than was her aunt. Aunt Maria apologized for this lapse, calling herself a "very negligent good for nothing relative," who must appear to her favorite niece as an "ungracious wretch." But the problem was understandable, for Aunt Maria happened to be an extremely active woman.[41]

Born in 1801, Lydia Maria Child was the youngest of five children. Her father, David Francis, moved his family to Medford a year before her birth. Francis was a baker, and his "Medford crackers" were extremely popular both in the United States and in Europe. Because his tasty crackers were much in demand, Francis retired at age fifty with cash assets worth more than $50,000. His daughter, Lydia Maria, according to those who knew her, was a "bright, impulsive warm-hearted and self-willed" child. These character traits remained with her throughout life. An early test of Lydia Maria's character came when her mother died in 1813. Maria's older sister cared for her until she married Warren Preston (Mary Stearns's father) and moved to Norridgewock, Maine. Francis then tried to keep up with his precocious daughter. Maria's elder brother, a student at Harvard College, sparked her interest in literature. This alarmed Maria's father. He sent her off to Maine to help her sister with a brood of children, one of whom was Mary. In later years, Maria could remember Mary, with her "little full moon face," sitting on her lap before bedtime as she listened to stories and asked for "more adin Aunt Maria." In her free time as a young woman, Maria read voraciously, whisking through *Paradise Lost* and *Decline and Fall of the Roman Empire*.[42]

Eventually, Maria returned to Medford to live with her older brother, Converse Francis, now a minister of the First Church of Watertown. In 1824 Maria published her first novel, *Hobmok*; soon after came other works, including children's books. On October 19, 1828, she married a Boston lawyer and state representative, David Lee Child. After the marriage, Child gave up his practice and turned to literature, editing the *Massachusetts Journal*. An ardent abolitionist, Child attacked the institution of slavery in a series of well-written open letters published in local papers. His wife shared his attitude toward slavery, for Maria had grown up in a family concerned with the plight of slaves in the South. In 1833 she published her famous pamphlet, "An Appeal in Behalf of That Class of Americans Called Africans." In the preface, Maria acknowledged the risks of the stand she had taken: "I am fully aware of the unpopularity of the task I have undertaken, but though I expect ridicule and censure, I cannot fear them."[43]

Lydia Maria Child did, however, fear Madam Stearns, who cared little for abolitionists. For several years, Aunt Maria edited the *National Antislavery Standard* in New York City. In 1849, she returned to Massachusetts to settle in Wayland at the home of her father-in-law. She occasionally visited her niece Mary in Medford. During one visit, Madam Stearns appeared and verbally attacked Maria Child. After the old woman had left, Maria remarked to George and Mary that she had never, in all her experience with hecklers at lectures, found it so difficult to prevent herself from losing her temper.

Sometime after Aunt Maria's departure, on November 21, 1850, Medford suffered, according to newspaper accounts, its "greatest and most distressing conflagration." Every building on Main Street and the surrounding neighborhood went up in flames, a total of over thirty-six buildings. Stearns happened to be at home that evening. He and Mr. Collins, his chief clerk, were discussing the account ledger when they heard fire bells ringing and saw flames rising from Main Street. Both men rushed to the scene and, as Frank Stearns remarked, "worked most of the night like common firemen." Many fire engines could not cross the Mystic Bridge because the west end was blocked by the fire. Fortunately for the fire fighters, other engines from towns to the south and west arrived and finally brought the blaze under control. Stearns believed that the losses incurred fell on those who could ill afford them. So he contributed to a general relief fund, which collected more than $1,335, and gave loans for rebuilding to men he could trust to repay.[44]

The following year, Medford suffered another disaster. Friday, August 22, 1851, was a lazy summer day, hot, humid, and oppressive. Little movement could be seen on the dusty streets, and most people were indoors. Toward late afternoon, the air became very still, and animals shifted nervously. At 5:15 P.M., Stearns returned from Boston and went to check on some recently planted fruit trees. The sun suddenly disappeared, causing him to glance toward the west. There he saw a thousand-foot~high funnel cloud racing down the southern slope of Arlington Heights. At that instant, as he recalled, its lower part, "writhing about like the trunk of an elephant," looked as if it would go right through his home. He ran to get Mary, who had also seen the inverted cone and had started searching frantically for the children. The destructive funnel suddenly veered to the northwest. The eighty-yard-wide swath of destruction raced up High Street and into West Medford, passing within two hundred yards of Madam Stearns's home. The wind caused considerable damage, lifting up a freight car and depositing it sixty feet away and demolishing homes and barns all across town. Rumors claimed that one elderly woman had been swept up and gently set down in a meadow outside town. After the storm passed, Stearns could see that his mother's home was still standing. Given her nature, however, he thought it best to check on her anyway. Sure enough, she met him and said that she would have "felt aggrieved" if he failed to check on her condition.[45]

At age sixty, the woman "felt her age heavily," relatives recalled. She had mentally survived the early deaths of both her husband and her daughter only to face the breakdown of her younger and favored son, Henry. His drinking problem had become so bad that in 1851 George committed him to an asylum in Somerville, where he languished for eight years. Madam Stearns became gloomy and taciturn after Henry was committed. George did everything he could to cheer his mother up; he even purchased a white horse, named Dolly, for her carriage, and drove her about whenever he could. Her depression was compounded by the fact she never fully recovered from the fall several years earlier in which she had broken a leg. According to Lucy Osgood the bone in her leg had been diseased for a long time and failed to knit properly. At times, Madam Stearns suffered dreadfully. Doctors proposed amputation, but George decided against it. In 1852 she hosted her last Thanksgiving dinner, which she cooked to perfection. That following spring, after an extremely painful winter, she died and was buried alongside her husband in the Old Medford Cemetery.[46]

After his mother's death, Stearns found a distraction in the visit to the United States by Hungarian patriot Louis Kossuth. For several years, Americans had followed his struggle against the Austrians. Abolitionists saw Kossuth as a representative of an enslaved and oppressed people. They were fearful, however, that he would ignore the plight of African-Americans in bondage in order to curry favor with politicians in southern-dominated Washington. Henry C. Wright, a noted abolitionist, wrote to a friend explaining that the proslavery administration would "avail themselves of his worldwide fame and influence to prop up American Slavery." Kossuth, understandably more concerned with his cause than with American domestic politics, attempted to sidestep the issue. When he did so, he brought down the Garrisonians' wrath. Garrison wrote a biting letter to the Hungarian patriot, reminding him that human rights were "not Hungarian, but universal," and that the United States was "too full of compromises and trimmers to need your presence."[47]

Never comfortable with Garrison or his radical philosophy, Stearns preferred to accept Kossuth for what he was, a patriot. In June 1852, George and Mary had the opportunity to meet him at a reception in Boston and came away favorably impressed. Stearns's friends often said he had the weakness of not looking beneath the surface to grasp the true character of many of the people he came in contact with. They claimed that because the Boston merchant was open and honest, he assumed people were that way with him. In this sense he could be called innocent and even perhaps gullible. Like other prominent men in Boston, Stearns purchased a substantial number of $10 certificates from Kossuth redeemable five years after Hungary's independence. In a letter to the couple, Kossuth expressed his thanks for the material aid given to him by the Stearnses in "such a kind, such affectionate manner."[48]

For a time, the Stearns family entertained and financially supported a number of Hungarian exiles. Three became constant visitors. The Reverend Gideon Achs, Captain Kinizsy, and a pianist named Zerdahelyi met regularly at The Evergreens. After dinner, over cigars, the men discussed politics, Hungarian history, and European affairs. Inevitably, Zerdahelyi played the piano. Stearns, who had a fondness for music, enjoyed this entertainment very much. Even when the group broke up and Kossuth left the country, Stearns continued to help the refugees who stayed in the United States. Among those he befriended were relatives of Kossuth, Madam Zulavsky and her three sons, for whom Stearns personally located and purchased a farm in Orange County, New Jersey. As late as 1858 Stearns gave one son a position in his counting room. Unfortunately, the young man stole money and when confronted admitted the theft, stating that his $800 yearly salary did not allow him to live like a gentleman. Stearns's temper flared and he dismissed the young Zulavsky. But Stearns was also forgiving, for several years later he obtained a commission for Zulavsky in a Kansas regiment, only to hear that the man later robbed an express office.[49]

Mary did not always think well of the objects of her husband's charity. While Aunt Maria was in New York, a friend's son, John Hopper, married the daughter of a man who made his fortune in the slave trade. The young man's father, Isaac T. Hopper, a Quaker and abolitionist, disowned him. Maria went to see Stearns about a position for the son. Mary made it clear that she did not care for the couple, and Stearns did not give young Hopper a job. He did, however, set him up as an agent for the New England Life Insurance Company.[50]

By the mid 1850s, Stearns maintained a comfortable status within his society. He had a reputation as an honest, hardworking, and concerned manufacturer. His business and social contacts were widening as he began to take a greater interest in politics and the plight of slaves. Little did George realize that he was moving with events that were to propel him toward taking a dangerous and unpopular public stand against the institution of slavery.

NOTES

1. Stearns, *Life*, p.36.
2. George L. Stearns to Reverend R.C. Waterston, November 10, 1842, Manuscripts, New York Historical Society, New York, New York (hereafter cited as Stearns MSS, NYHS).
3. Stearns, *Life*, p. 42.
4. Commonwealth of Massachusetts, Voting Records of Massachusetts by Town (1840); Stearns, *Life*, pp. 41-42.
5. Stearns, *Life*, p. 42.
6. Ibid., p. 36.
7. Wilson and Fiske, Appleton's, 4:547. Thomas Starr King to Randolph Ryder, June 4, 1849, quoted in Charles W. Wendte, *Thomas Starr King: Patriot and Preacher* (Boston: Beacon Press, 1921), pp. 23-24.
8. Stearns, *Life*, p.47.
9. Ibid.
10. Charles Henry Preston, "Descendants of Roger Preston of Ipswich and Salem Village," *Essex Institute Historical Collection* 65 (1929) :153.
11. Ibid., 63 (1927):175; Anna D. Hallowell, "Lydia Maria Child, *MHR* 3 (July 1900):97.
12. Caleb Stetson to Mary Elizabeth Preston, May 1843, quoted in Stearns, *Life*, pp. 47-48; George L. Stearns to Mary Elizabeth Preston, May 17, 1843, quoted in Stearns, *Life*, pp.48-49.
13. George Lindsey Stearns to Charles E. Heller, July 31, 1973, a letter from George Luther Stearns's grandson in the possession of the author; Stearns, *Life*, p. 51.
14. J. C. Furness, *The Road* to Harpers Ferry (New York: William Sloane Associates, 1959), p. 364; George L. Stearns and William A. Rhea, March 13 1845, file 45846, Middlesex County Registry of Deeds, Middlesex County Court House, Cambridge, Massachusetts.
15. The description of the estate is from a composite drawing done in 1899 and given to the author by George Lindsey Stearns; Stearns to Heller, July 31, 1973.
16. Harry Stearns to George L. Stearns, April 21, 1863, Stearns Manuscripts, Massachusetts Historical Society (hereafter cited as Stearns MSS, MHS).
17. Stearns to Heller, July 31, 1973; Sidney H. Morse, "An Anti-Slavery Hero," *The New England Magazine*, March 1891, p. 488. A number of letters concerning the Stearns family's relationship with the Concord literati appear in Ralph L. Rush, ed., *The Letters of Ralph Waldo Emerson*, vols. 4-6, New York: Columbia

University Press, 1939; and Richard L. Herrenstadt, ed., *The Letters of A. Bronson Alcott* (Ames: Iowa State University Press, 1969).

18. "Resolves," Samuel J. May Papers, vol. 1, May 29, 1845, Boston Public Library; Helen Tilden Wilde, "Female Union Temperance Society," *MHR* 12 (October 1906): 90; Henry C. De Long, "The First Parish in Medford," *MHR* 12 (October 1906): 78; Stearns, *Life*, p. 61.

19. Stearns, *Life*, pp. 61-62. Lucy Osgood to Caleb Stetson, November 7, 1849, Caleb Stetson Manuscripts, Massachusetts Historical Society (hereafter cited as Stetson MSS).

20. Stearns, *Life*, p. 63; Lucy Osgood to Caleb Stetson, March 15, 1850, Stetson MSS.

21. Thomas Harlow to Caleb Stetson, April 25, 1849, Stetson MSS; George L. Stearns to Samuel Johnson, November 28, 1848, quoted in Stearns, *Life*, pp. 63-64 (the letter was created from memory by Stearns's son Frank, and he has the date and the vote incorrect; Brooks and Usher, p. 217, confirms Harlow's letter); Samuel Johnson, "George L. Stearns," *The Radical*, April 1867, p. 612.

22. Harlow to Stetson, April 25, 1849, Stetson MSS.

23. Stearns to Johnson, November 28, 1848; De Long, "The First Parish," pp. 79-80; Stearns, *Life*, pp. 64-65; Johnson, "Stearns," p. 64.

24. George L. Stearns to E. C. Cabell, September 29, 1865, quoted in *The Right Way*, November 25, 1865.

25. Eric Foner, *Free Soil, Free Labor, Free Men* {New York: Oxford University Press, 1970), p. 78; Henry Wilson, *Rise and Fall of the Slave Power in America*, 3 vols. (Boston: Houghton Mifflin, 1872); *The Boston Commonwealth*, October 28, 1865.

26. Thomas H. O'Conner, *Lords of the Loom* (New York: Charles Scribner's Sons, 1968), pp. 64-65.

27. David Donald, *Charles Sumner and the Coming of the Civil War* (New York: Alfred A. Knopf, 1967), p. 161; Boston Whig, April 29, 1848; Frank Otto Gatell, "Conscience and Judgement, the Bolt of the Massachusetts Conscience Whigs," The Historian 21 (1958): 21; George L. Stearns to Andrew Johnson, October 8, 1865, Andrew Johnson Manuscripts, Library of Congress.

28. Boston Whig, June 10, 1848; Kinley J. Brauer, *Cotton Versus Conscience* (Lexington: University of Kentucky Press, 1967), pp. 3--4.

29. Donald, *Sumner*, p. 167.

30. Medford, Massachusetts, Selectmen's Records, 4:122, quoted in *MHR* 10 (April 1907):55; Boston Post, February 1, 1849; "The Towers of Medford," pp. 10-11.

31. Stearns, *Life*, pp. 53-54; Edwin T. Freedley, *Philadelphia and Its Manufacturers* (Philadelphia: Young, 1867), pp. 421, 423.

32. Albert S. Bolles, *Industrial History of the United States*, 3rd ed. (1881; reprint, New York: Augustus M. Kelly, 1966), p. 360; U.S. Patent Office, W. P. Tatham, "Making Lead Pipe," September 3, 1850, file 7,624.

33. Ibid.

34. Boston *Daily Evening Transcript*, March 16 and 19, 1848.

35. *National Cyclopedia of American Biography*, 1906 ed., s.v. "William Penn Tatham"; Trow's New York City Directory, 1863-1864 ed., s.v. "Benjamin Tatham"; Stearns, *Life*, p. 57.

36. Stearns, *Life*, pp. 53, 57.

37. Ibid., p. 54.

38. Ibid., p. 55. Brooks and Usher, *Medford*, p. 462.

39. Ibid., p. 57.

40. George L. Stearns, "Last Will and Testament," 1867, file 42218, Middlesex County Court House, Cambridge, Massachusetts (George Stearns's will was not itemized; he left everything to his wife, Mary); Mary E. Stearns, "Last Will and Testament," December 1901, file 57312, Middlesex County Court House, Cambridge, Massachusetts (cash assets totaled $161,643.24).

41. Stearns, *Life*, p. 56; Lydia Maria Child to Mary E. Stearns, May 13, 1850, Lydia Maria Child Manuscripts, University of Massachusetts/Amherst (hereafter cited as Child MSS).

42. Hallowell, "Lydia Maria Child," p. 90; Child to Stearns, May 13, 1850.

43. Hallowell, "Lydia Maria Child," p. 106.

44. Brooks and Usher, Medford, p. 345; *Stearns*, Life, p. 70.

45. "The Tornado of 1851," MHR 24 (June 1926):32-35; Brooks and Usher, *Medford*, pp. 343, 344: Stearns, *Life*, pp. 66-68.

46. Emily Porter to Caleb Stetson, October 22, 1849, Stetson MSS; Stearns, *Life*, p. 69; Lucy Osgood to Caleb Stetson, April14, 1852, Stetson MSS.

47. Allan Nevins, A House Dividing, 1852-1857, vol. 2 of *Ordeal of the Union*, (New York: Charles Scribner's Sons, 1947), p. 24; letters of Louis Kossuth concerning freedom and slavery in the United States quoted in Wendell Phillips Garrison and Francis Jackson Garrison, *William Lloyd Garrison* (Boston: Houghton Mifflin, 1894), 3:354.

48. Morse, "An Anti-Slavery Hero," p. 488; Louis Kossuth to Mr. George L. Stearns and Lady, June 17 1852, quoted in Stearns, *Life*, p. 72.

49. Stearns, *Life*, p. 75.

50. Lydia Maria Child to Mary E. Stearns, July 17, 1851, Child MSS.

3

Personal Growth, National Collapse

He belonged to a class of men who are called forth by national emergencies.

— Frank Stearns

For Stearns's society the decade of the 1850s began with a political crisis that was seemingly resolved and yet flared anew a scant four years later. Slavery was at the root of the problem, and many Americans, including George Stearns, saw the issue as a challenge to the basic tenets of democracy. Freedom for African-Americans was not the only issue at stake: so was the survival of democratic institutions in the United States.[1]

The most recent crisis had its roots in the war with Mexico. During the war the issue of slavery confronted the federal government. A young Democrat from Pennsylvania, David Wilmot, moved in the House of Representatives to amend an appropriations bill to read that slavery would be forbidden in all territory wrested from Mexico. The amendment passed, but the appropriations bill died when the 1846 session of Congress adjourned. Several years later, during the 1848 presidential campaign, both Whigs and Democrats sought to defuse the slavery issue by simply ignoring it. When political leaders did so, antislavery and antiextension men in both parties united with Liberty party supporters to form the Free Soil party.

When the call came for a convention to launch the new political party, Stearns attended a meeting called at Worcester, Massachusetts. He left the convention not completely convinced of the new party's sincerity. While the Liberty party, he believed, was "founded wholly on principle," the Free Soil movement, so he thought, originated as did most other parties, with the "union of self-interest with some political theory." How Stearns cast his vote in the election is unknown, but his later actions in conjunction with Free Soilers make it clear that they eventually captured his support. The Free Soilers obtained sufficient dissident Democratic votes to divide that party and thus ensure Whig contender Zachary Taylor's election.[2] The new president immediately faced the sensitive issue of territorial organization and statehood for the conquered Mexican provinces. The discovery of gold in California and the attending surge in population intensified the issue. Stearns saw the new source of wealth as the beginning of an unusual chain of events in the history of America. He believed society had begun to drift, lacking national purpose and direction, partly because of the prosperity the gold was bringing. In December 1849, President Taylor presented legislation that requested the admission of California as a free

state, yet allowed its citizens the right to determine, after admission, whether to become a slave state or to remain free.[3]

Daniel Webster supported fellow senator Henry Clay in the latter's efforts to reach a compromise on the slavery issue in the territories wrested from Mexico. In his famous speech on March 7, 1850, Webster attacked abolitionists and Free Soilers for causing dissension. The speech annoyed Stearns. This revelation of Webster's changing political philosophy was a surprise to the staid businessman. He had, on occasion, heard of the dark side of the senator's character, but had refused to believe the gossip. Stearns was especially shocked by rumors that the man ignored his debts. After all, "a man of his income," said the manufacturer, "ought to have been able to live within it." As the senator lost favor in his eyes, Stearns enjoyed repeating stories about what he called Webster's "impecuniosity."[4]

Stearns paid close attention to the arguments of William H. Seward, the senator from New York, who responded to Webster and compromise legislation proposed by Clay. Four days after Webster's March 7 speech, Seward declared that all "legislative compromise led to the surrender of the exercise of judgement and conscience on distinct and separate questions at distinct and separate times." Seward withheld his most biting argument on what many in the North considered the most odious piece of proposed legislation, the Fugitive Slave Law's strengthening. Seward echoed Stearns's sentiments when he declared the measure "unjust, unconstitutional, and immoral; and thus, while patriotism withholds its approbation the conscience of our people condemns it."[5]

The Fugitive Slave Law deeply concerned George Stearns. He saw the legislation, which denied an accused fugitive a jury trial, as a subversion of democracy's basic tenets, if not because the Constitution required due process of law for all men, then on technical grounds. If slaves were property, as Southerners claimed, common lawsuits involving property valued at $20 or more required a jury trial. Furthermore, the law did not require that a judge issue the order to send an African-American back into bondage; an appearance before a federal commissioner was enough to turn the fugitive over to his accuser. To make matters worse, the commissioner received twice as much money if the accused was returned to the claimant. The final insult, as Stearns saw it, rested in the stipulation that any federal marshal, deputy, or citizen who failed to assist in enforcing the law could be subject to a fine of $1,000.

Stearns, a cautious and respectful citizen, believed strongly enough about the law's injustice to express a willingness to violate it should the occasion arise. The full impact of the measure struck the wealthy manufacturer, his son Frank recalled, "like the blow of an assailant" and caused Stearns to buy a revolver. He vowed to his family that no fugitive slave who sought refuge at The Evergreens would be returned to slavery. From this time forward, Frank declared, his father's "political activity never ceased." Although for now he merely played a shadow role in the struggle to halt the spread of slavery, later events caused him to assume an active part in the struggle against the institution.6

The Fugitive Slave Law became the signal for general unrest throughout the nation. This legislation drove Stearns and others into an acceptance of resistance to the law as justifiable and morally right. When Stearns bought the revolver, his action echoed Reverend Theodore Parker's comment in a sermon given at the Music Hall in Boston, on the "New Crime Against Humanity." In the unusually strong sermon Parker declared that when politicians "enacted wickedness into a law which treads down the inalienable rights of man to such a degree as this, then I know no ruler but God nor law but natural justice . .

. ." Stearns believed that the slavery question would eventually be "settled by the Eternal Laws of God and as he directed Man will obey." When he referred to the "Laws of God," Stearns did not "mean those only to be found within the covers of the Bible." Reacting to the law as he did was putting into action words he expressed as Sunday School Superintendent, that Christian virtues should be applied to "every day life" and that people "must enforce ... precepts" they believe in by example.[7]

A Boston committee, whose members also believed that they must enforce precepts they believed in, swore to protect fugitive slaves who reached Boston. Stearns knew of the committee and its members: Henry Bowditch, Ellis Gray Lorin, Samuel May, Wendell Phillips, Francis Jackson, Samuel Gridley Howe, Thomas Wentworth Higginson, and two African-Americans, Lewis Hayden and Frederick Douglass. In October 1850, a few short months after the Fugitive Slave Law's passage, the committee rescued a slave couple, Ellen and William Craft. In February 1851, African-Americans in Boston, with the help of this committee, aided the escape of a slave named Shadrack (Fred Wilkins).

These rescues prompted increased vigilance by federal authorities in Boston. Stearns never joined or outwardly supported the committee's actions, but he had vowed that "no fugitive negro should be taken" who sought refuge with his family. Shortly after the Shadrack rescue, the Medford manufacturer had an opportunity to prove his sincerity.[8]

On the morning of April 4, 1852, Stearns drove into Boston and on the way to his counting room passed the city courthouse. When he drew up in the carriage there were a number of men guarding the building. To his amazement, iron chains were strung around the building. A bystander explained that a fugitive slave youth, Thomas Sims, had been seized that previous night. Angered by the news, Stearns proceeded down the narrow streets to his counting room. He began his normal routine with thoughts of Sims when a ship's captain entered the establishment. The man told Stearns he had a stowaway slave on board his ship and wanted no part in returning the fugitive to bondage. Stearns agreed to help. At eight that evening, the captain gave the crew shore leave. He then took the slave to the counting room, where Stearns had food, money, and clothing ready. Stearns drove the man to the railway station, where he boarded a train headed north to freedom in Canada. Sims, not as fortunate, was returned to slavery.[9]

Several years later, the master of a plantation near Snow Hill, Alabama, took his jockey, a slave named William Talbot, to Philadelphia. During the

51

races, Talbot managed to slip away. He found a collier captain in need of a deckhand and sailed to Boston. After the ship docked, Talbot made his way to the city's African-American section on Joy Street. Apparently fearing for the slave's safety, the free blacks then directed Talbot to the Stearns estate in Medford. Arriving late at night, the man sought cover in the Stearnses' barn, where George found him asleep the next morning.

The Stearnses sheltered him four or five weeks waiting for the vigilance to lessen. When strangers appeared, Talbot hid beneath a bathroom floor. During the time he spent with them, Stearns and his family became attached to the man. Stearns made no secret of the fact that Talbot was staying on his property. Theodore Parker went out to visit Talbot and referred to him in a sermon on "Conscience," and Medford held two public meetings to discuss the fugitive. Unsubstantiated rumors, that the estate had secret tunnels and that it was a station on the underground railroad, persisted around Boston. When the Stearnses were away, several deputy federal marshals appeared at The Evergreens, prowled about the grounds, and peered into the windows of the mansion, while poor Talbot lay cramped beneath the bathroom flooring. Stearns's groundkeeper confronted the intruders; according to Frank, the man was "fortunately not an Irishman but a Scotchman who showed them a bold front and gave them biting replies to their questions." Finally, the pair of slave catchers left the estate. After returning home and learning of the incident, Stearns realized that Talbot's freedom was in jeopardy. That evening Stearns drove the man to Lowell and placed him on a train to Montreal.[10]

Another antislavery advocate acquainted with Stearns was Charles Sumner. Sumner, a young lawyer with social connections, successfully challenged the Massachusetts Whig leadership and became a Conscience Whig leader. Stearns probably first met Sumner in 1848 at the Free Soil Convention in Worcester. Several months later, Stearns needed a lawyer to handle a business dispute and asked Sumner for his help because of the young man's reputation as, according to Stearns, "the whitest lawyer in Boston, a man for whom money had no value." After explaining the legal dispute, Stearns was impressed with the lawyer's response. Sumner told the businessman to settle out of court: "I advise all my clients not to go to law. "[11]

Stearns followed the young lawyer's career with interest. Daniel Webster's fall from grace in Massachusetts helped advance Sumner's political ambitions. When Webster joined Millard Fillmore's cabinet, his vacant Senate seat became a prize Massachusetts Free Soilers hoped to capture. Henry Wilson, the other senator from the Bay State, formed a coalition of Democrats and Free Soilers in an attempt to place Sumner in the seat. On November 6, 1850, Stearns attended a political rally at Faneuil Hall to ratify the nominations of Free Soil candidates. By this time, Wilson, with Sumner's approval, struck a bargain with the Democratic leadership: Free Soilers would support Democratic state office seekers, and they, in turn, would help obtain the Senate seat for Sumner.[12]

Totally unaware of this arrangement, the politically naive Stearns thought that Sumner's November speech at the Faneuil Hall rally won the seat. However, even Stearns's friends believed that before this time, the manufacturer encouraged Sumner to prepare to replace Webster, should the opportunity arise. Certainly, the speech against the despised Fugitive Slave Law helped, but so had the indication that he favored a coalition of Free Soilers and Democrats. Stearns, ever trusting, boasted that he was "one of the first, if not the very first" to tell Sumner of his impending nomination by the state legislature. George told his family of Sumner's surprise at the news: "What are you talking about, Mr. Stearns? Such an idea never entered my head. I am totally unfit for politics by taste, education and all my instincts." According to his biographer, Sumner was a far better politician than even his friends, including Stearns, believed, for "he knew the advantages of rowing toward his objective with muffled oars."[13]

George Stearns's personal ethics would not always allow him to be as circumspect as Sumner, so he continued to act on his convictions. Still, while maintaining an interest in national affairs, Stearns continued to seek ways to secure additional wealth. An indication of his success was moving the counting room from Water to Milk Street, a more prestigious location. Shortly after, agents of a New York based lead pipe concern attempted to cut into the wealth Stearns was so intent on accumulating. Most businessmen of the period agreed upon and maintained a fair price for their products in order to ensure a reasonable return. The New Yorkers began to sell their products below the market prices that Stearns and his local rival, the Boston Lead Company, maintained and quietly contacted Stearns's customers in an attempt to drive him out of business. Fortunately, several plumbers told Stearns about the prices the out-of-town agents were offering. Although Stearns, with his quick temper, became indignant at this behavior, his anger was short-lived-he merely told Mr. Perkins, his chief clerk, to reduce the price of finished lead pipe to within a half cent of pig lead, the raw material from which the product was made.[14]

Stearns stubbornly watched his product being sold at a loss. Clerks in the Boston counting room at 129 Milk Street posted first one $5,000 loss and then another. The New York agents, Stearns told Mary, "came to him on their knees" to beg for a restoration of the old prices. Without hesitation he agreed, but told them, "the moment I hear of your underselling me, down they will go again." Because the agents could not compete and their product had no advantage over his, they closed their office and returned to New York.[15]

Stearns never faced such a challenge again, and he continued to maintain control over his business territory while coexisting with Mr. Chadwick, owner of the Boston Lead Company. According to his contemporaries, because Stearns "had great executive skill, a clear method, and a just attention to all the details of the task at hand," the business could practically run itself. Over the years, he expanded his product line. He sold lead shot to the government situated as he was close to the Charlestown Navy Yard, and most certainly marketed lead ballast for the ships under construction. He also manufactured white lead paint. Finally, perhaps because the Tatham patent for lead pipe called for a use and a knowledge of hydraulics, Stearns fabricated and began to sell hydraulic "rams."[16]

The profits of Stearns and Company showed George to be "a man with boundless energy and with a mind never at rest." A friend of Stearns once said, "Wealth honorably earned seemed to flow into his hands by natural attraction." The desire to accumulate wealth was not the only thing that motivated Stearns, for his ambition also drove him to establish his family in the new social hierarchy of Massachusetts. He may have come to realize that the social order was changing, as those segments of society once in power were losing control over events. This realization partially accounted for his support of Charles Sumner, who challenged the established Whig aristocracy. By this time, however, business success was not, as it once had been, the sole criterion for admission to the upper social stratum. Now rising businessmen apparently had to add political and cultural activities to their financial success in order to gain acceptance into the upper classes. Stearns's striving for wealth was coupled with an increasing interest in politics and reform. Stearns's personality was a blend of new and old. Although he maintained old values that were, as his son said, "not corrupted by the Jeffersonian fiction of equality," he was very much in tune with the new social force of monied and paternal manufacturing interests.[17]

Devoted to expanding his business and keenly aware of economic shifts, George Stearns appeared to have a special ability to make the right decision at the crucial moment. His linseed oil mill went into production at the same time the shipbuilding boom began to peak, and he left this industry just before its decline in Medford. Stearns then entered the ship chandlery business at the height of the China trade and again left with profits intact before its decline. His move into lead pipe manufacturing came at the beginning of a decade in which capital investments in the United States almost doubled from $533,200,000 to $1,009,000,000 and prompted a building industry boom. This rate of growth surpassed even that of the next decade. Especially in Massachusetts, industrialism grew at a tremendous rate. In 1845 the value of manufactures there totaled $125,000,000. But by 1855, the figure had reached $350,000,000, marking an unprecedented growth. While this boom was occurring Stearns incorporated in 1850 and separated himself from the actual day-to-day operation of the mill in Charlestown, conducting business in the counting room in Boston.[18]

From his office on Milk Street, Stearns joined a business elite whose members had changed almost overnight from merchants to entrepreneurs. The best brains of America entered business; they were aggressive, quickwitted, visionary men who sometimes had questionable ethics. Although he usually made sound, ethical business decisions, Stearns was not completely above all of this elastic morality and was seduced by a scheme that might bring him great wealth in a short period of time. Whether the idea was his or the Tatham brothers' is uncertain, but Stearns decided to corner the market in pig lead and make a fortune with a single business transaction. Unfortunately for the Medford businessman, the scheme had little chance of success. At this time raw lead sold on the New York docks for about six cents a pound. The Galena, Ohio, mines produced some 42 million pounds a year, and imports from Spanish lead mines were almost as much. The imported lead determined the price, because the shipping charges across the Atlantic were less than those from Ohio to eastern cities. Shipments arrived almost daily, and it seemed an almost impossible task to make sufficient purchases to drive the prices up.[19] Bent on increasing his wealth, Stearns traveled to New York in July 1852. Once established at a hotel, he immediately began to purchase incoming cargoes of lead. Shipments continued. to arrive, and Stearns borrowed and bought on credit. Shortly thereafter, the prices began to rise, just as he had hoped. After three weeks, however, his cash and credit were exhausted, and yet lead cargoes continued to arrive. At that point, the Medford manufacturer began buying against himself. His only recourse was to sell, and, when he did, the bottom fell out of the market and prices fell drastically. In a panic he appealed to the Tatham brothers. They refused to help. However, there was little anyone could do. Within three weeks, Stearns had either spent or used as security all of his cash and property.[20]

Much shaken, Stearns returned to Boston. Unable to face his family, he took a room at the Tremont House. The morning following his arrival, he sent word to a neighbor and speculator, Peter Buder, to meet him at the hotel. When Butler entered the room, Stearns's appearance shocked him. There sat the usually meticulously dressed Stearns with his clothing rumpled and his face covered with several days' growth of whiskers. George explained he had not slept for three nights and had not eaten. Then the Medford manufacturer blurted out the story of his speculation attempt: "Butler, I wanted to blow my brains out in New York, but I thought of my wife and could not do it." Buder offered words of sympathy and ordered breakfast, which Stearns devoured. The speculator then discussed financial alternatives with his distraught friend. Butler told Stearns to list his assets and then asked what amount he needed to keep his business solvent and to support his family. The conversation over, Butler told Stearns to rest while he canvassed business acquaintances on State Street for loans. There was "no one in Boston who could raise money more quickly," and, of course, Stearns's business reputation helped. Amos A. Lawrence, the noted textile manufacturer, for example, once stated that he knew of Stearns's business dealings and believed him "entirely reliable." Butler raised an amount sufficient to carry Stearns through until the short term notes were paid and all personal and business expenses covered.[21]

His immediate financial needs met, Stearns now possessed the courage to return to Medford. It is difficult to imagine Mary's accepting the news calmly. She thought little of her husband's occupation, and now with a fine home and good life, the lead business might bring them to financial ruin. Stearns consoled his wife, his son later recalled, "as well as a man could with such a conscience." After two days' rest, his spirits partially restored, the lead pipe manufacturer returned to New York.[22]

Arriving in New York's bustling commercial district, Stearns, with a strategy worked out with Peter Butler, asked his creditors to a meeting. He addressed the assembled businessmen: "Gentlemen, if you force me into bankruptcy my property will be sold at a disadvantage." Stearns estimated that it would bring fifty cents on the dollar. Also, he "possessed a good business in Boston which [paid] fifteen or twenty thousand a year," and if the assembled men allowed him time, he would be able to pay off both principal and interest. Benjamin Collins, a prominent New York merchant and holder of the largest note, spoke up. Collins, whose son at one time had worked in Stearns's counting room, expressed confidence in Stearns. He intended to take Stearns's "notes for one, two and three years, and consider [the] loan . . . amply secured." The other creditors followed suit. Those with small notes were paid off with the cash Butler raised, and the others had notes secured by mortgages on The Evergreens and the mill in Charlestown.[23]

A wiser businessman now, Stearns, with his family, faced a frugal and economical time, but fortunately, these were boom years. The growing economy lightened Stearns's debts by increasing the money supply. In 1857 in the midst of a financial panic, Stearns told his family that the last of the debts incurred by the lead speculation was paid in full. This period of financial difficulty also marked a change in the Stearnses' social life. After purchasing The Evergreens, George and Mary had hosted many large evening parties, the largest of which occurred during the winter social season of 1851, when they invited nearly everyone in Medford society. The failure of the speculation attempt now put an end to large gatherings at the Stearns mansion. As the decade wore on, the couple's circle of acquaintances changed. Their visitors now came from out of town and were names known in politics, reform, and literary circles. The Stearnses also began regularly attending performances at the Boston Music Hall. The shy, retiring Stearns became quite taken with the beautiful Jenny Lind and traveled to Fitchburg to hear her sing. At the performance, in the midst of his rapture, the practical Stearns could not relax. P. T. Barnum had sold almost a hundred more tickets, or so it seemed to him, than the Fitchburg hall could safely hold. George noted that iron rods from the rafters were all that held the floor. He realized that if it collapsed, there would be no escape and thought that perhaps they should leave. He overcame his anxiety by calculating the stress on the rods and finally decided that they would support the mass of humanity around him.[24]

Ill health also caused Stearns's partial withdrawal from Medford society. Like his father, George had bronchial problems. His physician, Dr. Marshall

S. Perry of Boston, decided that the best method of protecting George's chest from drafts was for him to grow a lengthy beard. Before filling this unusual prescription, Stearns wore fashionable side whiskers. He tried several beard styles, but he and his barber gave up on the unruly, curly dark growth. The only solution seemed to be to allow the facial hair to grow to its natural length. The resulting patriarchal beard caused members of polite society to stare, and people who did not know him personally thought he was eccentric. With the new whiskers, Stearns appeared to Christian eyes as the stereotypical Jew; Stearns's son remarked that the mistaken identity was understandable because his father dressed with "simple tastes" and had "much of the old Hebrew prophetic spirit" that was a part of the "essential manliness and independence of his character."[25]

George Stearns's reactions to the events of 1854 were measures of his character. Perhaps, if it had not been for the political turmoil of the year, Stearns would have continued to spend most of his time working and improving the estate, while devoting what little free time remained attending to Mary and their boys. True, he had pledged himself to aid the antislavery forces after the passage of the Fugitive Slave Law in 1850, but his reactions to this legislation were not much different from those of many informed Northerners. Where he parted company with his fellow countrymen was in his rescue of the two slaves. One son commented that his father "belonged to a class of men who are called forth by national emergencies," a sentiment echoed by Ralph Waldo Emerson, the Concord, Massachusetts, literary figure, and other acquaintances.[26]

Stearns saw the passage of the Kansas-Nebraska Act of 1854 as just such a national emergency. Henry Wilson, a member of Congress and an acquaintance of the manufacturer, believed the legislation a "beacon giving warning of approaching danger." Introduced by Senator Stephen A. Douglas, this act called for the formation of two territories, Nebraska and Kansas. Douglas injected the slavery issue into the legislation by proposing that settlers residing in those territories resolve the question for themselves. This proposal renewed the slavery issue in Congress, caused considerable consternation, and upset many Northerners because it opened vast sections of the Louisiana Purchase territory to the expansion of slavery.[27]

The legislation in Congress convinced many Northerners, including Stearns, that the slaveholding South could accomplish whatever it undertook.

Moreover, the legislation created a crisis over the question of whether the rights of men, the freedom of American institutions, and the prosperity of a growing economy could survive a government dominated by slaveholding states. Stearns sensed this crisis and strongly believed that the slave system degraded labor everywhere and that, if allowed to expand, it would eventually destroy free labor and the free enterprise system, both of which Stearns treasured dearly.[28]

Conservative Boston merchants who once had shunned such men as Stearns for their antislavery sentiments and supported the Compromise of 1850 now condemned Douglas, the Kansas-Nebraska Act, and the slave power in the harshest terms. Stearns spoke for his fellow businessmen when he declared that "the Government had proved faithless" and that it now "behooved the friends of freedom to cast about for other help." Initially, he and other antislavery men had taken for granted that the Kansas territory would become a slave state because it lay on the western border of slaveholding Missouri. In speech after speech, Northern politicians spoke of the territory as already lost. The legislative act itself was an act of surrender, and "to surrender this vast territory," said Joshua Giddings, a member of the House from Ohio, "to slavery will exclude free men from it."[29]

One man who refused to believe Kansas was lost to slavery and sought help in preventing this was Eli Thayer, whom Stearns called a "friend of freedom." A native of Worcester, Massachusetts, the city that gave birth to the Free Soil movement, Thayer founded Oread Collegiate Institute, a women's preparatory school. A member of the Free Soil party, he won a seat in the Massachusetts General Court for the 1853-1854 legislative session. Anticipating that President Franklin Pierce would sign the Kansas-Nebraska Act, Thayer sought to promote Northern emigration to Kansas, as he said, "guided and guarded by a responsible business company." Thayer believed such a company could make capital investments to secure the settlers' comfort and protection, but that the people who emigrated to Kansas would have to be self-sacrificing, willing to risk their lives and property in order to establish freedom in the territory by their very presence.[30]

On March 11, 1854, Thayer broached his plan to the public in a speech at one of the many meetings held to protest the Kansas-Nebraska Act. The response was so favorable that Thayer set about drawing up a bill of incorporation to present to the Commonwealth's legislature. Thayer said that the Massachusetts Emigrant Aid Company was to be a "moneymaking affair as well as a philanthropic undertaking." Thayer envisioned the settling of about twenty thousand emigrants in Kansas. The company would make travel arrangements for groups of two hundred in order to obtain reduced fares on rail and steamboat lines. When emigrants arrived, a hotel owned by the company would provide rooms until families settled on plots of land. The new settlers could then build homes with lumber from company-owned sawmills. The company, he believed, should establish a weekly newspaper as an "organ of the company's agents." Agents hired by a board of directors were to manage all of the enterprises. Once the Kansas territory became a free state, all the company's property would be sold and a dividend paid to stockholders. The remaining assets then could be used to populate yet another territory.[31]

On April 26, 1854, a month before the passage of the Kansas and Nebraska bill, the Massachusetts governor signed the charter incorporating the Emigrant Aid Company. Capitalization was authorized at $5 million and Thayer set about recruiting stockholders. He and Edward Everett Hale began lecturing in New England and New York, obtaining editorial support on the way from such newspaper giants as the New York *Tribune*'s Horace Greeley, William Cullen Bryant of the New York *Evening Post*, and Thurlow Weed of the Albany *Journal*.[32]

While Thayer was marshaling support for the venture, the newly formed nominating committee for the board of directors was revising the original charter proposals. Thayer enlisted the support of Amos A. Lawrence, the extremely wealthy and influential textile manufacturer whose family established the manufacturing city of Lawrence, Massachusetts. Lawrence apparently did not feel comfortable with the endeavor's profit-making side. Known for philanthropic work, he wanted to discard the investment aspects and create what he called a "cooperative society" with unlimited membership and total dependence on donations. He believed that Boston businessmen preferred to contribute to the cause of freedom rather than buy stock in a venture that might never show a return. Membership would require merely a signature and nominal dues.[33]

On July 24, 1854, Lawrence and Thayer reached a compromise at a meeting in Boston. However, the idea to create a strictly philanthropic society did not obtain support from the board. Lawrence did win a reduction in the capitalization ceiling from $5 to $2 million, to be raised by selling $20 shares. Lawrence became both a trustee and the treasurer. Still, the tone of the new charter was less profit-oriented. Thayer was not altogether happy with the shift to what he called the "charity plan." Years later, acknowledging that they had to convince people that they were not influenced by pecuniary motives, he claimed the new direction made the company "one half as efficient as we would have been." The name, too, was changed, and the word *Massachusetts* was added in order to distinguish it from companies Thayer founded in New York and Connecticut.[34]

Stearns knew of the organization and even traveled to Worcester to talk with Thayer in the early stages of the company's development. However, he was preoccupied with business and domestic matters and did not choose to become a charter member. Mary, pregnant again and never a silent sufferer, took much of her husband's time. On June 26, 1854, Carl Stearns, the third and last child, was born at The Evergreens. That summer of 1854 passed quickly for Stearns as he tended to his family, estate, and business. As the colorful New England fall approached, even the feverish election campaign failed to arouse Stearns. He watched with disgust as Henry Wilson, a former tradesman, used the anti-Irish sentiment in the Bay State to his political advantage. Wilson abandoned the new Republican party, whose basic tenet was the protection of free labor, and joined a nativist movement, known as the Know-Nothing party. In November 1854, the Know-Nothings captured almost all Massachusetts political offices, so weakening the infant Republican party that Charles Sumner did not even campaign. After the election the Medford manufacturer expressed quiet pleasure at the Know-Nothing triumph. Although he had donated money for the Irish famine relief in 1848, he had little use for the Boston Irish and decried their wanting freedom for Ireland while objecting to conferring the blessing of liberty on African-Americans. After the votes were counted, Stearns left Boston that November evening and drove his carriage over the Medford pike to The Evergreens. Entering the mansion he strode over to the fireplace and stood before it to thaw out his large, bony hands. In what Frank called "very good humor," he recounted the number of regular party candidates who had lost to the Know-Nothings. This event, he believed, served a purpose by breaking "down the old boundary marks and that is what we want just now."[35]

For now, Stearns observed political events. In December he attended an evening lecture at the Medford Unitarian Church, where Ralph Waldo Emerson addressed an audience on "The Conduct of Life ." After the lecture and discussion that followed, Stearns invited Emerson to The Evergreens to spend the night. The next morning when the two elder Stearns boys descended the black walnut staircase, they stopped short when they saw, Frank recalled, a "remarkably thin, sparse looking gentleman warming his hands before the fire." George and Mary had not awakened, so Emerson engaged the boys in conversation. He gave them a short lecture on the solar system and the stars in the universe. Frank showed Emerson his toy locomotive, the Eagle, a prototype of an engine on the Boston Lowell Railroad.[36]

Emerson's visit thrilled Mary, who, with her increasing wealth, saw the family rising in society. She began to take an interest in the arts and became a patron of the Concord literati. She courted the Emersons after this visit, and a friendship sprang up between the two families. Immediately after Emerson left The Evergreens, Mary sent a holiday package of books for his children. Emerson wrote to acknowledge receipt of the gift and expressed "surprise and pleasure" at being remembered by her "good heart." Edward Emerson asked his father to draw Frank's locomotive, which was done, he said, on the "leaves of my MS." Edward "critically examined" the drawing and found fault with the "form or size of the chimney." As a result, Emerson explained he wanted the "rival engineers" to have an "early opportunity" to settle the "Technicalities" and suggested that either Frank visit Concord that spring of 1855 or Eddy visit Medford.[37]

In the spring, Mary Stearns wasted no time inviting Eddy to The Evergreens. Emerson wrote to tell her his son would be on the 7:00A.M. train from Concord on the first Saturday in June. Emerson said that after Eddy had enjoyed "all the privileges and happiness of the day," Frank could take him to the station for the 6:40 P.M. return train. Later that month, the Stearnses received an invitation to visit the Emersons. All the Stearnses, but especially Mary, looked forward to the visit with a great deal of pleasure. Stearns drove the carriage, loaded with the entire family, out to Concord. Although the men and children got along well, Mary was uncomfortable with Emerson's wife, Lilian. According to Mary, she "held strict Puritanical views on morals and religion" that did not fit with the Stearnses' liberal views. The Stearnses were amused upon discovering that Emerson called her "Queeny." They agreed that she certainly presided over the meal in what Stearns described as a "highly dignified manner."[38]

During the summer of 1855, while the Emersons and Stearnses were exchanging visits, Amos Lawrence approached Stearns with an offer to become an Emigrant Aid Company director. Lawrence had moved slowly to diminish Thayer's influence and insisted on handpicking new directors. He also decided to increase the number to thirty-eight in order to broaden the support for the organization. Selected along with Stearns was a friend, noted physician Samuel Gridley Howe. Under Lawrence, the membership comprised respected and substantial community leaders, such as the Samuel Cabots, Senior and Junior, and John Lowell, members of the old Boston aristocracy, where, according to contemporaries, "the Lowells speak only to the Cabots and the Cabots speak only to God." Stearns immediately pitched in, raising concerns about the company's image, and suggested that, when soliciting funds, they "not present the name of anyone who has openly espoused extreme views on the slavery questions." His leadership role was tangible evidence that finally Stearns had gained the entree to the society his father's early death denied him.[39]

Guided by Lawrence, the Massachusetts Emigrant Aid Company directors set to work encouraging emigration and arranging settlements in Kansas. In the summer of 1854 twelve emigrant parties reached the territory. Eventually, sawmills and gristmills sprang up in such towns as Lawrence, Topeka, Manhattan, and Osawatomie. Other settlers organized by companies similar to the Boston based group joined the Massachusetts emigrants. Proslavery Missouri residents viewed with alarm the increasing stream of northern emigrants. The territory's opening and the flood of emigrants caused President Franklin Pierce to send the first of a string of territorial governors to Kansas. In the fall of 1854, Andrew H. Reeder, a rotund Democratic lawyer from Easton, Pennsylvania, arrived at Fort Leavenworth, high on a bluff overlooking the muddy, twisting Missouri River. Reeder, who had never held an elected office, immediately set about organizing the governing of the territory. He appointed judges, established seventeen election districts, and drew up rules for the election of a congressional delegate.[40]

On election day, November 29, 1854, more than seventeen hundred Missourians in a holiday spirit crossed the river to vote in the Kansas election. Many of them were members of secret political societies known by such names as the "Friends Society," "The Sons of the South," and the "Blue Lodge." All of these organizations were, locals said, "sound on the goose," that is, intent on making Kansas a slave state. Of the 2,871 ballots cast, only 1,114 were legal. As a result, a proslavery Tennesseean, John T. Whitfield, became the territory's congressional representative.[41]

Even more shocking to Northerners like Stearns were the results of the territorial legislative election held the following year. Proslavery people decried the delay in holding this second election. They complained that Reeder was postponing the voting until more antislavery men arrived in Kansas. As a consequence, the election, held on March 30, 1855, caused a great commotion. Again, the polling places were flooded with strangers from Missouri. John Long of Leavenworth testified that he saw as many as two hundred former neighbors from Jackson County, Missouri, vote in the town's polling place.[42]

The results were predictable: a proslavery legislature was elected. The "Bogus Legislature," as it became known to Free Soil people, probably would have contained a majority of proslavery sympathizers even without the blatant interference of neighbors to the east. More than sixty-two percent of the eligible voters in Reeder's census were former Southerners. The new legislature refused to meet at Pawnee, near Fort Riley, where Reeder had invested heavily in land. The legislators decided instead to set up the territorial capital at Shawnee Mission, near Kansas City, Missouri. Once the legislative session began, the legislators expelled antislavery delegates and passed laws over Reeder's veto. That summer of 1855, the legislature petitioned President Pierce to remove Reeder. At the same time it became known that Reeder had compromised himself by making some questionable land deals at Pawnee, and Pierce had no choice but to relieve him.

The Free Soil leaders in the territory were usually company agents. Two, Martin F. Conway and Charles Robinson, reacted to the situation by calling for a meeting at Topeka on October 19, 1855, to draft a constitution to send to Congress. They also demanded that Kansas be admitted to the Union as a free state. The agents urged Free Soil men to boycott the October congressional election called by the Bogus Legislature. When they met, Andrew Reeder was elected to Congress, and the delegates began work on a constitution. The Free State party, as the Topeka legislature came to be known, declared that all laws of the Bogus Legislature were null and void and that, if Missourians continued to interfere in Kansas affairs, there would be violence. Finally, word spread that a proslavery man had murdered a free stater. Making the situation worse, Sheriff Samuel J. Jones arrested a friend of the murdered man at an antislavery meeting in Lawrence. The new territorial governor, Wilson Shannon, a Cincinnati, Ohio, attorney and a former governor, declared that Lawrence was in "open rebellion" and called out the proslavery militia. Free staters, including a man by the name of John Brown, accompanied by his sons, all looking formidable with an assortment of weapons, arrived in Lawrence to defend the town.[43]

Also with weapons in hand, proslavery men organized the "Law and Order party." Murder followed murder until the Wakarusa "War" broke out in December 1855. Actually, the war was more a paramilitary demonstration than a battle. Shannon arrived in Lawrence in time to prevent full-scale bloodletting by persuading both sides to sign an agreement to disband. The battle for Kansas, however, was merely postponed. Back east, another battle for Kansas raged. After his dismissal, Reeder returned to Boston to tell the company directors about the outrages taking place in the territory. He, his wife, and his daughter were the Stearnses' guests. While Reeder's daughter played Mrs. Stearns's new piano, he spoke to George about his Kansas experience, which "converted him from a Jacksonian Democrat to an Abolitionist." Reeder declared that he "felt more sorrow and pity" than anger for President Pierce. Pierce's problem was his inability to stand up against Democratic leaders such as Jefferson Davis. Reeder told Stearns that Davis was the "real president" and favored a southern invasion of the territory. Stearns later said that he had found his conversation with this former territorial governor "very interesting."[44]

Pierce, true to Reeder's assessment, made an effort to place the blame for the violence in Kansas on the Emigrant Aid Company, whose "extraordinary measure of propagandist colonization" prevented the "free and natural action of its inhabitants" to decide the territory's future. Massachusetts senator Henry Wilson reacted to Pierce's comments by introducing a resolution asking the president for details on the events in Kansas. His purpose was to show that the invasion of Missourians created the problems. In February 1856, debates on Kansas territorial government began in Congress.[45]

On March 17, 1856, Senator Stephen Douglas reported out a bill authorizing the Southern "Law and Order" territorial government to present a constitution in preparation for statehood. William Seward countered by demanding that Kansas be admitted as a free state under the constitution drafted in Topeka. With tempers running high, Charles Sumner rose to deliver a speech he called "The Crime Against Kansas." He asked the Senate to "redress a great wrong" in Kansas, "where the ballot box, more precious than any work in ivory . . . is plundered." The "rape" of a "virgin territory" was being committed because of a "depraved desire for a new Slave State." The senator continued reciting the compromises made to placate the South, ending with recent events in Kansas. The speech, even Sumner supporters claimed, was extreme, and, furthermore, the Massachusetts legislator attacked fellow senators Stephen Douglas, James M. Mason of Virginia, and Andrew P. Butler of South Carolina.[46]

Southerners were more upset over the speech's harsh tone and the personal insults against Mason and Butler than over Sumner's political views. Henry Wilson believed "things were called by their right names." Stearns, reading the speech, thought Sumner displayed "heroism" in telling the truth to "that bold and confident oligarchy." But his friend and former lawyer was to pay a price for speaking out. Senator Douglas, in the midst of the speech, muttered, "That damn fool will get himself killed by some other damn fool."[47]

The "other damn fool" turned out to be Representative Preston S. Brooks of South Carolina, a relative of Butler. On May 22, 1856, while Sumner sat writing at his Senate chamber desk, Brooks approached and said he had read the senator's speech several times and found it "a libel on South Carolina and Mr. Butler." With these words, he began to beat Sumner with a cane, knocking him to the floor of the Senate chamber "bleeding and insensible."[48]

In Boston, Stearns received word of the beating at his counting room. Extremely upset, he left and drove to Medford. Scattering the blossoms falling from a large cherry tree in the front yard, he entered the mansion, his son recalled, with "such a serious face" that those present became alarmed. George quickly told his family and visitors that Sumner was "at the point of death" after having been beaten by a "ruffian." Augusta King, a friend of both the Stearnses and Sumner, wept bitterly. Mary felt a deep sadness settle over her. Later the group discussed Sumner and Kansas, those, as Stearns said, "overwhelming subjects from which we cannot get away." John King said that the "South will always get the best of us," for they are united by "self interest and the north divided." Mary asked, "Who will show us any good?" Stearns listened to what he considered defeatist talk and declared,

> I admit that the sky looks dark . . . but I shall never give up . . . . The assault on Sumner will make a million of abolitionists . . . . [I vow] to do what one man can and to devote my life and fortune to this cause.[49]

Stearns's immediate concern was for his friend's health. In order to ensure Sumner received the best possible medical care, he asked Dr. Perry to tend to him. He would pay all expenses. George Sumner, unsatisfied with the local physician treating his brother, was relieved when Perry arrived and took charge. On May 26, George Sumner was able to write to friends in Massachusetts, "The crisis has passed and our noble fellow is safe."[50]

Before Perry left for Washington, Stearns, at Mary's urging, brought him a box of wine, his treasured Tokay, and asked him to give it to Sumner as a gift from a "Woman of Massachusetts." When Perry arrived back in Boston several weeks later, "lo it appeared," he told Stearns, the box was left, but he neglected to tell the Sumners of its contents. The doctor rectified the mistake by wiring Sumner. Mary then told a friend that she "humbly dared to hope it will please him one little bit. I know the wine will do him good."[51]

With Sumner recovering, George Stearns proceeded to fulfill his vow to do what one man could and to devote his life and his fortune to the cause of freedom.

NOTES

1. George L. Stearns, ed., *Universal Suffrage and Complete Equality in Citizenship,the Safeguards of Democratic Institutions* (Boston: George C. Rand and Avery, 1865), a pamphlet of articles discussing the threat posed by the denial of freedom for African-Americans to democratic institutions in the United States; George L. Stearns to E. C. Cabell, September 29, 1865, quoted in *The Right Way* (Boston), November 25, 1865; James A. Rawley, *Race and Politics* (Philadelphia: J. B. Lippincott, 1969), pp. 16, 25.
2. Stearns, *Life*, pp. 59-60.
3. Ibid., p. 97.
4. Ibid., p. 82.
5. George E. Baker, *The Life of William H . Seward* (New York: Redfield, 1855), p. 238.
6. Stearns, *Life*, p. 84.
7. Wilson, *Rise and Fall*, 2:304; Henry S. Commager, *Theodore Parker* (Boston: The Beacon Press, 1960), p. 207; George L. Stearns to Charles Sumner, January 3, 1861, Charles Sumner Manuscripts, Harvard University, Cambridge, Massachusetts (hereafter cited as Sumner MSS); George L. Stearns to R. C. Waterston, November 10, 1842, Stearns MSS NYHS.
8. Stearns, *Life*, p. 84.
9. Sidney Morse, "Anti-Slavery Hero," *The New England Magazine*, March 1891, p. 84.
10. Lucy Osgood to Caleb Stetson, March 21, 1851, Stetson MSS; Stearns, *Life*, pp. 88-89. For years rumors persisted in Medford that The Evergreens was

honeycombed with escape tunnels for fugitive slaves. *The Medford Historical Register* even carried several articles on the subject. In a letter to the author dated July 31, 1973, George Lindsey Stearns states, "Tunnels? There were none .... As an inquisitive youngster I will guarantee that."

11. Stearns, *Life*, p. 58.
12. Donald, Sumner, pp. 188-191.
13. Morse, "Antislavery Hero," p. 488; Stearns, *Life*, pp. 84-85; Donald, Sumner, pp. 186-190.
14. Stearns, *Life*, pp. 57-58.
15. Ibid.
16. Ralph Waldo Emerson, "Remarks on the Character of George L. Stearns, Given at Medford, April14, 1867," Stearns Manuscripts, American Antiquarian Society, Worcester, Massachusetts (hereafter cited as Stearns MSS, AAS); Johnson, "George L. Stearns," p. 614; Stearns, *Life*, pp. 57- 58; "George L. Stearns and Company," business card, Stearns MSS, MHS.
17. Emerson, "Remarks"; David Donald, "Toward a Reconsideration of Abolitionists," *Lincoln Reconsidered* (New York: Alfred A. Knopf Vintage Books, 1956), pp. 19-36; Frederick Caple Jaher, "The Boston Brahmans in the Age of Industrial Capitalism," in Frederick Caple Jaher, ed., *The Age of Industrialism in America* (New York: The Free Press, 1968), p. 190; Stearns, *Life*, p. 57.
18. Nevins, *A House Dividing*, 2:246.
19. Victor S. Clark, *History of Manufactures in the United States, 1607-1860* (Washington, D.C.: Carnegie Institute, 1929; reprint, New York: Peter Smith, 1949), 1: 330.
20. George Stearns's son Frank gives the year of his father's speculation as 1853; however, a review of the New York *Times* financial section failed to reveal any major price fluctuation. The following year, 1854, Stearns was involved in other matters; therefore, the correct year is 1852.
21. Stearns, *Life*, p. 92; Amos A. Lawrence to Edwin M. Stanton, August 26, 1863, Old Military Records Division, Bureau of Colored Troops and Records of the Adjutant General's Officer Commission Board, Record Group 94, National Archives, Washington, D.C.
22. Stearns, *Life*, p. 92.
23. Ibid.
24. Ibid., pp. 79-80, 86.
25. Ibid., p. 101.
26. Ibid., p. 81.
27. Wilson, *Rise and Fall*, 2:378.
28. Rawley, *Race and Politics*, p. 16; Stearns to Cabell, September 29, 1865, quoted in *The Right Way*.

29. Nevins, A House Dividing, 2:128; Eli Thayer, *A History of the Kansas Crusade* (New York: Harper & Brothers, 1889), p. 11.

30. Thayer, *Kansas Crusade*, p. 24.

31. Ibid., pp. 28-29.

32. Ibid.

33. Samuel A. Johnson, *The Battle Cry of Freedom* (Lawrence: University Press of Kansas, 1954; reprint, Westport, CT: Greenwood Press, 1977), p. 25; Horace Andrews, Jr., "Kansas Crusade: Eli Thayer and the New England Emigrant Aid Company," *New England Quarterly* 25 (Spring 1962): 499.

34. Thayer, *Kansas Crusade*, p. 59.

35. Stearns, *Life*, p. 100.

36. Lucy Osgood to Caleb Stetson, April 14, 1852, Stetson MSS, MHS; Stearns, *Life*, p. 94; Ralph Waldo Emerson to Mary E. Stearns, January 8, 1855, in Ralph L. Rusk, ed., *The Letters of Ralph Waldo Emerson* (New York: Columbia University Press, 1939), 4:482.

37. Ralph Waldo Emerson to Mary E. Stearns, January 8, 1855, in Rusk, *Letters*, 4:482.

38. Ralph Waldo Emerson to Mary E. Stearns, May 28, 1855, in Rusk, *Letters*, 4:511; Stearns, *Life*, pp. 94-95, quotes the same letter incorrectly dated 1852.

39. Johnson, *Battle Cry*, p. 31; William Lawrence to George L. Stearns, June 30, 1856, Samuel G. Howe Manuscripts, Massachusetts Historical Society, Boston.

40. Nevins, *A House Dividing*, 2:312; U.S. Congress, House, Kansas Affairs: Report of the Majority and Minority, Report 200, 34th Cong., 1st sess., July 1856, p. 3.

41. Alice Nichols, *Bleeding Kansas* (New York: Oxford University Press, 1954), p. 29; Nevins, *Ordeal of the Union*, 2:313.

42. "Testimony of Leander Ker, May 31, 1856," quoted in U.S. Congress, House, *Kansas Affairs*, p. 859; "Testimony of William H. Miller, May 21, 1856, Ibid., p. 863; "Testimony of John Long, May 6, 1856," Ibid., pp. 202-203.

43. New York *Times*, December 4, 1855; Stephen B. Oates, *To Purge This Land with Blood* (New York: Hatper Torchbooks, 1972), p. 106.

44. Stearns, *Life*, p. 105.

45. Wilson, *Rise and Fall*, 2: 476.

46. Charles Sumner, "The Crime against Kansas," May 19-20, 1856, quoted in C. Edwards Lester, *The Life and Public Services of Charles Sumner* (New York: United States Publishing, 1874), pp. 263-264.

47. Wilson, *Rise and Fall*, 2:481; Stearns, *Life*, p. 114; Donald, *Sumner*, p. 286.

48. Wilson, *Rise and Fall*, 2:481.

49. Stearns, *Life*, p. 114; Mary E. Stearns to Augusta G. King, June 8, 1856, Boyd B. Stutler Collection (microfilm, Yale University, New Haven, CT), hereafter referred to as the Stutler Collection; Stearns, *Life*, p. 115.

50. Donald, *Sumner*, p. 313; George L. Stearns to Henry Wadsworth Longfellow, May 29, 1856, Charles Sumner Manuscripts, Houghton Library, Harvard University, Cambridge, Massachusetts.

51. Mary E. Stearns to Augusta G. King, June 8, 1856, Stutler Collection.

4

Kansas Business

Although the Border Ruffians cannot drive them out, and our government dare not
they cannot resist hunger and cold.
                                                    – George L. Stearns

Even before the attack on Lawrence, the increasing violence and harsh living conditions that faced free state settlers in Kansas aroused the concern of many Northerners. In late winter 1856, Kansas aid committees sprang up in towns and cities throughout the North. These organizations reawakened public support for efforts to send free state settlers to and maintain them in the embattled territory.

That February, the Kansas Free State delegation, together with Emigrant Aid Company representatives, toured Massachusetts. They organized public meetings in quaint farming towns and bustling industrial cities. Both delegates and company representatives spoke to the assembled crowds. Stearns attended a number of these meetings in the Boston area but remained in the background to observe and gauge the audience's mood. When the speeches concerning the situation in the territory ended, the sale of company stock began. Those people moved by the plight of settlers were also encouraged to form charitable relief committees. Stearns found the response so heartening that he urged the company directors to call a mass meeting in Boston as a method of centralizing Kansas relief efforts in the Commonwealth. On March

12, 1856, as concerned citizens, Stearns and other company officers held a meeting in Faneuil Hall. The gathering was a larger version of the earlier local gatherings, except that this time the organizers did not mention the sale of Emigrant Aid Company stock. During the carefully orchestrated meeting, Kansas Free Soilers testified to Missouri "ruffian" "outrages." Stearns noted that it was a meeting with "conservative overtones." Soft felt hat in hand, he sat in the rear of the hall with director LeBaron Russell, attracting little attention except by his long beard. The other directors also maintained a low profile once the meeting began, "lest it should prejudice some persons who might have any feelings against the company," as Russell explained. Samuel H. Wally, a conservative Whig businessman and acquaintance of Stearns, offered several resolutions.[1]

From these resolutions sprang the Boston Kansas Relief Committee or, as people commonly referred to it, the Faneuil Hall Committee. The men chosen for the committee included Patrick T. Jackson, Ingersoll Bowditch, and Samuel G. Howe, all members of the Emigrant Aid Company. Howe initially expressed his apprehension about the possibility of civil war in Kansas, "from which nothing but disaster and downfall to Republican Liberty and to Human Liberty can result." He suggested sending only food and clothing to the settlers. The doctor believed that if they forwarded "more money and more munitions of war," "heated and furious competition" between free staters and proslavery forces would result. The members of the committee, for the most part, shared these sentiments, and the group immediately set to work collecting relief supplies and funds for nonviolent purposes.[2]

When Howe called on Stearns to make a contribution, he gave liberally of both money and advice, and although not a member, he even began to make collections for the committee. Money flowed in, but the energetic Stearns did not consider it enough. In May following Sumner's beating, news of the attack on Lawrence reached the Senate chamber. Shrewdly realizing that these events would breathe new life into relief efforts, Stearns could no longer contain some ideas he formulated while collecting funds. He heard complaints that the local committees were inefficient and had no plan of operation. Stearns blamed this situation on the fact that well-meaning members lacked business sense and, as he told friends, had "no sufficient idea of what they [were] to do." His scheme envisioned the coordination of the activities of all the Bay State's Kansas aid committees. Stearns hoped to centralize and to direct their efforts from one office, his counting room. He also wanted to broaden the base from which to draw support. At a meeting of the Faneuil Hall Committee, Stearns spoke slowly and deliberately as he outlined several ideas to raise funds after consolidation of the local committees. "If we cannot obtain money from the rich," he said, "we must apply to those who are not rich." The key, as Stearns saw it, was to encourage small donations from many people: "If every Republican voter would give us a quarter, we could raise a hundred thousand dollars."[3]

The committee members listened intently to Stearns and decided to act on his suggestions. They called a convention of all Kansas aid committees and others interested in the territory. Stearns wrote to former Governor Andrew Reeder about their plans, and the portly gentleman agreed to be the keynote speaker. On June 25, citizens from all over Massachusetts gathered in Boston to discuss the proposals put forth by Stearns and to decide on a unified course of action. This meeting created the Massachusetts State Committee. Because Stearns both indicated a willingness to devote all his time to this cause and had proved himself to be one of the most successful fundraisers in Boston, they named him chairman. Patrick T. Jackson became treasurer, and the organization absorbed all the members of the Faneuil Hall Committee. Most of Stearns's acquaintances did not know that he held stock in the Emigrant Aid Company, and although he was a director, he continued to remain relatively inconspicuous. So the spirit of noninvolvement of the company in a charitable organization prevailed at least outwardly, and Stearns could coordinate the efforts of the new organization.[4]

Businessman Stearns proceeded to build a network of influential people to help establish the organization. William Lawrence, brother of Amos, wrote to the new chairman in regard to a list of names Stearns sent to him. Lawrence went over the individuals with Mr. Rogers, whom he described to Stearns as an "old conservative Whig." Although both of them respected all the men on the list, they thought that some should be removed. Those who had, according to Lawrence, "openly expressed extreme views on the Slavery question" and those who had voiced support of the Emigrant Aid Company's work would not be able to gather support from the general population. Lawrence thought it would be "more advantageous if only those serve who heretofore have been in the background." With his list trimmed, Stearns then contacted influential men around the state, asking them to recommend people who would make "good (county) agents for canvassing this state properly, organizing Town Committees, (and) making appeals to Communities." Stearns specifically wanted men who were, he told Lawrence, "well booked up in territorial matters" and had the ability to discuss present affairs in Kansas in their "true light." Of course, fair compensation would be paid for their services.[5]

This involvement in the Massachusetts State Committee did not detract from Stearns's attention to his family. About the time he received the committee chairmanship, Mary complained of sciatic neuralgia. Dr. Perry visited The Evergreens to treat her. Perry suggested that a trip to the shore would help the suffering woman. The best medicine he had, however, was a letter recently received from George Sumner, which mentioned Mary's gift of Tokay to the stricken senator: "Whether it was that," George's note said, "or the cheering words of Mrs. Stearns note ... one or all of these causes worked a marvelous change." Mary beamed with delight, happy that she had aided Sumner's recovery.[6]

Stearns wanted to continue to develop his organization, but Mary convinced him that he could not do much for Kansas during the hot, humid northeastern weather. He agreed, for too many people were away trying to escape the heat. To please Mary, Stearns took his family to the North Shore of Massachusetts. However, at Beverly Farms, everything seemed to annoy Stearns. He remarked sarcastically to his middle son that "there was no telling what people had to suffer in search of pleasure at the seashore." After a few weeks of unsuccessful attempts to enjoy himself, Stearns returned to Medford.[7]

Two letters awaited the Stearnses when they returned. The first was from their friends, the Emersons. Mary, prior to their departure, wrote to invite Eddy to The Evergreens. Emerson replied that Eddy would be in New York for a while, but that upon returning, he would be delighted to visit. Emerson explained that Eddy would "answer for himself." The other letter was from Stearns's new lawyer, George E Hoar. Stearns was being sued for the delivery of faulty pipe and wanted Hoar to settle out of court. The "last offer for a settlement," Stearns told Hoar, had not elicited the response he hoped to receive. Hoar, Stearns believed, had not shown enough initiative, and the businessman wrote to him with some annoyance, "I presume nothing has been done." When the lawyer wrote in the affirmative, Stearns said to "drop the matter" and advise him of the "present state of affairs." Evidently, Stearns settled, as he had wished, out of court.[8]

The following month, both Stearnses were ready to turn their attention to Kansas affairs. Settlers' descriptions of the harsh Kansas winters inspired both of them to collect supplies and funds with a fervor. While Stearns kept several clerks busy writing letters to establish his network of agents, Mary, as she told a friend, was motivated by "the divine spirit" and decided to get relief work moving on her own. One morning, after seeing her husband off at the train station, known locally as Stearns Steps, she gathered up little Carl and reluctant Frank and placed them in her carriage. Mary headed into Medford center to see whether she could, as she related to Augusta King, "drum up women enough to call a meeting." She proposed to have "some able speakers ... make an address" to a gathering of women interested in Kansas relief. Then, after Theodore Parker or Henry Ward Beecher finished elaborating on the evils of slavery, she planned to "take up a subscription" for the destitute settlers. Despite her spirited enthusiasm Mary met a cold response from many women in Medford. Mrs. Porter said she would like to help but did not think Kansas would ever become a free state regardless of what Northerners did. Another "quiet homebody," as Mary described her, said that she "never meddled with such things." At this point, Mary had heard enough. She indignantly rose to her feet and told the woman that if "firesides continue[d) to be desecrated in Kansas," she might not have the opportunity to decide whether she should become involved. Mary returned home vowing not to be "beaten off." That evening she wrote to her friend Dotty (Augusta) King that she was determined to "have [her] own meeting, and get [her] own money."[9]

Her husband was far more successful. Mary's attempts were spontaneous and emotional, but George's moves were calculated. From rented rooms at 17 Niles Block in Boston, Stearns directed his statewide organization. Each county had a relief agent hired by Stearns. He wanted to continue to reach into every community and recommended that the county agent select a reliable person in each town. The town agents would then secure a collector in the school districts. Perhaps thinking of Mary's efforts, Stearns suggested that "ladies [would] do the work most faithfully." He wanted reports from the county agents sent either to him or to his secretary, Samuel Gifford. The first report had to include the town agent names for the record. After all the initial reports were filed, the committee would publish a list of the names to be used in public appeals. Stearns told the county agents to "stimulate the delinquent [town agents] to a prompt performance of their work 'by making a personal visit' or as a last resort, 'admonishing them by letter.' "The money needed for Kansas relief, he believed, could be acquired only by continuous efforts and by a "thorough canvass of the State."[10]

On the basis of personal experience, Stearns believed the county agents would have more credibility when soliciting if they had knowledge of the present relief situation in Kansas. The people who contributed, he told agents, had a right to know exactly why aid was needed and how food, money, and clothing reached settlers. Stearns told his agents that in order for them to "answer questions frequently asked," he would provide information. "I can state," he advised in a letter, "that there are 'from 2,000 to 3,000 Free State Men' in Kansas who are 'bona fide settlers.'" These men and their families had "expended all their property," and therefore, the Massachusetts Committee and other aid societies must furnish them food and clothing until crops were harvested. Stearns stated, "Although the 'Border Ruffians' cannot drive them out, and our government dare not, they cannot resist hunger and cold." He went on to assure the agents that donations would be used wisely by relief agents in Kansas, who were "known to us to be reliable." Not everyone expressed the same confidence in the selection of these men. A Greenfield, Massachusetts, resident wrote to Patrick Jackson after an interview with Stearns. During their talk the Medford manufacturer had informed the gentleman that he had recently hired "Colonel" L. W. Eldridge to distribute goods in Kansas. The Greenfield man declared his shock at the selection and said the committee was "deceived in your man." He wrote that if it were known in the county that they had hired Eldridge, nothing could help "raise the first dollar," for the man, a former railroad conductor, was totally unreliable. Still, many people, such as George's friend Samuel G. Howe, believed that Stearns had established a "systematic organization of good business capacity."[11]

Stearns's own lead pipe business continued to operate smoothly, as smoothly as his relief organization. In fact, he decided to use business contacts to solicit additional relief funds. In almost every city and town in New England, tinsmiths and plumbers used Stearns's products. His clerks prepared appeals to send out to customers. In this way, he hoped to make the common man aware of the situation in the Kansas territory and call the relief organization's work to the attention of a larger portion of the population. Stearns achieved good results from the effort to raise funds, food, and clothing. Within five months, from August to December, he alone obtained more than $48,000 for Kansas settlers.[12]

After her initial disappointment, Mary organized enough women to feel, she wrote to Dotty, "buoyant with triumph." On October 17, 1856, she declared to a friend that her "Medford Kansas La bon[ne] Guerre" raised money to the "tune of six hundred and fifteen dollars!!!" Mary, always the martyr, let everyone know that she worked hard for Kansas. All who would listen were told that she "went out those days to collect money" after attending to the "whole work of the house," for the housekeeper had recently quit. Of course, Mary explained to friends, she had no wish to glorify herself, but she did want them to understand why, during the past few months, she had neglected to contact them. Her efforts were well rewarded, however, and she could hardly contain her exuberance over her success. In addition to the money raised, Mary also began forming societies to contribute clothing. Within a few months, these organizations sent $30,000 or more in supplies of various kinds to the destitute settlers in ·the Kansas territory.[13]

By the end of October, Stearns's network reached its maximum efficiency. Armed with letters of introduction from "Mr. Durfee, which would aid me materially," Stearns began to travel in order to offer assistance and to coordinate the activities of other states' relief organizations. One of his first such trips was to New York, "this time on Kansas Business." The Tatham brothers also became involved in Kansas relief and rented rooms at 110 Broadway to the American Settlement Company and the New York "Kansas League." Stearns stopped by to apprise these emigrant organizations of his relief work and to discuss the activities of the New England Emigrant Aid Company.[14]

After a few days in New York, Stearns returned to Boston to find the city in an uproar, preparing to welcome home Charles Sumner. On November 3, Mary and a friend called for Stearns at work in his rooms on the Niles Block. He then escorted the women to the parade being held in Sumner's honor. Stearns drove the chaise slowly through the crowds a few blocks to the State House on Beacon Hill. Mary read aloud the signs displayed as the carriage bumped its way over the cobblestone street: "Massachusetts Loves, Honors and Will Sustain Her Noble Sumner and Welcomes Freedom's Defender." Outside the gold-domed structure, the three listened to the cheers come closer and closer as Sumner's carriage proceeded up Beacon Hill. When the senator arrived at the steps leading to the State House, the waiting band broke into "Home Sweet Home." Mary and Augusta King wept with emotion. As George later recalled, Sumner, "pale and weary," looked over the crowd until his eyes rested on the Stearns party. He nodded to George and doffed his hat to the ladies. Seeing Sumner, a victim, he believed, of southern arrogance, made Stearns even more determined to press on with his work to aid Kansas Free Soilers.[15]

By the end of November, Amos Lawrence received word concerning the impact of Stearns's Kansas aid efforts. The influx of goods and money showed decided results in relieving the sufferings of those in pressing need. Amos Lawrence now wanted the emphasis shifted from direct relief to the appropriation of money for employment. The wealthy and practical business leader saw a double purpose in stimulating the territory's economy: not only giving relief to the settlers, but also providing a permanent benefit to those for whom the work would be done. Also, with Stearns's success, it seemed to Lawrence that the State Committee might one day overshadow the company. He wanted to lead the State Committee back to using the Emigrant Aid organization to carry out the original plan.[16]

Stearns, however, seemed carried along with the momentum of his own organizing efforts and resisted attempts to shift the Committee's emphasis. He believed every dollar, every barrel of clothing and food was another blow struck for freedom. Stearns went on the road again, to Philadelphia and then to New York, where he attempted to influence businessmen and politicians to support Kansas relief. He obtained pledges of support from influential men in both cities in the hope that, as he said, "when we have them the money will come." He wrote to Samuel G. Howe from New York to thank the doctor for a copy of a letter from Senator Henry Wilson to presidential candidate John C. Fremont supporting Stearns's work. This sort of letter would overcome his greatest problem in fund-raising, convincing men like Fremont that the money donated would be handled by responsible people. Still, Lawrence and others in the Emigrant Aid Company increasingly saw Stearns as a liability.[17]

Charles Robinson wrote to Stearns on the company's behalf and as a personal favor to Lawrence. He pointed out to the stubborn businessman, as others had, that there was reason to believe that a good portion of the relief funds and supplies was now not reaching the truly destitute among the settlers in Kansas. Robinson indicated that many agents hired by the State Committee were either incompetent or corrupt. Complaints were coming in from free state community leaders who reported that the indiscriminate distribution of charity was leading to the recipients' demoralization. An eastern newspaper correspondent, James Redpath, wrote, "Instead of Aid Societies we need Aid Companies; not charitable associations but monied corporations."[18]

Lawrence hoped Robinson's letter would motivate Stearns and his committee to "go to work in the [right] direction." Stearns ignored the pleas. Exasperated, Lawrence wrote to Robinson about a December 17 meeting with Stearns, who was, he said, "so unwilling to do anything to stop the 'relief' agency." Lawrence thought that Stearns withheld information from his Kansas committee and key donors. Stearns, Lawrence declared, remained "backward in showing anything which goes to prove that the time for that [relief] has gone by .... "Fortunately, Lawrence maintained control over most of the Emigrant Aid Company directors. He influenced those on the Executive Committee to agree to suspend all relief work and, instead, to invest a total of $1,000 to rebuild the Free State Hotel in Lawrence. This project would provide a goodly number of jobs for destitute settlers. Stearns remained unmoved. Now, for the first time, he held direct control of an organization involved in supporting the fighters for freedom in Kansas. Stearns found a great deal of personal satisfaction in being in charge of an organization that was having a direct impact on events in far-away Kansas.[19]

Knowing that Stearns was establishing local Kansas relief committees Emerson had introduced him to Frank Sanborn, a schoolmaster and Concord neighbor. A young romantic, Sanborn became caught up in the struggle for Kansas and joined the Middlesex County Kansas Relief Committee. He became secretary and corresponded regularly with the Massachusetts Kansas Committee before Stearns became chairman. In late September 1856, Stearns offered Sanborn the position of committee secretary. Sanborn suited Stearns's purpose, for the young man had experience with a county committee, where he kept meticulous accounts, and even visited Kansas on relief business.

In January 1857, Frank Sanborn took a visitor to Stearns's office who would give the Boston businessman an opportunity to have an even greater influence on freedom's fight in the Kansas territory. As he strode into Stearns's office this cold, windy day, Sanborn was in a jubilant mood. Excitedly, he told Stearns that someone from Kansas was waiting in the counting room and wanted to meet him. Stearns came out and shook hands with a gaunt man with piercing eyes by the name of John Brown. Brown had gone to Boston seeking material aid in forming "a company of men for the protection of Kansas." He had with him impressive letters of introduction from Charles Robinson; Gerrit Smith, a former New York congressman and wealthy landholder; and Senator Salmon P. Chase of Ohio. Before visiting Stearns, the Kansas "hero" visited Unitarian minister Theodore Parker, antislavery editor

William Lloyd Garrison, and Amos Lawrence. All of these men gave Brown encouragement, and after a lengthy discussion about the situation in Kansas, Lawrence even offered to support his family while he battled for freedom in Kansas.[20]

George Stearns met John Brown, Stearns's son Frank recalled, "like the iron and the magnet." Frank said that each "recognized the other at first sight and knew him for what he was worth." Stearns asked Brown to wait while he quickly gathered the other members of the committee. Stearns, Howe, and the others listened intently as Brown gave a grim appraisal of the Kansas struggle. Brown, at times, distorted the picture of events in Kansas. He argued, for instance, that the federal government harassed free state settlers and violated "all law, and all right, *moral* and *constitutional*, for the *sole and only purpose of forcing* slavery upon that Territory." Stearns asked what Brown thought would happen next in Kansas. Brown paused and then told him that the present calm would last only till spring. Then heavily armed Missourians would burst into the territory to destroy everything in their path. Brown said he could defend Kansas, but only if he could obtain weapons and funds.[21]

Howe responded first to Brown's emotional appeal. The doctor had served alongside Greek patriots in their struggle for independence from Turkey. In 1856 he traveled west on behalf of the National Kansas Committee. Now, like Amos Lawrence, Howe wanted to end relief and to do something more to aid the free staters in Kansas. He believed the committee should provide Brown funds. Stearns agreed and told him that although he was convinced that there was a danger to the territory, the committee needed to meet again to decide on a course of action.[22]

Stearns spoke of John Brown as a "Cromwellian Ironside introduced in the nineteenth century for a special purpose." The more Stearns talked to Brown, the more he became impressed with his wisdom, courage, and integrity. When Stearns called the committee together again, he urged the members to make Brown an agent. They readily agreed and proposed to give Brown two hundred Sharps rifles purchased by Stearns and enough funds to purchase ammunition for the defense of Kansas. In addition, the committee voted Brown $50 to pay his personal expenses. Later, before Brown left Boston, the men authorized an additional $500 and gave him authority to sell one hundred rifles, if necessary, for ready cash.[23]

After Brown finished his business with the Kansas Relief Committee, Stearns suggested that he talk with Reverend Thomas Wentworth Higginson.

That fall, Higginson, a Worcester Unitarian clergyman and strident abolitionist, had, after joining the Massachusetts and the National Kansas committees, visited the disputed territory. His newfound interest brought him into contact with Stearns, whom he believed was a "noble and self-devoted man." When they met in Boston, Brown and Higginson discussed plans to defend Kansas. The clergyman expressed strong support and assured Brown he would do all he could to rally friends in Worcester to the cause.[24]

That Sunday, after Higginson left Boston, Stearns invited Brown to dinner at The Evergreens. Friends John and Dotty King joined the Stearns family to greet Brown. As the meal progressed, one of the company asked Brown to tell about his fight at Black Jack in Kansas. He gladly did so with, the family later recalled, "a grim kind of humor" that Stearns enjoyed. Stearns then asked what "sort of a noise a Sharps rifle bullet made." In a solemn tone, Brown replied, "It makes a very ugly noise, Mr. Stearns." Augusta King, her eyes wide with the talk of fighting and killing, asked Brown about several free state leaders. The guest shook with a silent laugh and said, "As a rule, Miss King, the higher the officer, the less of a soldier." He said he thought of himself as merely "a plain captain" always ready for a fight, while James Lane, a free state forces "colonel," would fight if Governor Charles Robinson "allowed him." And then there was Samuel Pomeroy, who, Brown said jokingly, "[was] a general and there [was] no fight in him." Stearns joined in the laughter. Here, finally, was a man of action in contrast to do-nothing politicians and all-talk abolitionists. After dinner, Harry, the Stearnses' eldest son, timidly approached Brown with a request. "Captain Brown," the twelve-year-old boy said, "I wish you would tell me about your boyhood." Everyone laughed, and Brown patted the young man affectionately and said, "My son, I cannot do that now, for I fear it would weary the ladies." He did, however, promise to write Harry an account of his childhood. When Brown began to bid farewell, Harry went to him again. This time the boy gave the man his savings to pass along to a destitute child in Kansas.[25]

After the visit Brown left for New York, where he tried, unsuccessfully, to obtain additional funds from the National Kansas Committee and wealthy land speculator Gerrit Smith. After a brief stop at North Elba, New York, to visit his family, Brown returned to Boston, where Stearns and Sanborn arranged to have him speak on February 18 before a Massachusetts General Court joint committee. Stearns hoped that Brown would convince the legislators to apportion $100,000 to the latter because of the interest

Massachusetts citizens had in Kansas. After Brown spoke to the lawmakers, Stearns listened to what he called a "great deal of patriotic speech making" only to have the legislators vote down a motion to grant the request. Stearns tried to console Brown by telling him that "large bodies of men act more from instinct than reason, and are proverbially shortsighted." He believed that the Massachusetts politicians hoped Kansas would be saved by James Buchanan's new administration.[26]

Undaunted by the vote, Brown left Boston and crisscrossed New England, making occasional side trips to New York. Unknown to Stearns, Brown began contracting for arms, including the forging of a thousand pikes. Later, in New York, Brown met an English soldier of fortune, Hugh Forbes, and commissioned him to write a tactics manual and to train a company of men Brown had waiting in Iowa.[27]

On April 3, Brown again returned to Boston. Howe persuaded Superior Court Justice Thomas B. Russell to take Brown in, for he had received word that at least one U.S. marshal was looking for the man. Once hidden away at the Russells' home, Brown composed a short discourse, which he called "Old Brown's Farewell to the Plymouth Rocks, Bunker Hill monuments; Charted Oaks; and Uncle Tom's Cabbins." He intended to arouse sympathy in this crafty farewell, in which he bemoaned his plight and that of his cause. He sent word through George for Mary Stearns to go over what he had written. Brown had made a shrewd analysis of Mary's hero worship of him and of her devotion to the Free Soil cause in Kansas. Mary believed her hero to be, as she explained to her father, a "Noble and refreshing specimen of mankind" and a gallant warrior who "saved Lawrence from destruction." In an easterly storm, Mary drove at once to the Russells' home, where Brown greeted her warmly. In a tone and manner that captivated her, Brown explained that he wanted his "little address," as he called it, read by Theodore Parker next Sunday at services. She told her Kansas hero that although Parker would like it, for "it rings the metal he likes," his congregation might miss the point. Mary, however, suggested Brown send it anyway and asked for a copy. Brown now had Mary in the emotional state he wanted her in and sprang the trap. "If I could have the money," he mused, "that is *smoked away* during a single day in Boston, I could strike a blow which would make slavery totter from its foundation." Overwhelmed by Brown's "moral magnetism," she later told Frank Sanborn, Mary bade him good-bye and drove back to The Evergreens.

Here she was, she said to herself, "living in luxury while such a man was struggling for a few thousand to carry out his cherished plan."[28]

Mary awoke the following morning with her mood so heightened by the "splendor of spring sunshine" and "everything . ... so beautiful" that the "wish rose warm in my heart," she confessed to her father, "to comfort and aid John Brown." While poor George slumbered on, Mary made plans to sell his beloved estate. When he awoke, Mary unfolded her plan. If George was not fully awake when she began, he certainly must have been when Mary finished. He loved Mary and throughout their marriage had tried to please her. Silently reflecting on her plans, he finally thought of a reason best calculated to dissuade her. He explained that selling The Evergreens would not be fair to their boys. He did promise, however, to see what could be done to provide Brown additional funds. After breakfast, Stearns returned to Judge Russell's home and presented Brown a note authorizing him to draw on his account for $7,000 to be used for the defense of Kansas. When George returned home, Mary, still harboring guilt, wanted to sell the carriage and horses to make the donation a total of $8,000. George put his foot down and said no. He told her that he would urge the committee to increase its financial support to Brown. By this act, Stearns became totally committed to John Brown and stood ready to support his efforts to destroy slavery.[29]

NOTES

1. Stearns, *Life*, pp. 116-118; LeBaron Russell to Edward Everett Hale, June 30, 1856, New England Emigrant Aid Company Papers, Kansas State Historical Society, Topeka (hereafter cited as NEA, KSHS).
2. Samuel G. Howe to Massachusetts Kansas Committee Member Robert Winthrop, June 25, 1856, Howe MSS, MHS.
3. Franklin B. Sanborn to "A Friend," June 14, 1856, Franklin B. Sanborn Manuscripts, Concord Free Public Library; Stearns, *Life*, pp. 118-119.
4. Stearns, *Life*, p. 118: Johnson, *Battle Cry*, p. 213.
5. Stearns, *Life*, pp. 118-119; Johnson, *Battle Cry*, p. 213.
6. William Lawrence to George L. Stearns, June 30, 1856, Howe MSS, MHS; Thomas H. Webb to Martin F. Conway, August 23, 1856, NEA, KSHS.
7. Ibid.

8. Ralph Waldo Emerson to Mary Stearns, August 19, 1856, in Rusk, *Letters*, 5:31; George L. Stearns to George F. Hoar, August 18, 1856, Stearns MSS, MHS.

9. Mary Stearns to Augusta G. King, September 16, 1856, Stutler Collection.

10. George L. Stearns to Agent, Franklin County Kansas Aid Committee, September 22, 1856, Antislavery MSS, Boston Public Library (hereafter cited as BPL).

11. Ibid.; Samuel G. Howe to Patrick T. Jackson, September 12, 1856, Massachusetts Kansas Committee Manuscripts, Massachusetts Historical Society (hereafter cited as MKC MSS, MHS).

12. Stearns, *Life*, p. 118; U.S. Congress, Senate, *Reports of the Majority and Minority of the Select Committee on the Harper's Ferry Invasion, with the testimony accompanying, and other Papers*, Report 278, 36th Cong., 1st sess., June 21, 1860, pp. 227-228 (hereafter cited as U.S. Senate, "Mason Report").

13. Mary Stearns to "Dearest Kathy," October 17, 1856, Stutler Collection.

14. George L. Stearns to Samuel G. Howe, November 9, 1856, MKC, MHS.

15. Donald, *Sumner*, p. 319; Stearns, *Life*, p. 125.

16. Amos A. Lawrence to Colonel Walker, November 19, 1856, NEA, KSHS; Johnson, *Battle Cry*, pp. 200-221.

17. Stearns, *Life*, p.121; George L. Stearns to Samuel G. Howe, November 24, 1856, MKC, MSS, MHS.

18. Amos A. Lawrence to Charles Robinson, December 17, 1856, NEA, KSHS; William Hutchinson to A. H. Shortleff, Fall 1856, NEA, KSHS, quoted in Johnson, *Battle Cry*, fn., p. 218; New York *Daily Tribune*, December 23, 1856.

19. Amos A. Lawrence to Charles Robinson, December 17 and 26, 1856, NEA, KSHS; Johnson, Battle Cry, p. 221.

20. Jeffrey S. Rossbach, *The Ambivalent Conspirators*: John Brown, *the Secret Six, and a Theory of Slave Violence* (Philadelphia: University of Pennsylvania Press, 1982), pp. 75-77; Franklin B. Sanborn, ed., *The Life and Letters of John Brown* (Boston: Roberts Brothers, 1891), p. 347; Oates, *To Purge This Land*, pp. 183-184; Franklin B. Sanborn to Thomas W. Higginson, January 5, 1867, Thomas W. Higginson Manuscripts, Houghton Library, Harvard University, Cambridge, Massachusetts (hereafter cited as Higginson MSS).

21. Stearns, *Life*, p. 129; Oates, *To Purge This Land*, p. 187; Sanborn, *John Brown*, pp. 332-333.
22. Ibid.
23. Stearns, *Life*, p.129; U.S. Senate, "Mason Report," p. 227.
24. Thomas W. Higginson, *Cheerful Yesterdays* (Boston: Houghton, Mifflin, 1898), p. 215.
25. Stearns, *Life*, p. 133.
26. Oates, *To Purge This Land*, p. 159; Stearns, *Life*, p. 135.
27. Oates, *To Purge This Land*, p. 195.
28. Mary Stearns to Warren Preston, March 13, 1857, Stutler Collection; Mary Stearns to Frank Sanborn, April 1885, quoted in Sanborn, *John Brown*, pp. 509-510.
29. Mary Stearns to Frank Sanborn, quoted in Sanborn, *John Brown*, p. 510; Stearns, *Life*, p. 159.

5

Financier of Insurrection

Having put his hand to the plough tumeth not back.
— Franklin B. Sanborn

From their first meeting forward, George Stearns believed in John Brown because he wanted to believe in him. Brown became the vehicle to destroy the greatest threat Stearns saw to his democratic and capitalistic society, the institution of slavery. Stearns came to have such an absolute faith in the merits of Brown's opposition to slavery that he overlooked the feasibility of the latter's plans to destroy the institution. Eventually, Stearns stood ready to support this man even when the modus operandi included violence. Stearns never questioned Brown's involvement in the rumored brutal slayings of five proslavery men at Pottawatomie, Kansas. The businessman made a deliberate decision to give money and to encourage others to contribute so that Brown could be an instrument of his personal desire to rid the nation of slavery. In Stearns's view, Brown "could never be a failure." He believed Brown to be a nineteenth-century Cromwell whose mission in life was that of "social regeneration."[1]

On April 11, 1857, several days after Brown left Boston, Stearns called a Kansas Aid Committee meeting. He paced back and forth while the members took their seats. Stearns joined them at the table and, after calling the meeting to order, told the men that Brown required additional funds to prepare his band and other free staters to repel an invasion of Kansas by Missouri ruffians. Stearns moved to allow Brown to proceed to sell half the Sharps rifles now in his control to prepare for an attack. The committee approved the motion. Stearns suggested they give an additional sum of $500 to Brown, should the need arise. Some members voiced dissatisfaction with the arrangement and Stearns had to use a great deal of persuasion to carry the motion. As a compromise, Brown would become a Kansas Aid Committee agent. As such he would be required to account for funds allocated to him.[2]

On April15, 1857, Stearns sent a letter to Brown informing him of the committee's decisions. He instructed Brown to sell one hundred rifles "at a price not less than $15 each" and to "account for the same agreeably to his instructions for the relief of Kansas." Once in the territory, Brown was authorized to request from P. T. Jackson, the committee's treasurer, $500 if necessary. Stearns was not certain how strong the support for Brown was in the committee and appended a personal note, stating, "On looking at the votes I think it is clear that you had better draw the money" right away. If Brown did so, Stearns believed there would be "no questions asked." Stearns also included a personal draft for $100.[3]

At The Evergreens Stearns told his family about the support given to Brown and expressed concern over whether the money would be adequate. That evening, Stearns retired to the study. Presently, the door opened and there in the firelight stood his son Harry. The boy walked over and gave his father thirty cents for Kansas relief. George asked him whether he was certain he wanted to part with such a large sum. Harry said yes. Then Stearns finished composing a letter to Brown, asking whether he had received the earlier note concerning the actions of the committee. But most of the letter spoke of the enclosed donation. Stearns was proud of Harry's sacrifice. He told Brown that it was the boy's "own decision to give the money not prompted by his parents." Stearns asked Brown whether if he would be so kind as to "write a note to him acknowledging the receipt of it."[4]

Brown received this letter at the Massasoit House in the western Massachusetts manufacturing city of Springfield. After leaving Boston, Brown sought to buy revolvers. Several arms dealers could provide them, but not, according to Brown, "*in time*." Here in the Connecticut River valley, Brown found an arms manufacturer, north of Springfield, in Chicopee, from whom he could immediately obtain revolvers similar to Colts. The firm's agent, "Colonel" T. W. Carter, told Brown that the Massachusetts Arms Company would charge only $1,300, for they "mean it to be a donation, in part from them." Colonel Carter explained he "did not want the thing be made public." Brown wanted these arms badly. Unfortunately, he took the wrong tack with Stearns. He asked Stearns to see whether the people in Boston would give him additional funds so that he might at least be well armed.[5]

Stearns's temper flared at this insinuation that he and the others were not doing enough. Stearns was also annoyed because this letter came on the heels of another request from Brown for personal funds. In this request, Brown asked that a subscription be taken to purchase the home he now rented from Gerrit Smith in North Elba, New York. Brown explained in separate letters to Stearns, Lawrence, and Sanborn that his Kansas service was placing an increasing hardship on his family. He would be relieved by knowing they would be provided for should he fall in defense of Kansas.[6]

Stearns wrote to Brown that he and Lawrence had recently discussed the request for personal funds. Stearns told Brown, "Mr. Lawrence has agreed with me that the $1000 shall be made up." He assured Brown that Lawrence would write to Gerrit Smith to tell him he could depend on the money. Several days later, Lawrence spoke to Stearns and said he had written Smith as promised. Lawrence, however, changed his mind about contributing the full amount and asked Smith to take $600 down and to obtain a mortgage from Brown for $400. Stearns, embarrassed, wrote to Brown to ask him whether the new arrangements were satisfactory and, if not, to write.[7]

Brown was not satisfied and lost no time in telling Stearns so. The response upset Stearns, and he immediately drove to Lawrence's counting room. There the two men argued about who had said and promised what. Stearns left Lawrence without settling the issue entirely. The next day he wrote to Brown, explaining that Lawrence would pay the $600 immediately and that he, Stearns, "would be responsible for one half of the deficiency if he [Lawrence] would provide the other half." Stearns told Brown that Lawrence had left for a trip west. When Lawrence returned he would tell him to fulfill the agreement. Brown wrote again to request even more money; Stearns curtly told him he "had better accept the proposition to mortgage for $400" and let it go at that.[8]

On June 1, Lawrence returned to find a note from Stearns. The Emigrant Aid Company president responded, indicating that there was a misunderstanding between the two businessmen. Lawrence wrote, "My dear sir. I did not intend to do any more than write a 'heading' for a subscription for Capt. Brown." He would like to "do the whole" but he was "behindhand in everything." Lawrence thought Stearns must have misunderstood, for he would "be held for the $1000 only if Capt. Brown sh' be killed or disabled." After some further wrangling, Stearns managed to persuade Lawrence to donate $335. Stearns put himself down for $285 and then had business acquaintances pledge the balance. All the money was finally collected late in November 1857, and Stearns, having received more from one subscriber than pledged, sarcastically returned $25 to Lawrence.[9]

Stearns found it easier that spring of 1857 to arrange for the purchase of the revolvers than for Brown's homestead. On May 4, Stearns informed Brown that he had placed an order for the revolvers from "Colonel" Carter. Stearns showed a streak of the hard driving business side. "If I pay for those Revolvers," he told Brown, "I shall expect that all the arms and ammunition, Rifles as well as revolvers, *not used* for the defense of Kansas shall be held as pledged to me." As almost all the recent letters to Brown ended, he asked, "When do you go to Kansas?" Stearns explained the free state leaders needed him in the territory to coordinate planning.[10]

Stearns also believed other people needed to be talking about the defense of Kansas. So, on May 10, he wrote to the National Kansas Committee, headquartered in New York City. He carefully explained that, in his judgment, Kansas needed one year of "quiet and prosperity." If peace could be secured, he said, a "large influx of Northern and Eastern men will secure the state for freedom." In order to gain the stability needed for continued migration, Stearns said that the following three actions were necessary: first, an appropriation of $100,000 from the Massachusetts legislature to be placed with discreet persons (his committee) to use for relief work; second, the organization of a secret defensive force, commanded by John Brown, to "repel Border-ruffian outrage"; and, third, the continuation of donations of food, clothing, and money to settlers who "from misfortune are unable to provide for their present wants." Stearns told the New Yorkers of his confidence in Brown's courage, prudence, and good judgment. Brown, as an agent of the Massachusetts Kansas Aid Committee, would maintain "control of the whole affair," and, by implication, Stearns controlled Brown. Stearns also told them that he lacked confidence in the present free state leaders, who were too interested in land speculation. Brown, on the other hand, would not be sidetracked by other interests and could be counted on to "hold to the original principle of making Kansas free."

Stearns closed by echoing the intent of the letter, an appeal for money to aid Brown or, if funds were not forthcoming, for continued aid to settlers in the territory.[11]

On May 22, 1857, on his way to Kansas, Brown reached Cleveland, Ohio, where he took time to catch up on correspondence, for Stearns demanded reports on a regular basis, just as he did from other agents. Brown wrote to Stearns mostly about personal money matters. He complained about Gerrit Smith, who was in no position to help financially, since "last year's efforts for Kansas had embarrassed him." According to Brown, Smith offered "no encouragement of any help." Brown mentioned that he had used his own money to pay "Colonel" Carter for the weapons' primings, a cost not anticipated.[12]

Stearns acknowledged the letter, but was weary of Brown's continued efforts to obtain additional money. The businessman had other pressing matters on his mind. Brown might keep Missourians at bay, but sustaining the free state settlers in the territory was still a concern. Stearns's agent, Martin F Conway, informed him that the plan to ration clothing, "not especially designated for private individuals," for later sales to the needy at a low rate on one-year credit met "approbation both from donors and recipients." Fortunately, through Stearns's efforts, the various relief organizations agreed to place clothing into a common stock to facilitate the sales. The advantage was consistency to prevent complaints which might arise if one aid organization gave some items away while another sold donated goods. Conway urged Stearns to continue to work toward cooperation with the various relief groups, especially the Emigrant Aid Company.[13]

Conway answered questions Stearns raised regarding aid money. He explained they "bought 700 Bushels of red potatoes and 500 barrels of oats, 50 boxes of garden seed." Later in the year Conway hoped to purchase spring wheat, seed com, and field beans. "I know," he declared, "of nothing that will give greater joy" than the arrival of seeds. Still, if emigration continued at its current levels, that might create a food shortage next year. Conway said they had to convince established settlers to "plough largely" and to make certain "large crops are put in." The letter pleased the Massachusetts Kansas Relief Committee chairman. Stearns believed this news vindicated him. It was obvious Lawrence was wrong and aid work must continue.[14]

Stearns and others watched the political and economic situation in Kansas. The assumption of the presidency that January 1857 by James Buchanan left both proslavery and Free Soil supporters in doubt as to territorial issues. Each side—Free Soilers meeting in Topeka, proslavery advocates in Lecompton—claimed its government was the legitimate legislative body. The last territorial governor, John W Geary, appointed by President Franklin Pierce in late summer 1856, had managed to bring an end to the bloodshed in the territory. He had also tried to merge the two legislative bodies. But the "bogus" proslavery legislature, as the free staters called it, was desperate to maintain Kansas as fertile ground for slavery. Threats were made on Geary's life. General Persifor Smith, commanding federal troops at Fort Leavenworth, refused to support the governor. On March 4, fearful for his life and frustrated by the thankless task, Geary resigned.[15]

Buchanan's replacement for Geary was excellent. A Northerner by birth currently residing in Mississippi, James Walker harbored strong Unionist sentiments. Although Lawrence believed the appointment would make Kansas a slave state-an opinion Stearns shared-Walker's main's goal was to bring the territory into the Union under the political control of free state Democrats. When the free state legislature met at Topeka in June, the delegates passed resolutions condemning Walker's upcoming constitutional convention and adjourned. However, the territory's future was not going to be decided by politics or violence. Emigration held the key to the future. On April 11, 1857, the Lawrence *Herald of Freedom* estimated that there were a thousand new arrivals in the territory each day. During the following months, the population of Leavenworth, for example, increased by four thousand. In addition to the New Englanders, many of the new arrivals were from the Middle Atlantic and prairie states. At least nine tenths of the emigrants were from free states. Unfortunately, these new arrivals were forbidden to vote in the next election for convention delegates. As it turned out, the June election became a farce, for in protest, many of the free staters who could vote did not.[16]

For a time, it appeared Stearns had grown weary of Kansas politics, and with the coming of warm weather, the urgency associated with relief work faded. At Mary's insistence, the family turned to pleasurable activities. At the end of June the Stearnses drove out to Concord to spend an evening with the Emersons. It was a delightful visit, and the family, basking in the brilliant moonlight, was enraptured by a late ride back to Medford. The following months, while Medford languished in the humid summer heat, Stearns decided that his business and Kansas relief could do without him for a while. With his usual meticulous planning, he arranged for a family expedition to the White

Mountains of New Hampshire. On the way, Mary's two sisters and their husbands joined the Stearnses. When the contingent arrived at Gorham, New Hampshire, there standing on the train station platform to give them a cordial welcome was George's old friend Thomas Starr King, now a clergyman of note. That evening in a nearby lodge, King, with Stearns listening attentively, gave a discourse on the mountains they were about to tour. Several days later, the party ascended the peak of Mount Washington on horseback. When someone asked upon their return whether they had seen any bears, Stearns must have chuckled when one of his brothers-in-laws responded, "It's all bare up there." This jesting set the tone for the stay. During their several weeks' stay in the cool mountains, they experienced, one relative declared, not even a "superficial ruffle of unpleasantness. "[17]

Things were quite different when the family arrived back in Medford. Although there had been undercurrents of an impending financial crisis, the rumors seemed louder and more persistent that August. Earlier, Stearns had prepared for the eventuality of a financial crash. He had possessed the good sense to observe the overextension of credit, the western land speculation, and other indications of an overheated economy. So, the previous month he had begun to call in notes due, to sell stock in shaky corporations, and to convert many of his assets into gold. John Brown, writing from Tabor, Iowa, was apparently unaware that the impending financial crash would take a toll on his backers; he either ignored it or was too intent on his plans. In any case, Stearns must have expressed some annoyance at another Brown letter complaining about a lack of funds, especially his inability to pay his son-in-law for the construction of a house in North Elba. Another letter from Brown addressed to Harry Stearns cast a warm glow over the entire family. As he promised, Brown sent the boy an autobiography, although he referred to it as a "short story of a certain boy of my acquaintance." Written to Harry, the story appears to be an attempt to convince George and Mary of his worthiness and of his degree of success in accomplishing his objectives, for, Brown declared, "our plans are right in themselves." Brown discussed his long war with slavery and the willingness to risk his life in the struggle against this evil. On August 10, Brown wrote to Stearns again, and this time he did not refer i:o any specific need for money but told the businessman that he was in immediate need of $500 to $1,000 for what he called "secret service with no questions asked." With peace growing in Kansas, Stearns puzzled over the request's wording.[18]

Stearns asked his young friend Sanborn to respond to Brown. The manufacturer was now distracted by the possibility of a financial crash. Sanborn told Brown that Stearns did receive his letter and the "account of a boy named John." He went on to suggest that Brown was needed in Kansas to guarantee the peace and should go regardless of whether additional funds were available. Stearns, fearing a run on the banks, told Sanborn to tell Brown that if he had not cashed the draft, he "had better do so now." Stearns advised his agents to use caution in regard to their funds. Thomas]. Manti responded that he would pay only bills "as I think you will approve" and would not "encourage any expenditures that do not seem to be absolutely necessary."[19]

On August 11, the New York flour and grain firm of N. H. Wolfe declared bankruptcy. Then the large Ohio Life Insurance and Trust Company failed. Stearns dated the beginning of the Panic of 1857 from these events. He watched one company after another go down, like, he said, "the successive detonations in a thunderstorm." For the moment Stearns tried to leave public affairs to others so that he could pay attention to his own business. But by then he was committed and could never totally remove himself from Kansas affairs.[20]

That fall Stearns managed to find time to correspond with agents in Kansas. Martin E Conway wrote to ask Stearns's opinion on whether he should vote in the October 5 territorial convention. Stearns cautiously refrained from taking a position. He told Conway that, being so far removed from the Kansas political scene, he found it "impossible to form a decided opinion." On the basis of the few facts at hand, Stearns told him that he had better vote, rather than divide the Free Soil party. Stearns warned that he was "open to conviction or correction." He said he just did not know what was best, for "our world is now engrossed" in the financial panic. "If it would snap the South," Stearns declared, "I would welcome it, so much do I hate the present state of affairs."[21]

In Tabor, Brown was also bemoaning the present state of affairs as he saw peace in Kansas and the panic eat away at his financial backing. In ill health with barely enough money for food, Brown wrote blaming the Massachusetts Committee for his destitute state. Busy at his counting house, Stearns asked Sanborn to respond to Brown. Sanborn explained that, yes, Stearns had received the request for the $500, but as matters stood, the committee could not send that amount. "Money," he explained, "is very tight here." The committee treasury was exhausted, and new donations were needed. He reminded Brown that it was not easy to raise money during a national financial panic. However, Sanborn told Brown that an agent of the committee, E. B. Whitman, was in Boston and some funds might be available by the time he returned to Kansas.[22]

At the end of September, Whitman returned to Kansas with instructions to give John Brown, when available, $500 from committee funds. Stearns told Whitman that if the transfer of funds created any difficulty for him, he should draw the amount on Stearns's personal account. Unfortunately, Whitman found that it was, "impossible to negotiate a draft on any terms" and told Stearns he could not "get the money on yours or any other individual's credit." When Brown wrote to Whitman, the agent told him that no funds were available.[23]

Stearns renewed his interest in Kansas politics and took a more positive stand as the October 5 election approached. Now Conway's reluctance to participate bothered Stearns, for he feared other free staters would not cast their ballots. Agent Thomas Marsh wrote to Stearns that his fears were groundless. All those who opposed slavery were united in earnest and would vote. The territory was, according to Marsh, "saved. to freedom." The election would be peaceful, Marsh explained, for they were relying on Walker's promise to require six months' residency as the only qualification for voting.[24]

Marsh was correct in his assessment. Six days after the election, the returns indicated a victory for the free state party. Governor Walker discarded all fraudulent ballots, and a free state candidate was elected to represent the territory in Congress. The party claimed thirty-five of the fifty-two seats in the territorial legislature. The vote took the heart out of the proslavery movement for the moment. Whitman wrote Stearns that all was peaceful in the territory and likely to remain so in the near future.[25]

Whitman also reported that he was distributing clothing and expected to complete the work within six weeks. He expressed concern about charging for it, as previously agreed. Some of the clothing had been specifically donated for free disbursement. Whitman asked Stearns whether he thought it would be better to put aside an assortment of equal value for free distribution later in the harsh winter months to truly destitute settlers. Traveling throughout Kansas distributing goods, Whitman prepared settlers for the coming winter. Upon arriving in Wyandotte, the agent found a messenger from Brown and relayed the information to Stearns: "Poor Mr. B is badly disappointed at being thus kept back." But the agent thought it best because of the election results. He assured Stearns, once more, that all was peaceful in the territory.[26]

However, soon afterward the political climate changed. Apparently some constitutional convention members meeting in Lecompton still had visions of creating a southern style society in Kansas. A move was afoot to draft a proslavery constitution but not submit it to a vote. Free staters were up in arms, and Whitman wrote to Stearns the "plot was thickening." Brown was to meet with the Free State Central Committee. Militant territorial senator James Lane, described by some as a "hatchet faced political opportunist," offered Brown a commission in the territorial militia.[27]

In November 1857, with the territorial slavery issue still in doubt, Stearns contacted Brown. He wrote, "The Free State Party should wait for the B.R. [Border Ruffians'] moves and checkmate them." Stearns emphatically declared, "Don't attack *them*, but if they attack you, 'Give them Jessie and Fremont besides.' You know how to do it." Basing his opinion on recent reports from Whitman and other agents, Stearns believed that if the free staters let the Democrats play their games in Kansas and in Congress, they would do themselves more harm than their opponents could. He closed the letter by telling Brown that Mrs. Stearns had received $15 for a slave's chain that Brown had left with her. He explained she could only get this price from a "good Kansas Man." In any event, Mrs. Stearns extended her heartiest wishes in the hope that Brown would be in their neighborhood soon and that his family was well and bearing up under the troubles sweeping the nation.[28]

The following week Stearns received a letter from Whitman, whom Brown was badgering for money. The agent told Stearns he was presently using his own funds for relief work. The harried Whitman explained that he was "willing to work, wear out, die if need be in the cause" but that he could not "make brushes always without straw." Stearns responded by sending authority to draw $2,345.34 from various sources. As for Brown, he was to receive $500 from the sale of clothing. Irked by Brown's claim that he was due more money, Stearns told Whitman that it was wrong to suppose he was "under any obligation to] . B. either expressed or implied." Stearns reminded the agent that in all instances when he "had the management of money for the use of Kansas he exceeded the amount pledged and that J. B.'s case was no exception." Also, Stearns explained, Brown was only authorized to draw on him for funds in a "certain contingency, [and] that contingency has not occurred." The relief chairman believed it would be very unwise for Brown or anyone else to attempt to establish order by force. Stearns was not willing to have any of his money used for that purpose. According to him, the best policy for free staters was to "meet the enemy at the polls and vote them down." There was no doubt in his mind that they could do this and only defend themselves, as he told Brown, "if attacked, but by no means attack them."[29]

Stearns, however, was increasingly distracted away from events in Kansas by the deepening panic as it began to strike close to home in the waning months of 1857. "We are in such a crisis here," a business acquaintance wrote, that only those who went through the 1837 panic could realize how severe conditions really were. He said,"]. K. Mills and Company and many stronger houses have gone and other larger ones on Milk Street only exist by sufferance." Stearns was safe because of his keen business sense. The underlying cause of the panic, he believed, was the "power given to banks to issue currency for their own benefit, and at their own convenience." Actually, events far more complex than his interpretation took into account had brought about the current financial crisis. In the 1850s, the nation underwent tremendous growth in western lands under cultivation, followed by sizable railroad expansion financed from abroad. With the Crimean War came an increase in the exports of grain to Europe. When the war ended and Russian grain exports revived, the demand for American agricultural products fell off sharply. Simultaneously, the powerful Bank of France increased its demand for specie payments by its debtors. This placed a severe strain on English banking houses. Because American businesses and foreign trade relied heavily on European loans, especially from England, the French demand had a ripple effect in the United States. Banks began calling in their loans and limiting the supply of notes, hence Stearns's comment. The Ohio Life Insurance and Trust Company's failure then signaled the beginning of a period of contraction that resulted in significant numbers of business failures, including those of Stearns's friends and acquaintances.[30]

One panic victim was Peter Butler, who had saved Stearns from financial ruin after his aborted speculation in lead. Butler was heavily invested in railroad stock prior to the crash and now found himself in a serious financial situation. Stearns devoted the better part of a week poring over Butler's ledgers. At first, he thought Butler was headed for bankruptcy. Then, one evening at dinner he told the family that there was a way to rescue his friend. He and another Milk Street businessman would lend Butler the money needed to remain solvent. Stearns's contribution was more than $5,000. Obviously, although the panic caused Stearns some anxious moments, his early precautions had left his wealth intact.[31]

George and Mary enjoyed the financial position his timely, accurate, and straightforward dealings brought. Money allowed for indulgence. For example, he had an eye for horses and stylish carriages. He purchased several Black Hawk mares, which were not particularly fast yet remarkable for their form and grace. The conveyance the mares pulled came from the famous carriage maker who had built a similar vehicle for Boston Brahmin Charles Francis Adams. At fifty, financially secure, Stearns found life very satisfying. Kansas relief work was a decided success and brought him recognition. The Stearnses were known in society, and among his friends and acquaintances were some of the most influential people in the Northeast. None questioned his business integrity. The New York financier August Belmont once told Stearns, "You have only to show me your note, and I hand it to the cashier." Whether on political State Street or in the financial centers of New York and Boston, Stearns was a notable figure.[32]

Socially ambitious, Mary never ceased nagging George to be more stylish in his appearance. But he could be called good looking, and even at fifty, his ruddy brown beard and lighter hair did not show any white. His large hazel eyes, though solemn, were full of humbleness. To some he often seemed ingenuous as a child. Frank thought of his father as not a particularly reflective or observing person, but one who could apply tremendous concentration to any business at hand. Some people might have called Stearns self-absorbed. To a great extent, the more Stearns became involved in public service, the more he seemed to drift away from his family. Mary complained that he should make a greater attempt to advance his interests and those of his family in society. He meekly endured her criticism and, on at least one occasion, replied, "I think considering all things, I have done very well." If he had any influence, it was because people knew he had no wish to further his own interests.[33]

This sometimes dull merchant did, however, take a delight in music and theater. On almost any Wednesday that winter of 1858, one could have found Stearns at the Boston Music Hall symphony rehearsals. He not only enjoyed music, but also took pleasure in watching people. The young women who secretly met their beaux at the Music Hall amused him, as did the older women of fashion who frequented the hall to put themselves on display. But what pleased him most of all was Fanny Kemble, and her dramatic Shakespeare readings. He had admired Fanny from the very beginning of her first American tour in 1832. Now, as a wealthy businessman, Stearns could afford the luxury of a box seat to listen to her perform. He enjoyed the artist's work so much that in one two-week period he traveled to Boston twelve times to listen to her. Not a good public speaker himself, Stearns was thrilled with, he said, her "perfect mastery over voice and action" when she lost herself in the character. At George's urging, Mary Stearns arranged a bouquet for Fanny's table every evening that season. Fanny's agent tried to arrange a meeting between the actress and the Stearnses, but for some unexplained reason it never materialized. Conservative in his own manners, Stearns overlooked and was faintly amused at the actress's eccentric behavior, such as throwing a glass through a closed window for fresh air. When he and Mary praised her artistic virtues to Emerson, they met rebuff. Emerson called Fanny Kemble a "great exaggerated creature" and told the couple that he "felt a kind of satisfaction to know that the ocean rolled between us." Stearns told Emerson that his criticism was severe and that he was "too hard on human nature." To Mary, George remarked, "It is not everyone who has such cool blood in his veins as Ralph Waldo Emerson."[34]

Stearns did not have such cool blood flowing through him. In that bleak winter of 1858, his generosity reached not only the settlers in Kansas. The wealthy manufacturer believed that men of his class should take a direct interest in relieving the suffering of the poor. "He gave," Frank said, "because he could not endure to see others suffering." While touring the estate, Stearns discovered a small lad of ten years with ragged clothes and bare feet, sitting in the orchard. After much prodding the boy gave his name, Stark MacGregor. The boy lived in Charlestown with his father and a stepmother, who beat him severely and regularly. Stearns took the boy back to the mansion where he was bathed and clothed. He confirmed Stark's story through his mill foreman. Stearns spoke to the father and eventually arranged to send the youngster to a country school.[35]

Although Stearns could not be called a cheap or stingy person, he never gave presents to acquaintances and rarely to relatives. He did attend some of the children's parties and the boys received gifts at appropriate times, but their father disliked Christmas and other occasions on which gifts were customarily exchanged. Stearns's relationship with his sons seemed a combination of his father's gentleness and his mother's coldness. He sent the two older boys to boarding school to prevent their becoming "soft and effeminate," but later regretted doing so. The boys received no allowance without performing chores, such as hoeing the garden. As for guiding his sons toward a profession, he believed it wrong for a parent to determine an offspring's destiny. He did believe, however, that if a son did not decide on a career at the proper time, it was a father's duty to coerce the offspring into selecting a suitable profession. As the decade of the 1850s drew to a close, one thing was certain about Stearns: he was about to have less time to spend with his family.[36]

As the year 1858 began, the peaceful situation in the Kansas territory relieved Stearns. In January free staters effectively blocked the proslavery Lecompton constitution. For John Brown the pressure was not relieved because slavery still flourished elsewhere. Peace in the territory meant taking his war against the institution elsewhere. At the end of January, having removed his men and supplies from Kansas to Iowa, Brown visited free black Frederick Douglass; he wrote to his Massachusetts supporters: Frank Sanborn, clergymen Theodore Parker and Thomas Wentworth Higginson, doctor and philanthropist Samuel Gridley Howe, and George L. Stearns. Each received a different letter, but all the letters revealed a plan to rid the nation of slavery. Stearns received his letter forwarded from Boston while he was on a business trip to New York City. His letter, like all the others, mentioned arrangements for an operation that would require additional, "secret service" money and asked whether Stearns would meet him at Gerrit Smith's home in Peterboro, New York, to discuss the matter.[37]

Stearns was in no mood to see Brown. Apparently, the British soldier of fortune Hugh Forbes had had a falling out with the Kansas hero over money. Brown must have placed the blame on eastern supporters, for Forbes wrote several, Stearns said, "abusive letters" to Charles Sumner, Frank Sanborn, and others. On February 4, while still in New York City and so mad that he could not wait to return to Boston, Stearns wrote an angry letter to Brown in Rochester. Whitman was to give him $500 because Stearns thought Brown needed money for the winter and not because of an obligation. Stearns repeated much of an earlier letter to Whitman, telling Brown that the true course of action in Kansas was now to "meet the enemy at the ballot box." Now that free staters controlled the territorial legislature, the contingency which required more money no longer existed. Stearns said he wanted the money returned "without conditions" and that if he were in error, he would "be glad to be enlightened" by Brown. Then, oddly, the letter's tone changed. Stearns told him that he was not indifferent to his request for a meeting and that Brown's advice and encouragement were of great importance. Stearns suggested that perhaps a trip to Boston would give Brown a much better chance of success than a meeting at Peterboro. Stearns promised to aid Brown as far as it was proper and told him that "Mrs. Stearns would send an encouraging word," if she knew that he was writing. Stearns also asked Brown whether Forbes's claim of a "positive contract to pay him money based on promises from the New England men" were true.[38]

One of the New England men did accept Brown's invitation to meet at Peterboro. Frank Sanborn received two letters from Brown in which he spoke of a plan but did not give any details. Sanborn arrived at Gerrit Smith's mansion on February 23. That evening, Sanborn listened while Brown revealed his plan to invade the South to obtain recruits for an African-American army of liberation armed with weapons seized from a federal arsenal. With a large enough force of escaped slaves, Brown proposed to launch a guerrilla war from a stronghold in the Allegheny Mountains. The following day Sanborn left Peterboro unconvinced of the plan's merit. Arriving in Boston, he sought out Howe, Stearns, Parker, and Higginson and revealed the plan to each, as Brown had instructed. Sanborn said that Brown very much wanted to see his friends and would be in Boston, at Stearns's expense, the first week of March.[39]

As scheduled, Brown arrived on March 4 and immediately sent word to Sanborn, Howe, Stearns, Parker, and Higginson to meet with him at the American House the following Friday evening. No sooner had they assembled than questions concerning Forbes from the five men flew at Brown. All of the inquiries showed their concern about Forbes's "abusive letters." Brown adroitly explained away the letters and downplayed their impact. When he shifted the conversation to request funding he left the men with the feeling that withholding their support was equivalent to betrayal and desertion. Then Brown revealed his plans for a slave insurrection. He did not, however, share with them the exact location for his "Rail Road business on a somewhat extended scale." He told the five men that even if a rebellion lasted for only a few days, it would be enough to set the South ablaze. Here was another agenda. Regardless of his immediate success or failure, an attack with the purpose of liberating slaves might well provoke an insurrection, a sectional crisis, or both. Then, too, Brown, if captured or killed, would become a martyr for the abolitionist cause. Brown's words stirred his audience, and the men decided to support him despite some lingering doubts. What finally might have led Stearns and the others to accept the plans for armed insurrection was Brown's preliminary work over the past year. He had demonstrated that he held the same values they did and the strength of character to carry out his objectives. To reject Brown at this stage, one modern historian stated, "would have been to reject themselves." Although the situation in Kansas was improved, it appeared to the group that President James Buchanan, who had recently called on Congress to admit Kansas as a slave state, would tear the nation apart, and when that happened, treason would not be treason much longer, but patriotism. Higginson had told Brown earlier that he was "always ready to invest money in treason." Stearns was caught up in the moment. He saw now that Kansas was merely one battle in the war against the slave power and that Brown had made a correct assessment of the current situation. Like Brown, Stearns was not a thinker, but a doer, and Buchanan's efforts to force slavery on the territory, the majority of whose residents rejected the institution called for action. All five visitors and later Gerrit Smith came around to Brown's convincing argument that because peaceful alternates against the slave power conspiracy failed to halt it, violent revolution remained an option. Stearns was no fool. Since their initial meeting, he had carefully gauged Brown in business terms and believed in him. And Brown had done everything possible to convince Stearns of his reliability. Brown, like Stearns, had always shown himself to be decisive and impatient. They both agreed slavery was immoral, a cancer destroying the society that had blessed Stearns and his family with a good life. To preserve what Stearns had achieved for his sons, he believed he must contribute to the destruction of slavery. Brown was the vehicle to accomplish this objective.[40]

Stearns had traveled a long road to reach this decisive point in his life. Events such as the Fugitive Slave Law, the Kansas-Nebraska Act, Sumner's caning, and Buchanan's efforts to foist a proslavery government on Kansas settlers all contributed to his growing willingness to support violence. For the quiet, unassuming businessman, the time had come to travel a dangerous path. He could not fill the role that Brown played, the soldier of freedom. Brown could, for no one else had offered to do so much. Still, Stearns's decision to support violence had an aura of innocence and childhood adventure in it. Stearns, in midlife, longed for adventure, the kind his friend Samuel G. Howe had experienced while fighting in Greece. As in his earlier attempt to comer the market in lead, Stearns now became impetuous and daring, hoping in one gamble, in which he risked all, to achieve his objectives. Brown revealed a plan that appeared to be a calculated risk. If Brown's insurrection strategy did not succeed, it might start a chain of events that would lead to the destruction of the institution of slavery by igniting a sectional crisis. The impression Stearns had, according to Frank Stearns, was that whether Brown "succeeded or failed, living or dead, the results would be the same." Yes, Stearns must have thought, the time for him and for the nation had arrived. The United States could no longer endure the contradiction of slavery in a democracy.[41]

Putting into action their decision to support violence, on March 12, 1858, the five Massachusetts men met to form the Secret Committee of Six, which included Gerrit Smith, who earlier had agreed to participate. Without hesitation, Stearns assumed the chairmanship and became treasurer of the organization. Sanborn became the secretary. Their initial objective was to raise $1,000 for what the six men referred to as Brown's "business operations." At this first meeting, each member pledged to raise at least $100. The conspirators decided not to reveal the nature of the business to others, even those in sympathy with their cause, including close friend Wendell Phillips. In less than a week's time, on March 18, Stearns notified the members of a meeting to be held at Howe's office at the Blind Asylum on Bromfield Street at noon the following Saturday. Thus far, the group had raised or donated a little more than $100. Sanborn and Higginson would be responsible for only their own $100 contributions, and the others would become the fund raisers, in addition to providing their personal donations. As the men discussed ways to obtain the money, Stearns shrewdly announced his decision to up his personal contribution by $200. As Stearns expected, both Howe and Parker offered to increase theirs.[42]

Quite unexpectedly, for Brown had assured the Secret Six in March that the Forbes issue was dead, the British soldier of fortune brought the group's fund-raising activities to an abrupt halt. On May 1, Howe and Sanborn told Higginson that they had received letters from Forbes stating that Brown's business should be halted and that he had disclosed everything to Senator Seward. Forbes must have, indeed, revealed some of Brown's plan, for rumors were circulating in Congress. Senator Wilson wrote to Howe and told him that he "better talk with some few of our friends who contributed money to aid old Brown." Wilson said that if the arms they gave Brown for the defense of Kansas were "used for other purposes, as rumor says they may be, it might be of disadvantage to the men who were induced to contribute." The Massachusetts senator advised them to regain control of the weapons. The following Sunday, Sanborn, Stearns, and Howe met in the latter's office to discuss this new development. Howe brought out several other letters recently received. From the letters, the conspirators were shocked to learn that Forbes knew not only Brown's plan but also, what was worse, all their names. In

Washington, Forbes was where he could do a great deal of harm because, as one of the conspirators put it, "his exact knowledge makes it appear that there is a leak somewhere in our boat." Stearns argued that "the matter must stop," and Howe, Parker, and, finally, Sanborn agreed. Gerrit Smith's position on the matter was similar to theirs, but fiery Thomas Wentworth Higginson argued against delay, for if the action were postponed now, it would be ended permanently. Forbes, he said, could do as much damage the next year as this year. Sanborn wrote to Higginson telling him that protesting against delay was fruitless because Stearns, Parker, Howe, and Smith were each large stockholders and would halt "the raising of the mill" by refusing to solicit additional funds.[43]

Stearns took prompt action to placate Senator Wilson and anyone else concerned about Brown's activities. The shrewd businessman wrote Brown what amounted to a public letter, stating that the arms in Brown's possession were exclusively for the defense of Kansas and belonged to the Massachusetts State Kansas Committee. Stearns told Brown that it was his duty to warn him "not to use them for any other purpose, and to hold them subject to my order as chairman of said committee." To reassure Wilson and other members of the Massachusetts congressional delegation, Stearns had his clerks prepare copies and send them out to the anxious politicians in Washington.[44]

Brown, too, was doing his best to allay fears. To Higginson, he declared, "I do not know what to do that none of our friends need have any fears in relation to hasty or rash steps being taken by us." Brown urged his eastern friends to "keep clear of F[orbes] personally." Brown also asked for additional funds, "pledging ourselves not to act." Still, Stearns wanted one of the Secret Six to talk to Brown. Because he could find no one else, he told Brown to meet him in New York at John Hopper's home. Hopper was the young man Stearns had befriended many years earlier by setting him lip as an insurance agent. In the meantime, Stearns helped Howe draft an adroit letter denying everything to baffle Forbes. Then Stearns was off to New York, as he said, "to settle matters finally." Concerned about losing his backers, Brown met with Stearns at the Hopper residence, as requested. The two agreed that Brown would retain custody of the rifles as an agent not of the Massachusetts State Kansas Committee, but of Stearns.[45]

After they reached this agreement, Stearns immediately returned to Boston and called the Secret Six together. Only Higginson refused to attend. Gerrit Smith, usually absent from the meetings, was in Boston to address, of all organizations, the American Peace Society. On the afternoon of May 24, the five conspirators met with Brown in Smith's room at the Revere House and discussed Forbes's revelation and courses of action. Although the mood in the room was anxious, not one of the five men was in a panic. Their letters to Brown and to one another revealed neither fear nor timidity. The men believed that the disclosures, although placing them under scrutiny, might well be dismissed if the attack were delayed. Brown used the opportunity to ask for even more funds. The conspirators agreed merely to postpone the attack and to send Brown off to Kansas, one of them said, to "blind" Forbes while the Secret Six raised the $2,000 to $3,000 requested. Brown left the meeting both relieved that his plan was still alive and upset at the delay.[46]

Brown went immediately to Worcester to confer with Higginson, who was furious when he discovered the results of the Revere House meeting. "Postponement is abandonment," the minister told Parker. "The more I think of postponement," he declared, "the more annoyed I am." But because Higginson, like Brown, realized that Smith and Stearns held the purse strings, he could only defend his position for immediate action to the extent of his investment. In confidence, Brown told Higginson he thought that Gerrit Smith was a timid man, that Stearns and Parker "did not abound with courage," but that at least until now Howe "had more." Brown confided in Higginson that it was essential that they should not think him reckless, for he was "penniless without them" and could not "raise the mill."[47]

Brown returned to Boston and took a room at the American House, where Stearns called a meeting of the Secret Six on June 2. At this meeting they confirmed the earlier decisions: to postpone the operations until the following spring or winter, to send Brown to Kansas to mislead Forbes, to raise $2,000 to $3,000, and to give Stearns personal ownership of the Sharps rifles. The change in ownership of the rifles showed no lack of courage in Stearns. The group also decided in the future the Secret Six were not to know of Brown's exact plans. Brown left Boston the next day with a $500 advance in gold, retention of the arms, his delayed plan still intact, and good spirits.[48]

Stearns was also in good spirits, for he believed that they had narrowly averted a crisis. Earlier, Howe had written to Wilson that the Kansas Committee gave no countenance to Brown for any operations outside Kansas and that Brown was off to the territory to "take part in the coming election, and throw the might of his influence on the side of the right." As for Forbes, because no raid would occur in the immediate future, his story would be discredited. So, although the past few months had been trying, Stearns now thought that the conspirators were safe and the "mill raising" proceeding.[49]

Later that June, after observing that his "mill-wheels were rolling as steadily as ever" and that Kansas affairs were progressing favorably, Stearns decided to indulge himself by enlarging his home. Although the old mansion was roomy enough on the ground floor, it was much too narrow and contracted on the upper levels. One evening he sent for his carpenter. Sitting in their shirt sleeves at the dining room table, the two men discussed what was turning out to be a difficult problem. Finally, as the hall clock struck ten, the carpenter told Stearns that in order to do what he proposed, "every stick of lumber" in the house would have to be taken out and that, if he decided to go ahead with his plans, he should consult an architect. Stearns hesitated, for he had never had any planning done by contracting it out. He did it himself and then supervised local help. "If I should have this house rebuilt by contract," Stearns told Mary, "I should not feel that the lives of my wife and children were safe while I was away from home." George seemed to think that the system of contracting work caused "bad flues and leaky roofs." He said that he preferred to be "cheated in my pocket rather than on the work that is done for me." But the job still required outside help, so Stearns reluctantly obtained the services of an architect.[50]

Stearns let his first contract to a relatively unknown architect, Charles Follen, a young man who was, according to Stearns, of the "most perfect good taste in his dress, manners and conversation." Stearns was careful in selecting the inexperienced Follen instead of a man of established reputation. He preferred a young man who would honestly express his own ideas rather than attempt to patronize a client as so many successful architects did, or so Stearns believed. He must have enjoyed his fatherly role, perhaps thinking of his old benefactor, Deacon Train. Stearns and Fallen must have made an interesting pair, taking measurements, walking through the house, and engaging in serious conversation about which materials best suited the project. Practical and modest, Stearns limited the ornaments in the construction and wanted to have no "ogee curves, no white ceilings, and no marble fireplaces," Frank declared. Finally, the plans were drawn, and the craftsmen selected.[51]

In August the Stearns family moved to a neighboring cottage, where they would live humbly and economically until The Evergreens renovation was completed in May. As in past summers, Stearns withdrew from Kansas affairs and business matters to relax with his family. This year, however, the Stearnses planned no major outing, although they did make frequent trips to Concord to visit the Emersons. At the end of August, Stearns became entranced with the appearance of Donate's comet. It became a regular event for him to go out on the cottage porch and watch it grow from a small "star in the handle of the Big Dipper" in August until the beginning of October, when it "filled the western sky from the horizon nearly to the zenith," as he described it. Apparently the event caught the imagination of the manufacturer. He speculated on the popular superstition that the appearance of large comets was followed by devastating wars. Not a superstitious person, Stearns thought there might be "some occult influence in cometary matters . . . apart from the visual effect upon the mind." As a consequence, he read everything he could find concerning comets and then decided to pay no attention to it as a sign or an omen.[52]

That fall of 1858 signs did indicate that no further relief work was needed in Kansas. In September, Stearns called the Massachusetts State Kansas Aid Committee together for a final meeting. The agents were paid off, Sanborn gave a final report, and the books were closed. Brown's weapons remained Stearns's personal property. To dilute Forbes's revelation even more, the committee announced its demise to all the senators Forbes had contacted earlier in order to, Stearns believed, leave them "without any further ground for complaint." Unknown to the senators, however, the Secret Six continued their clandestine meetings that fall. Brown sent the group two letters informing them of his activities in Kansas. In answer to a letter probably written by Sanborn, Brown told them that Forbes had disappeared. Brown also wrote that little else could be "accomplished until we get our mill into operation." But, after the conspirators in Boston talked the matter over, there was no decision to allow Brown to proceed.[53]

Although he continued to raise funds for the "mill," Stearns did not appear very concerned with Brown's activities. In January 1859 the Stearnses joined the Emersons and Henry David Thoreau in a notable skating party at Concord on Walden Pond. Gliding like a youngster over the smooth as a mirror ice, Stearns enjoyed the exercise as much as he might have thirty years earlier on the Middlesex Canal. On returning to Medford, Stearns received word of a raid Brown and his men had conducted late in December on two plantations in Missouri. The raiders made off with slaves, wagons, horses, mules, and other property. One planter was killed, a fact that did not seem to move Stearns. On January 20, Brown had led eleven liberated slaves north to freedom. Property and slaves disposed of, Brown left Kansas for Tabor, Iowa, where he began in earnest to finalize his arrangements to "set his mill in operation." He wrote to Sanborn on February 10, 1859, that his plans included a trip east for the same purpose. Again Brown asked for funds. Sanborn told the others that they should give him the money "as a reward for what he has done .... At any rate I think he means to do the work."[54]

Although Stearns was more than willing to support Brown in fomenting revolution, he also continued to work the political system. As it happened this spring of 1859, the Medford manufacturer received an invitation to join an organization known as the Bird Club, which evolved in 1850 as a political supper club that dined initially at the Parker House and later at George Young's in Boston. The host, Frank W Bird, was a wealthy manufacturer who owned several paper mills in East Walpole. By 1856, with an amorphous membership of one hundred, the club was a large and powerful body of men. As with all of Stearns's ventures, his joining the Bird Club coincided with its ascending to power in Massachusetts. The club stood, as one member declared, "for ideals as the guides of political action [and] leadership in a democracy [with an] adherence to a theory, a plan, an inward vision . . . beyond the accommodation of the moment." In 1859 the club directed its energies to propelling one of its members, Stearns's lawyer, John Andrew, to the Massachusetts governor's office.[55]

Membership in the Bird Club acted as a tonic for the taciturn Stearns. Although, as he burst into the dining room for a meeting, he was usually applauded by the group, he paid no attention while finding a place at a table. "Waiter, bring me some minced fish with carrots and beets," the normally reserved businessman would shout. The political debates stimulated him so much that years later, Frank could remember his father's coming home late Saturday night "looking so full of force that he seemed as much like a steam-engine as a man." Stearns confided in his family that, although the conversation during the Bird dinner was to his liking, "the fish was not served in the way our grandmothers made it." Stearns remained a member of this club the rest of his life, enjoying his association with people with "force enough to threaten and alarm the great parties."[56]

In May 1859 Stearns anxiously awaited another force he hoped would also threaten and alarm the great parties, John Brown. Brown's primary purpose in paying a visit to Boston was again to raise funds. The Secret Six arranged to have Brown solicit contributions from other individuals. One evening, for instance, he talked to some orthodox clergymen, a meeting that appeared fruitless. The following morning, however, one of the ministers sought him out and put five $20 gold pieces in his hand. Because of The Evergreens renovation, Stearns was unable to entertain Brown at his home. They did, however, dine together at the Bird Club, where Brown became embroiled in a heated argument with Henry Wilson, who believed that Brown's Missouri raid had harmed the antislavery movement in Congress. Stearns later told Sanborn that the raid was a good thing for it would confuse Forbes and it proved Brown's plans had a chance of succeeding.[57]

Four of the Secret Six held a series of meetings to discuss Brown's plans. Still annoyed at the delay and probably ashamed at his lack of financial support, Higginson did not attend. Parker was absent because of consumption and left for Europe to recover. At these meetings, Brown confidently gave more details of his plans. As Brown was about to leave the last meeting, he reached into his belt and withdrew a pearl handle Bowie knife taken from "Border Ruffian" H. Clay Pate. Brown slowly handed it to Stearns and said, "I am going on a dangerous errand and we may never see each other again."[58]

On June 3, 1859, Brown set out from Boston with "$800 from all sources except from Mr. Stearns, and from him the balance of $2,000," according to Sanborn. From the very beginning, Stearns spoke and acted with his purse, giving John Brown more money for his activities than any other contributor. Sanborn told Higginson that Stearns was a man who "having put his hand to the plough turneth not back." In fact, Stearns left Boston to go to New York to make final arrangements of an undisclosed nature for Brown.[59]

On Stearns's return to Boston, Charles Fallen called on him at the Milk Street counting house to announce that the renovation of The Evergreens was completed. Stearns spent most of the summer of 1859 enjoying the comfort of the place, "planting elms on his avenue and the like," Frank recalled. Friends came out from Boston to spend an evening on the piazza, watching the lights of Medford wink while enjoying Stearns's favorite Hungarian wine, according to Frank, a "cup that cheers but not inebriates." Stearns also found time that summer to read. He brought home a small book, Hinton Helper's *Impending Crisis of the South*. "Here is a book," Stearns told his son, "written by a Southerner against slavery as a practical institution, from the white man's standpoint." This argument was very much in agreement with Stearns's practical, business oriented view, for it proved statistically that slavery was an economic burden for the southern states. Stearns let out a deep rumbling laugh, and said that Horace Greeley, who amused the businessman with his original ways, "has got hold of it and is making the most of it." Stearns did acknowledge that Helper, in making his argument, failed to consider differences such as climate and geography. Stearns attributed his financial success to the availability of labor in the North through immigration. Slavery, Stearns believed, as did Helper, discouraged free labor from moving south. As a consequence, artisans had to be imported from the North, but their wages, the capital for industrial growth, and they themselves eventually returned to their own region.[60]

Among the visitors to The Evergreens that summer was John Brown, Jr., who was in the Northeast seeking additional capital for his father's plans, which he called "hiving the bees." The son arrived in Boston on August 10 and shortly thereafter dined with the Stearnses. As he left that evening, his host said, "We have the fullest confidence in Brown's endeavor, whatever may be the result." The young man reported to his father, "I have met with no man on whom, I think, more implicit reliance can be placed." Unfortunately, the same could not be said of Higginson. Brown's request for yet more money, $300, had Stearns's support, but apparently Higginson had not backed his fiery statements with cash. Perhaps seeing a way to stifle the constant criticism that flowed from the Worcester clergyman, Stearns told Sanborn to contact Higginson. So Sanborn wrote, "You must raise $50, if possible. You see the emergency and how others have met it." Four days later, on September 8, Stearns wrote to Higginson, "We have done all we could and fall short another 50 as yet." Sanborn waited a week, and when no money was forthcoming, wrote again. A week later, Sanborn told Higginson that his share had been made up and sent to Brown by messenger and that the "business operation" was to begin the next Saturday, October 15, 1859.[61]

In the early morning hours of Sunday, October 16, 1859, John Brown struck. Within a relatively short period, Brown and his band seized the Harpers Ferry arsenal and occupied the fire engine house. Here he would either ignite the South with a slave rebellion or, failing this, precipitate a sectional crisis, the outcome of which would be civil war and the ultimate freeing of the slaves. When Brown's men stopped a train and allowed it to proceed, word of the siege spread. Stearns anxiously awaited news of Brown's activities. On October 19, a Boston morning paper reported that a "band of lawless ruffians had seized Harpers Ferry, Virginia." Stearns's reaction to the news must have been one of elation, for he believed that the invasion of the South had begun.

Eager for even more news, Stearns probably spent the night pacing up and down at The Evergreens. The following morning he drove off to Boston to await further news. The news brought the shock of Brown's capture and "business operation[s]" failure. Shaken, Stearns drove to Howe's office and found the doctor very much agitated. He begged Stearns to flee to Montreal with him. Stearns insisted that they consult his lawyer, John Andrew. Apparently, the two conspirators did not reveal the true extent of their involvement, for Andrew took the matter "quite coolly," according to Stearns, and said he would "look up their case." Stearns dropped off Howe and returned to his counting room. He wrote letters to two of the "boldest jayhawkers" in Kansas, offering them financial support if they thought it feasible to rescue Brown. Then Stearns waited to hear from Andrew.[62]

On Friday, after researching the issue with great care, Andrew wrote to Stearns, "I see no possible way in which any one can have done anything in Massachusetts for which he can be carried to another state. I know nothing for which you could be tried even here." Unfortunately, Brown left letters from the Secret Six at a farm near Harpers Ferry, and the newspapers published the names mentioned in the incriminating documents. Because Massachusetts Governor Nathaniel Banks was known to be hostile toward the Bird Club in particular, and unsympathetic to abolitionists in general, Stearns and Howe decided to "take themselves out of the way until the excitement . . . subsided." The two men hurriedly put their affairs in order and left on October 22 for Canada. Parker was still in Europe. Sanborn visited the Brown family in North Elba, and then left for Quebec. Higginson remained in Worcester, making plans to see Brown. The New York landowner Gerrit Smith apparently suffered a nervous breakdown and was admitted to the State Asylum for the Insane in Utica, New York, where he stayed until the furor died down.[63]

Initially, people in Massachusetts, in other parts of the North, and in the South reacted to the news from Harpers Ferry with horror and condemnation. Even William Lloyd Garrison's *Liberator* called Brown's efforts "misguided, wild and apparently insane." Both Democratic and Republican newspapers were strident in their criticism of Brown and the conspirators, even in radical Massachusetts. Within a short time, however, some abolitionists in Massachusetts began to moderate their hostile attitudes as it became apparent that Virginia's trial of Brown would be a farce, with legal procedures ignored or violated in an attempt to obtain a guilty verdict in the shortest time possible. The reaction was more in sympathy with Brown's personal condition than with his motives. Virginia's governor Henry Wise did not help matters by describing Brown as a "bundle of the best nerves I ever saw cut and thrust bleeding in bonds," a man of "clear head, of courage, fortitude and simple ingeniousness."[64]

George Stearns was correct in his earlier assessment that Brown could never be a failure. Brown's raid electrified the nation, and although few were to realize it initially, its effects widened like the ripples of a rock thrown into the Potomac at Harpers Ferry, until the waves reached the walls of Fort Sumter in Charleston Harbor. Writing to her niece to offer help while Stearns was away, Lydia Maria Child remarked, "I honor Brown's motives, but he made a great mistake . . .. The effects may be favorable to freedom in the long run; but it is impossible to foresee the consequences." Personally, she was "certain slavery or freedom must die in the struggle." A Southern journal, *DeBow's Review*, echoed those sentiments, calling the raid "the first act in the grand tragedy of emancipation . . . the vanguard of the great army intended for our subjugation." Sympathy for Brown began to grow in Massachusetts among abolitionists. Mary Stearns, acting on her own, if not on behalf of her husband, attended a meeting in Concord at which Henry Thoreau praised and canonized Brown. When word came of Brown's death sentence, Mary commissioned sculptor Edwin Brackett to prepare a bust of her hero. Brown at first objected, but when Brackett explained who sent him, he said, "Anything Mr. and Mrs. Stearns desire I am well pleased to agree to." Mary also sent small comfort items and a letter to Brown with Judge and Mrs. Russell when they visited. From the safety of Canada, Stearns continued to attempt to mount a rescue operation. Regardless of personal feelings toward Brown and apprehensions over his own safety, Stearns remained a businessman first. In the midst of all the turmoil, Stearns sent a lawyer, George Sennott, to Harpers Ferry to set about collecting Brown's weapons and equipment for shipment to Boston. The most expensive arms were the Sharps rifles, one hundred of which were, according to Sennott, "safe as yet, and may be recovered." Unfortunately, the balance of the rifles were "carried off by Baltimore 'Plug Uglies,'" Sennott said, and the pikes Brown obtained in Connecticut "plundered and are scattered everywhere." The agent told Stearns that if the one hundred rifles were recovered, he should consider it clear profit. The agent also advised Stearns to "prevent meddling just now," for if anyone went to Harpers Ferry to claim his rights, the Virginians would "break open the boxes and scatter their contents all over his Northern neck." Unless the request were made quietly, Sennott said, Stearns would "never see a rifle come back." "Speaking of coming back," Sennott added, "let me take a liberty and ask you to come back yourself."[65]

Stearns was not yet ready to return. His efforts to mount a rescue failed and John Brown was executed on December 2. On that same day, George Stearns said he "escaped from Dr. Howe," and spent a morose day at Niagara Falls, the falling waters of the cataract sounding a dirge for his martyred hero. Mary Stearns attended a memorial service held for John Brown in Concord and then spent the day with the Emersons. In memorial, Stearns again pledged his life and fortune to slavery's destruction. He became uncomfortable with the enforced idleness and could no longer remain in Canada. He now had work to do. Public opinion had shifted. Now extradition to Virginia was only a remote possibility. A week after the execution, Stearns returned home. As he approached Boston, late Indian summer weather turned first cloudy and raw and then into a severe snowstorm. Stearns finally reached The Evergreens just before midnight on December 12. The hollow sound of the great door knocker roused the household, and the door was thrown open to the "great rejoicing of his wife, children and servants." Yet, the homecoming's pleasure was marred by Brown's death. Stearns could not help thinking that ground might have been lost by the raid's failure. However, through the immediate gloom he saw, as he had predicted when their paths had first crossed, that in the long run Brown "could never be a failure." The Boston businessman was more ready than ever to put an end to slavery.[66]

Stearns basked in his family's warm welcome. They were indeed happy to have him home. It had not been easy for Mary, and George realized that. She did not have her husband's authority when it came to the servants. The coachman, whom Frank called brutal, also had responsibility for tending the steam furnace at The Evergreens. In Stearns's absence the man neglected to replenish water in the boiler. Fortunately, Harry had an interest, much like his father's, in mechanics. The boy diagnosed the lack of heat and called other servants to extinguish the fire before the boiler exploded. When Stearns heard about the incident, he promptly dismissed the errant coachman. He also had other matters to attend to upon his return, but after having taken care of the family and business matters, his thoughts turned south to Virginia.[67]

On December 14 Stearns began a campaign to have two of Brown's men's unclaimed bodies returned north. He wrote to abolitionist J. Miller McKim requesting "prompt measures might be taken to procure the bodies of Copeland and Green and have them properly interred in their native

Pennsylvania." Stearns offered to pay the necessary expenses. McKim, however, was not interested. Stearns became furious at the man's "neglect in this matter." He told the Reverend Samuel May, Jr., that he planned to display McKim's refusal in the antislavery office for reference, for he did not want to be accused of not doing the right thing for Brown or his men. He and Mary discussed the matter and hoped that John Brown's remains would be taken eventually to Mount Auburn Cemetery near Cambridge, where a "suitable monument [would] be erected to his memory and that of his noble associates." Stearns also wanted the African-Americans with Brown recognized for their heroic actions: "Let not the world say we honored the white but forgot the colored brethren."[68]

Nor did Stearns intend to forget the Brown family. He and Mary wrote several letters to Mary Brown expressing concern. Ruth Thompson, Brown's eldest daughter, responded to Mary because she had heard her "dear Father speak of [her] and Mr. Stearns as being his very dear friends that helped him so much." She also told Mary that, although they had never met, she did not think of herself as a stranger, for her mother shared their recent letter "full of heartfelt sympathy for Mother and respect for My dear lost Father." In his cell, Brown had written a farewell letter to George and Mary. His wife sent it to the Stearnses soon after Christmas, saying her husband had placed it in a book that she had brought home from the Charlestown, West Virginia, jail. "May God forever reward you and all yours. My love to all who love their neighbours," Brown wrote, telling the Stearnses that he had asked to be "*spared* from having any *mock*; *or hypocritical prayers made over* me when I am publicly *murdered*." Tears must have welled up in Mary's eyes as she read Brown's request that "*my only religious attendants* be poor *little, dirty, ragged,* bare *headed, and barefooted, slave Boys*, and Girls led by some old grey headed *Slave Mother*. Farewell." The letter devastated the Medford couple, and they both resolved to continue assisting Brown's widow and children.[69]

John Andrew, Stearns's lawyer and now a Republican candidate for governor, was holding funds donated for Mrs. Brown's use. He transferred them to the lead pipe manufacturer "as the person who would be able to apply them to the best advantage." Stearns personally saw that Brown's two younger daughters received an education. He arranged for them to attend Frank Sanborn's Concord school. "They were good girls," he said, "but with dreary expressions, as if their lives had been hard and joyless." The rest of his life, Stearns maintained a fund for the Brown family.[70]

113

When Stearns ventured back into the Boston business world, he received a rude shock. Merchants who had known him all his life, he said, "passed him on State Street without recognition." Commenting on Stearns's giving arms to Brown, Lawrence told a friend that "this was not the only impudent act of this committee." Stearns heard himself "cursed by others of the meaner sort who had nothing to hope or fear from him." The treatment received from his bank became intolerable, and he moved the accounts to another that had "an abolitionist for a cashier." At the Bird Club, Wilson gave Stearns a "rather biting compliment, which met with an equally sharp rejoinder," according to one of the members. But even though Frank Bird was a "trifle cool to him," said Stearns, a majority of the club, led by their candidate for governor, John Andrew, stood by him. Stearns had other supporters. His customers, plumbers and tinsmiths, admired John Brown as a national hero. In speaking of their heartwarming support, Stearns said, in answer to Wilson's fear that events at Harpers Ferry would kill Republican presidential chances, "Those are the men who carry our elections, and not college graduates, of whom a large proportion never go to the polls." Still, many Republicans were concerned when the Senate voted to appoint a committee to investigate the Harpers Ferry matter. Some abolitionists and northern politicians believed the committee's Democrats hoped to implicate leading Republicans in the affair and thus damage the party's presidential prospects. The committee began to summon "witnesses from the North," Republicans claimed, "with a view to get at the facts of the *great conspiracy* as they pretend to think it."[71]

Stearns, Sanborn, and Howe each received a summons to testify. Howe went first, appearing the last week in January 1860. Sanborn declined, and Stearns prepared to answer his summons to appear on February 17, 1860. He believed that testifying last put him at a disadvantage, for it "subjected his statements to a cross fire from the evidence that had already been taken." However, there was little to worry about for Howe did not make any statements incriminating Stearns. Howe told the Harpers Ferry committee chairman, James M. Mason of Virginia, that he had confidence in Brown but that it was "utterly absurd to infer from that any responsibility for his acts." Still, Stearns hesitated and asked Mason for a postponement on personal grounds. The chairman agreed. "It is certainly not expected," he wrote Stearns, "that you should leave home under the circumstances mentioned in your letter." Mason asked him to travel to Washington when he could, giving the committee one-day notice by telegraph. Massachusetts judge E. Rockwood

Hoar reassured Stearns that, even if an attempt were made to hold him, he would petition the Boston courts to issue a writ of habeas corpus.[72]

Stearns finally decided to appear. On February 20, he arrived in New York with Mary and their youngest son, Carl. The other two boys, Frank and Harry, stayed at home with the servants. George left Mary in John Hopper's charge and took the sleeping car to Washington. Arriving at six in the morning, Stearns went to Willards Hotel, where he wrote his name in the register, "as large as life." After a hearty breakfast, the lead pipe manufacturer visited first Charles Francis Adams and then Charles Sumner. After talking with the two Massachusetts men, Stearns called on Mason to arrange a meeting with the committee the next morning at eleven. He lunched at Willards with Sumner, who said, "You will of course say what you think of Slavery." Stearns replied, "I probably shall." Sumner responded, "I know Mrs. Stearns would." Stearns must have smiled and answered, "Yes, she would." The senator leaned over and said, "Tell them the whole truth, Stearns." Writing to his wife that evening, Stearns told Mary of his conversation with Sumner. Stearns also said that he was glad she had stayed in New York, for the trip would have been uncomfortable for her and embarrassing to him. He closed the letter "Love to all who love me and the rest of mankind."[73]

The next morning Stearns walked to the Capitol reflecting that the city was "the meanest hole in creation"; Congress, "the meanest part of Washington." He entered the committee room just before eleven. After taking the oath, Stearns began his testimony. He had no intention of following Sumner's advice, because he believed that "common prudence dictated" he be "reticent as possible concerning his own affairs." He wanted to be freer, but, as he told Dr. Howe later, "I was afraid they might bring me up with a round turn if I was careless." The opening questions concerned his involvement with the Kansas Committee and the initial meeting with John Brown. The questions shifted to the arms, revolvers and Sharps rifles captured at Harpers Ferry. Stearns responded in his halting manner, becoming more hesitant as the committee fired questions. Finally, the businessman asked the committee whether he might give them a statement on paper because, he said, "I am unaccustomed to speak in public, or even give evidence for it is seldom that I have been in courts to give evidence." Stearns told them that if he were allowed to read a statement, the testimony would be clearer and more condensed than he could make it any other way. The committee members agreed to allow reading of the notes he considered an answer to the questions at hand. Stearns tried to respond this way about the Kansas Committee's arms in Brown's possession. Then the businessman again requested that he be allowed to read the prepared statement. "That would open the whole question," Stearns declared, "and give you a better understanding. These questions involve my connection with Kansas affairs, and hence it will be as well to give the whole statement." The committee members consulted and then agreed to allow Stearns to read his statement. He began with his early involvement with Kansas and went on to the initial meeting and financial support of John Brown. Everything Stearns addressed was the truth, but the statement revealed more in what it did not include, such as Stearns's knowledge of Brown's insurrection plans. When asked pointed questions, Stearns did not hesitate to lie. He denied the fact that he wrote or referred to Brown as "Isaac." He refused to admit that he told John Brown, Jr., to tell the Kansas hero that he maintained "the fullest confidence in his endeavor whatever may be the result." The former Kansas Relief chairman also denied that he sent someone to reclaim the Sharps rifles Brown had taken to Harpers Ferry. When the two southern Democrats, Mason and Jefferson Davis, attempted to link the Bird Club's Republican membership with John Brown, he refused to admit that Brown dined or met with the members. Stearns also did not reveal whether any club member gave Brown money.[74]

At this point in the testimony, Jefferson Davis of Mississippi entered into a dialogue with Stearns. He asked about the Parker House. Stearns told the senator that it was "one of the best eating houses in the town." Davis responded, "Are select dinners given there?" Probably relieved at the divergent questions, Stearns responded, "Yes, sir; it is a place where everybody goes for a good dinner." Davis pursued the issue and asked whether it was a place where "fine and expensive dinners are given." The businessman told the senator that the Parker House served "the rarities of the season, and cooked in the best manner."[75]

Feeling more comfortable, Stearns let his guard down when addressed by the only Republican on the committee, Jacob Collamer of Vermont. Stearns expected the Northerner to be at least neutral, if not sympathetic. Instead, the businessman said, Collamer was "rough and surly." In his naive way, Stearns failed to realize, his son Frank later pointed out, that Mason and Davis were "courteous and respectful in order to draw him out and give him a false sense of security." Collamer sensed the questioning's drift and tried to make Stearns reserved and reticent. Unfortunately, just the opposite occurred. Collamer's harshness irritated him, and he became careless ... The Vermont senator asked whether Stearns had any intimation, any idea, that Brown would make a "forcible entry upon Virginia, or any other State." Stearns hesitated and said, "No, sir." He then went on to say, "Perhaps I do not understand you. I did suppose he would go into Virginia or some other State and relieve slaves." Collamer continued, "by force?" Hurting himself further, Stearns replied, "Yes, sir; by force if necessary." The senator pressed further, and finally Stearns hesitantly replied that he "never supposed that he contemplated anything like what occurred at Harpers Ferry." Stearns did his best to keep clear of any indication that he knew in advance of Brown's plans. He admitted an awareness of Brown's opposition to slavery, but he considered the man "as one who would be of use in case such troubles arose as had arisen previously in Kansas." Stearns also said that he did not "suppose he [Brown] would do anything that [Stearns] should disapprove of." To support this claim, the businessman introduced the November 7, 1857, letter to Brown telling him not to attack border ruffians unless they attacked first. Stearns went on to explain that all of the arms given to Brown were intended for the defense of Kansas and nothing more. By introducing the letter, Stearns defused the issue. A number of desultory questions followed concerning the knowledge the other Massachusetts Kansas Relief Committee members might have had concerning Brown's plans. Stearns parried these effectively, and at the end of the three hours, Mason excused the witness.[76]

While Stearns gathered his papers together, the committee filed out of the room, except Mason and a clerk. The senator walked over to the businessman, handed him a bright new Sharps rifle, and asked with a smile whether Stearns had seen it in Massachusetts. Stearns said no, that they were not manufactured in the state. The clerk, not realizing that the two men were beginning to spar, volunteered the information that the weapons were made in Connecticut. Stearns explained that they were boxed and sent directly to Chicago. Mason got to the point: "Don't your conscience trouble you, for sending these Rifles to Kansas to Shoot our innocent people?" Stearns, surprisingly quick, responded, "Self defense. They began the game. You sent ... arms before we sent any from Massachusetts." Sarcastically, Mason replied, "I think when you go to that lower place the old Fellow will question you rather hard about the matter." Stearns shot back, "Before that time comes ... he will have about two hundred years of Slavery to investigate, and before he gets through will say

'We have had enough of this business, better let the rest go.'" Mason laughed and left the room.[77]

Stearns followed Mason out and visited Charles Sumner, who made, the businessman said, "free of his room at all hours, and was of great use to me." The two men discussed the hearing, and Sumner said, "I feel now perfectly easy with regard to Slavery: it has received its deathblow." Stearns told Sumner that the committee members were civil and did not press him at all and that, as for his part, he answered freely and they had taken all he had said in good faith. Bidding Stearns a good evening, Sumner promised to prepare a speech that would do justice to the affair, including the Senate committee.[78]

The following day, Stearns returned to the Senate, where he reviewed the transcripts. He spent an hour and a half reading through his testimony and later said that he "did not want to change one word." He did, however, add several revealing lines to his answer to Jacob Collamer's question "Do you disapprove of such a transaction as that of Harpers Ferry?" Stearns had initially declared, "I should have disapproved of it had I known of it," after which he had submitted the letter telling Brown not to attack unless attacked first. He now asked the clerk for pen and paper and wrote after the one-sentence answer, "But I have since changed my opinion; I believe John Brown to be the representative man of this Century, as Washington was of the last—the Harpers Ferry affair, and the capacity shown by the Italians for self government, the great events of this age. One will free Europe and the other America." There is no record of the committee's response to the change.[79]

Stearns then left to visit the Massachusetts delegation, but found "nothing worth reporting." His observation of Congress was expressed in a letter to Howe. He found men of both parties "split up into petty cliques, each intent on grinding its own little axe, and trying to prevent all others from using the grindstone." If the men walking the halls of the Capitol, he told Howe, "are our Representatives we are indeed of a low type." If they "go on as they do now a few years more, we shall have to abolish the govt. and let the States take care of themselves." "If I had my way," the businessman declared, "I would put a hundred barrels of powder under the capitol, and if Congress did not clear *out*, blow *them* and it Sky high."[80]

Stearns was relieved when he arrived home. Despite anxiety over the trip, he told Howe he had a good time, especially talking to Sumner about the slavery question. A recent speech by William Seward, he declared stood "up to the mark well for a politician." But the New York senator was angling for

118

the Republican presidential nomination, and Stearns thought that the antislavery forces needed "one who believes a Man is greater than a President . . . to raise this question above the Political slough, into its true Position." Stearns said he wanted Sumner "to take up the Gauntlett." A letter from Sumner arrived several days later. The senator promised to see that Stearns was reimbursed for expenses. Unfortunately, Sumner explained "with mortification," he had lost all of Stearns's bills and receipts and asked whether copies could be provided.[81]

Stearns responded to Sumner's request on March 10, 1860, enclosing his "bill vs. Mr. Mason signed as you requested." The businessman had matters other than money on his mind for the eastern newspapers had printed his testimony. He said it was very meager and garbled in the *Tribune* and better in the *Herald*. The entire report was in the *Traveller*. Stearns was surprised at this interest. He expected "friends would be satisfied . . . but was not Prepared to meet the large number of Street acquaintances who have thanked me heartily for what they call bold speech." Stearns informed the senator that the public response confirmed what he had said to Wilson, who kept bemoaning the damage the Harpers Ferry raid had done to the Republicans. Stearns optimistically told Wilson that the "Harpers Ferry affair has sank deep into the hearts of our people." Despite the initial reaction, it "raised the tone of the Political Conventions and Governor's Messages and will force the Republican Party upward." Stearns urged Sumner to take a position on the slavery issue that "when property interferes with the rights of humanity that property must give way, because no amount of law can legalize a wrong."[82]

Stearns seemed obsessed with the Mason committee's legality. He wrote to Sumner thanking him for the "wages of . . . [his] testimony" and commenting that public opinion was slowly taking the right direction in viewing the raid, which he said, "the Senator has dignified into an insurrection." Stearns remarked that persons accused of the crime should be tried by the Courts and until the existing laws have been found insufficient . . . neither State nor National Legislature have any right to inquire into criminal offenses. All of the individuals involved in the raid have been punished. If southerners wanted to go further they should have made the attempt to punish the supposed conspirators in Mass.[83]

With tongue in cheek, Stearns speculated, "I am told these persons if found could have been reached by Process from the Federal Courts." Stearns declared openly that the Senate was wrong and the courts would like to hear an argument on it. Sanborn ignored the Senate summons, and Stearns said that "they will be sure to have the opportunity [if he] is arrested."[84]

Several weeks later the opportunity arrived. Authorities made a comic opera attempt to apprehend Sanborn. Two federal marshals arrived in Concord, seized the schoolmaster, and tried to spirit him off in a carriage. He resisted, and the commotion brought all of Concord to his rescue, including Judge Hoar with a writ of habeas corpus. The following day, April 4, the case was tried in the Massachusetts Supreme Court, and Sanborn was freed on a technicality because an arrest on the order of the Senate must be executed by a member of that body and not by an officer of another branch of the federal government. The marshals were in turn indicted for felonious assault. To Stearns, this episode seemed an "afterpiece to the Harpers Ferry Raid."[85]

NOTES

1. Mary Stearns to Richard J. Hinton in Richard]. Hinton, *John Brown and His Men* (New York: Funk and Wagnalls, 1894; reprint, New York: Arno Press, 1968), p. 724; Stearns, *Life*, pp. 137, 129.
2. George L. Stearns to John Brown, April15, 1857, NEEA, KSHS.
3. Minutes of the Massachusetts State Kansas Committee, April 15, 1857, Stutler Collection; George L. Stearns to John Brown, April 15, 1857, Stutler Collection.
4. George L. Stearns to John Brown, April18, 1857, Stutler Collection.
5. John Brown to George L. Stearns, April26, 1857, John Brown Collection, Library of Congress, Washington, DC (hereafter cited as Brown Collection, LC).
6. Franklin B. Sanborn to John Brown, April 26, 1857, John Brown MSS, Trevor Arnett Library, Atlanta University (hereafter cited as Brown MS, TAL).
7. George L. Stearns to John Brown, April 29, 1857, Houghton Library, Harvard.
8. George L. Stearns to John Brown, May 4, 1857, Stutler Collection.
9. Amos A. Lawrence to George L. Stearns, June 3, 1857, Stutler Collection; Subscription form with Stearns's note at the end, June 3, 1857, November 5, 1857, Stutler Collection.
10. George L. Stearns to John Brown, May 4, 1857, Stutler Collection.
11. George L. Stearns to the National Kansas Committee, May 10, 1857, Stutler Collection.
12. John Brown to George L. Stearns, May 23, 1857, Studer Collection.
13. George L. Stearns to John Brown, April 15, 1857, Stutler Collection; Martin F. Conway to George L. Stearns, March 2, 1857, Studer Collection.
14. Martin F. Conway to George L. Stearns, March 2, 1857, Stutler Collection.

Financier of Insurrection 117

15. Nevins, *Prologue to Civil War, 1859-1861*, vol. 3 of *The Emergence of Lincoln*, p. 137.

16. *Herald of Freedom*, April 11, 185 7.

17. Stearns, *Life*, pp. 140-141.

18. John Brown to George L. Stearns, August 8, 1857, Stutler Collection; Oates, *To Purge This Land with Blood*, pp. 208-209; John Brown to Harry Stearns, July 15, 1857, Stutler Collection; John Brown to George L. Stearns, August 10, 1857, in Stearns, *Life*, p. 144.

19. Franklin B. Sanborn to John Brown, August 28, 1857, Brown Collection, TAL; Thomas J. Manti to George L. Stearns, August 7, 185 7, George L. Stearns Collection, KSHS.

20. Stearns, *Life*, p. 145.

21. Ibid., pp. 141-142.

22. Franklin B. Sanborn to John Brown, August 28, 1857, Brown Collection, TAL.

23. E. B. Whitman to George L. Stearns, September 26, 1857, Stearns Collection, KSHS.

24. Thomas Marsh to George L. Stearns, September 28, 1857, Stearns Collection, KSHS.

25. E. B. Whitman to George L. Stearns, September 26, 1657, Stearns Collection, KSHS.

26. Ibid.

27. Nevins, *A House Dividing*, 2:230-231; E. B. Whitman to George L. Stearns, October 24, 1857, Stearns Collection, KSHS; Oates, *To Purge This Land with Blood*, p. 101.

28. George L. Stearns to John Brown, November 7, 1857, Stutler Collection. An edited copy of this letter in the Massachusetts Historical Society is incorrectly attributed to Franklin B. Sanborn.

29. E. B. Whitman to George L. Stearns, October 25, 1857, Stearns Collection, KSHS; George L. Stearns to E. B. Whitman, November 14, 1857, Stearns Collection, KSHS.

30. J. Forbes to Edward Cunningham, September 28, 1857, quoted in Sarah Forbes Hughes, ed., *Letters and Recollections of John Murray Forbes*, 2 vols. (Boston: Houghton, Mifflin, 1899), 1:167; George L. Stearns, *A Few Facts Pertaining to Currency and Banking; Adapted to the Present Position of Our Finances* (Washington, D.C.: Gibson Brothers, 1864); Douglas C. North, *The Economic Growth of the United States*, 1790-1860 (New York: W. W. Norton, 1966), pp. 212-213.

31. Stearns, *Life*, p. 145.

32. Ibid., p. 147.

33. Ibid., p. 150.

34. Ibid., p. 151-152.

35. Ibid., 154.

36. Ibid., p. 155.

37. John Brown to Thomas Wentworth Higginson, February 3, 1858, John Brown-Thomas Wentworth Higginson Collection, BPL (hereafter cited as Brown-Higginson Collection).

38. George L. Stearns to John Brown, February 4, 1858, Stutler Collection.

39. Franklin B. Sanborn, *Recollections of Seventy Years*, ed. George G. Badger, 2 vols. (Boston: Gorham Press, 1909), 1:154-155, 177; Franklin B. Sanborn to Thomas Wentworth Higginson, February 11, 1858, Brown-Higginson Collection; Franklin B. Sanborn, *Samuel Gridley Howe, The Philanthropist* (New York: Funk and Wagnalls, 1891), pp. 257-258; George L. Stearns to John Brown, February 12, 1858, Stutler Collection; John Brown to George L. Stearns, February 17, 1858, Brown-Higginson Collection.

40. John Brown to Thomas Wentworth Higginson, March 4, 1858, Brown Higginson Collection; Franklin B. Sanborn, ed., *The Life and Letters of John Brown, Liberator of Kansas and Martyr of Virginia* (Boston: Roberts Brothers, 1891), p. 440; Oates, *To Purge This Land with Blood*, pp. 229, 234; John Brown to Thomas Wentworth Higginson, February 12, 1858, Brown-Higginson Collection; Franklin B. Sanborn to Thomas Wentworth Higginson, February 11, 1858, Brown-Higginson Collection; Thomas Wentworth Higginson to John Brown, February 8, 1858, Brown-Higginson Collection; Stearns *Life*, pp. 129-130; Rossbach, *Ambivalent Conspirators*, pp. 145-146; Stearns, *Life*, pp. 189 and 191.

41. Stearns, *Life*, pp. 129- 130.

42. Oates, *To Purge This Land with Blood*, p. 234; Stearns, *Life*, p. 189; Oswald Garrison Villard, John Brown, 1800-1859: *A Biography Fifty Years After* (Boston: Houghton Mifflin, 1910), pp. 224-235; Franklin B. Sanborn to Thomas Wentworth Higginson, March 8, 1858, Higginson-Brown Collection; Franklin B. Sanborn to Thomas Wenworth Higginson, March 14, 1858, Franklin B. Sanborn MSS, Concord Free Public Library, Concord, Massachusetts (hereafter cited as Sanborn MSS); Franklin B. Sanborn to Thomas Wentworth Higginson, March 21, 1858, Brown-Higginson Collection; Villard, *Brown*, p. 326; George L. Stearns to Thomas Wentworth Higginson, April 1, 1858, Brown-Higginson Collection.

43. Franklin B. Sanborn to Thomas Wentworth Higginson, May 1, 1858, Brown Higginson Collection; Samuel G. Howe to Thomas Wentworth Higginson, May 1, 1858, Brown-Higginson Collection; Henry Wilson to Samuel G. Howe, May 9, 1858, Stutler Collection; Franklin B. Sanborn to Thomas Wentworth Higginson, May 7, 1858, Brown-Higginson Collection; Franklin B. Sanborn to Thomas Wentworth Higginson, May 11, 1858, Brown-Higginson Collection;

Thomas Wentworth Higginson to Samuel G. Howe, May 7, 1858, Brown-Higginson Collection.

44. George L. Stearns to John Brown, May 14, 1858, Stutler Collection.

45. John Brown to Thomas Wentworth Higginson, May 14, 1858, BrownHigginson Collection.

46. Franklin B. Sanborn to Thomas Wentworth Higginson, May 18, 1858, Brown-Higginson Collection; Sanborn, *Life and Letters of John Brown*, p. 464. Financier of Insurrection 119

47. Thomas Wentworth Higginson to Theodore Parker, May 18, 1858, and Higginson's notes on a meeting with John Brown, June 1, 1858, Brown-Higginson Collection.

48. Telegram, George L. Stearns to Thomas Wentworth Higginson, June 2, 1858, Brown-Higginson Collection; Higginson's notes, June 1, 1858, Brown-Higginson Collection; Sanborn, *Life and Letters of John Brown*, p. 464. Some discrepancies exist in the sources as to the actual dates of this last meeting with Brown.

49. Samuel G. Howe to Henry Wilson, May 12, 1859, quoted in Stearns, Life, p. 170, and Sanborn, *Life and Letters of John Brown*, p. 462.

50. Stearns, *Life*, p. 175-176.

51. Ibid, p. 177.

52. Ibid., p. 178.

53. Ibid., p. 179; John Brown to Franklin B. Sanborn, September 10, 1858, in Sanborn, *Life and Letters of John Brown*, p. 477; Franklin B. Sanborn to Thomas Wentworth Higginson, October 13, 1858, Brown-Higginson Collection.

54. Stearns, Life, p. 181; Franklin B. Sanborn to Thomas Wentworth Higginson, March 4, 1859, Brown-Higginson Collection.

55. Sanborn, Howe, fn. 252; Henry Greenleaf Pearson, *The Life of John A. Andrew: Governor of Massachusetts*, 2 vols. (New York: Houghton, Mifflin, 1904), 1:60.

56. Frank Preston Stearns, *Cambridge Sketches* (Freeport, NY: Books for Libraries Press, 1905; reprint, Essay Index Reprint Series, 1968), p. 257; Pearson, John Andrew, 1:60.

57. Samuel G. Howe to [?]. May 25, 1859, Howe MSS, MHS; Oates, *To Purge This Land with Blood*, pp. 270-271.

58. Thomas Wentworth Higginson to John Brown, May 1, 1859, Brown-Higginson Collection; Stearns, *Life*, pp. 181-182.

59. Franklin B. Sanborn to Thomas Wentworth Higginson, June 4, 1859, Brown-Higginson Collection.

60. Stearns, *Life*, p. 183.

61. Hinton, *John Brown*, p. 261; George L. Stearns to Thomas Wentworth Higginson, September 8, 1859, Brown-Higginson Collection; Franklin B.

Sanborn to Thomas Wentworth Higginson, October 6, 1859, Brown-Higginson Collection.

62. Stearns, *Life*, p. 187; Oates, *To Purge This Land with Blood*, p. 229.

63. John A. Andrew to George L. Stearns, October 21, 1859, Stutler Collection; Stearns, *Life*, p. 188.

64. *Liberator*, October 21 and 28, 1859; Betty L. Mitchell, "Massachusetts Reacts to John Brown's Raid," Civil War History, March 1973, pp. 65-79; New York *Herald*, October 26, 1859, quoted in Richard A. Scheidenhelm, ed., *The Response to John Brown*, William R. Taylor and Arthur Zilversmit, gen. eds., The American History Research Series (Belmont, CA: Wadsworth Publishing, 1972), fn. p. 4.

65. Lydia Maria Child to Mary Stearns, November 3, 1859, Stutler Collection; *DeBow Review*, January-May 1860, quoted in Oates, *To Purge This Land with Blood*, p. 323; Stearns, *Life*, p. 193; George Sennott to Samuel G. Howe, November 15, 1859, Howe MSS, MHS; George Sennott to George L. Stearns, November 26, 1859, Stutler Collection.

66. Stearns, *Life*, p. 198.

67. Ibid.

68. George L. Stearns to J. Miller McKim, December 15, 1859, J. Miller McKim Collection, Cornell University, Ithaca, New York (hereafter cited as McKim Collection); George L. Stearns to Reverend Samuel May, Jr., December 26, 1859, Antislavery MSS, BPL.

69. Ruth B. Thompson to Mrs. George L. Stearns, December 27, 1859, Alexander W. Armour Collection, Library of Congress, Washington, D.C. (hereafter cited as Armour Collection); John Brown to Mrs. George L. Stearns, November 29,1859 (photocopy), Brown MSS, TAL

70. Source unknown, quoted in Jules Abels, *Man on Fire: John Brown and the Cause of Liberty* (New York: The Macmillan Company, 1971), p. 395.

71. Stearns, *Life*, pp. 200-201; Amos A. Lawrence to Judge Collamer, December 9, 1859, NEEA, KSHS; Samuel]. May, Jr. to R. D. Webb, December 27, 1859, Antislavery MSS, BPL.

72. Summons to George L. Stearns Concerning Harpers Ferry, February 9, 1860, Stutler Collection; Stearns, Life, p. 202; Samuel G. Howe to James M. Mason, February 11, 1860, Howe MSS, MHS; James M. Mason to George L. Stearns, February 15, 1860, Stutler Collection. Frank Stearns, in his father's biography, claims the date set for the hearing was February 24, 1860.

73. Stearns, *Life*, pp. 202-203; George L. Stearns to Samuel G. Howe, February 27, 1860, Howe MSS, MHS; George L. Stearns to Mary Stearns, February 23, 1860, Stutler Collection.

74. George L. Stearns to Mary Stearns, February 23, 1860, Stutler Collection; Stearns, *Life*, p. 203; U.S. Senate, "Mason Report," pp. 225-226, 235.

75. U.S. Senate, "Mason Report," p. 239.
76. Stearns, Life, p. 208; George L. Stearns to Samuel G. Howe, February 27, 1860, Howe MSS, MHS; U.S. Senate, "Mason Report," p. 242.
77. George L. Stearns to Samuel G. Howe, February 27, 1860, Howe MSS, MHS.
78. Ibid.
79. U.S. Senate, "Mason Report," p. 242.
80. George L. Stearns to Samuel G. Howe, February 28, 1860, Howe MSS, MHS.
81. George L. Stearns to Samuel G. Howe, February 28, 1860, Howe MSS, MHS; George L. Stearns to Charles Sumner, March 1, 1860, Sumner MSS, Houghton; Charles Sumner to George L. Stearns, March 2, 1860, in Stearns, *Life*, p. 214.
82. George L. Stearns to Charles Sumner, March 10, 1860, Sumner MSS, Houghton.
83. George L. Stearns to Charles Sumner, March 20, 1860, Sumner MSS, Houghton.
84. Ibid.
85. Stearns, *Life*, pp. 216-218.

6

Emancipation, Black Soldiers, and the Major

> Mr. Stearns is the man who indomitable energy and great business capacity has been brought to bear on the organization of the Firth-four and Fifth-fifth [sic] Regiments.
>
> – Springfield *Republican*

In 1860, countless Americans joined with Stearns in viewing the Harpers Ferry raid as an omen, for some a frightening look into the future. John Brown's prophecy was coming true. Even if the raid failed, it would create a sectional crisis leading to civil war and ultimately slavery's destruction. The South's violent reaction guaranteed the nation was on ,the road to these eventualities. Indeed, the hysteria was so great that any political compromise between Southerners and Northerners appeared less likely than at any time previously. Stearns's generation sensed that the slavery issue had finally reached a crucial point. That point would manifest itself in the 1860 presidential election. The issue hung over the land that spring like the dark clouds of a Kansas tornado.[1]

The storm struck first in April at the Democratic Convention in Charleston, South Carolina. The Platform Committee issued a majority report declaring Congress had no right to abolish slavery in a territory or to pass any legislation to impair the right to own slaves. The minority report declared the Supreme Court should decide the slavery issue. When southern delegates failed to reach a consensus on several resolutions concerning slavery and the selection of a candidate became deadlocked, no alternatives remained but adjournment and division. Meeting separately, northern Democrats nominated Stephen A. Douglas. Proslavery men in Baltimore pinned their presidential hopes on John C. Breckenridge. The Saturday following the Democratic schism, Stearns dined at the Bird Club and shared in the great rejoicing at what he called the Democrats' "political smashup." The gloom that had hung over Stearns since John Brown's execution in December began to lift as the prospects of a Republican party victory brightened. Sumner expressed confidence that any candidate nominated by the Republicans in Chicago in May would be elected. Most of the men at the table, including Stearns, believed that Senator William Seward would receive the nomination. But Stearns believed that principles were more important than men and the party platform would determine the issue of slavery.[2]

To ensure Republican delegates were thoroughly educated to the issues, Stearns convinced Mary's uncle, David Lee Child, to write a tract for distribution at the Chicago convention. Stearns contracted Child to meet with the Massachusetts congressional delegation and obtain approval for the concept. On April18, 1860, Child told Stearns the men in Washington agreed to a tract that was to highlight the following:

1. Gather the most striking outrages upon, Persons, upon Private Right, the Freedom of Speech, the Press and the Post Office.
2. Great omnifest Political wrongs and outrages, having a National hearing, violating the Federal Compact and involving wholesale destruction of lives and property and the degradation of the moral character and honor of the country.
3. Crimes and aggressions of Diplomacy War and Filibustering.[3]

Child reported back that if this met his nephew's in-law's approval, the tract would be ready by the first of May. Should Stearns find it acceptable, then Child would, he said, write "one or two more on the other classes of slaveholding crimes." Stearns accepted the outline but asked Child why he intended to write a series of tracts. His wife's uncle responded that a series would be best because, after viewing the first tract, the "thing could be pursued or abandoned as the friends of the cause and the authors judge best." Stearns agreed. He would personally circulate the first tract at the Republican

Convention after visiting the territory that had been so much a part of his life for so many years—Kansas.[4]

Stearns planned the Kansas trip not only for sentimental reasons. Although the Massachusetts Kansas Committee had ceased operations, Stearns wanted to settle the outstanding relief matters with his agent, E. B. Whitman. He timed the trip to be present at the Republican Convention when it opened. However, he had no intention of staying more than a day or two, such was his confidence in a Republican victory. Once that victory was obtained, Stearns wanted to create a political lobby for African-American emancipation. The methodical businessman also planned to stop in New York, Philadelphia, and Washington, to meet with conservative abolitionists and antislavery politicians to discuss his plans for emancipation.

Before leaving, Stearns invited the Reverend David A. Wasson to spend a year at The Evergreens. Stearns had first met Wasson in 1856 and supported his candidacy for the Medford Unitarian Church ministry. Eventually Wasson was removed from the pulpit because he held strong antislavery sentiments. The purpose of his stay at The Evergreens was to tutor Frank. for admission to Harvard. Stearns had not attended college because of his father's early death. He was determined that at least one son would have the opportunity to do so. Wasson was a philosopher, a poet, and a prose writer, as well as a teacher. Stearns was in complete agreement with Wasson on "religious, political, and social subjects," according to Frank. The businessman initially admired Wasson's "perfect sincerity, his keen penetration, and absence of eccentricity." However, with Stearns's increasing political activity came a divergence and an impatience with Wasson's habit as a philosopher of weighing the pros and cons of a question. Stearns took this habit to be a sign of indecision and weakness. Mary came to disapprove of Wasson's feminine friendships, according to Frank, and just before Stearns's departure for Kansas, a "certain Boston lady," a noted flirt, visited The Evergreens, a visit that caused "Mrs. Stearns great annoyance."[5]

I

On April 26, 1860, Stearns prepared to leave for Kansas. Mary planned to accompany him as far as New York and after a brief stay return to Medford. Frank and Harry Stearns were visiting the Emersons. George wrote to them to return home the following evening to take care of their younger brother,

Carl, and to "let him sleep with you." He closed his note to them in a paternal way: "Be good boys. Your loving father."[6]

On May 1, having left Mary in New York, Stearns wrote from Philadelphia, hoping she "got safe and comfortably home." He had expected Howe and Frank Bird to meet him in Philadelphia; however, Howe became too ill to travel. Stearns and Bird planned to leave that evening after a round of discussions with Philadelphia abolitionist J. Miller McKim. The abolitionist approved of Stearns's plans to lobby for emancipation and thought that after the elections wide support could be obtained.[7]

Traveling west, Stearns and Bird eventually arrived in St. Louis, where they boarded a steamboat for Kansas City. From there, they hired a carriage and drove to Lawrence, Kansas. Stearns arrived during what was normally the most beautiful season in Kansas. Instead of the flatness he and other Easterners envisioned, he found rolling hills and heavy thick woods in the ravines and along the stream banks. The redbud trees were in bloom, their crimson blossoms, although covered with dust, contrasting nicely with the white of the dogwood trees. This year the territory was suffering from a drought, and the countryside, normally emerald green, was barren. According to Stearns, the corn did "not even swell in the ground." Still, Stearns said he found it a "beautiful country." Breaking through from a patch of wood, Stearns must have been startled to see the town of Lawrence sandwiched between the Kansas River and a surprisingly high hill. In town, the businessman received a cordial welcome and declined suggestions of a public ovation. At a gathering that evening in the rebuilt Free State Hotel on Massachusetts Street, the leading men crowded around Stearns and entertained him in a "homely manner," as he recalled. He said it was fortunate he could "drink whiskey cocktails," for the rough and ready Kansas men plied one another and their guest with many. He spoke to Jim Lane at length concerning John Brown, but Charles Robinson, who became the territory's first state governor, avoided contact with Brown's backer. Stearns wrote to Mary about the "sturdy race" of abolitionists represented by James Lane and Jayhawker James Montgomery. He reported that all was quiet and that apparently it would remain so in the near future. His only complaint was the dust, samples of which he sent in the writing paper. Stearns wrote to Charles Sumner declaring that he found the Free Soilers in Kansas the "sturdiest race of Freemen in our land" and that if the federal government did not declare the territory a free state, they would "take it." He would help them, if necessary, and offered funds to Lane and Montgomery for "operations in that quarter." Still, Stearns had not given up on the political process and pinned his hopes on the Republican Convention and the upcoming election.[8]

Stearns left Kansas on May 10 for Chicago, accompanied by the territorial delegate, Judge Martin E. Conway. When they arrived in Chicago, there was a carnival atmosphere. As the somber Stearns strode through the flag-bedecked streets, cheering arose from campaign organizations, and at every corner men argued and buttonholed delegates. Although Seward was still the leading contender among a host of other candidates, Stearns heard one name more than others, "Old Abe" Lincoln of Illinois. On May 16, Stearns was in attendance when Governor E. D. Morgan of New York called the convention to order. The crowd sensed the occasion's importance, and many observers remarked on the bonding of delegates and spectators in a common purpose.[9]

On the second day, the convention adopted the party platform, all of which appealed to Stearns: free homesteads; high protective tariffs; internal improvements, including support for a railroad to the Pacific; daily mail; immediate admission of Kansas into the Union; and a telling declaration that all territories were free and that legislation was needed to ensure they remained free. Stearns left Chicago on the third day, before nominations for the presidential candidate began. If he favored any candidate it was Senator Salmon P. Chase of Ohio, a former Liberty and Free Soil party man, but Stearns, according to Frank, "knew politics too well to expect his nomination." Still, he had almost enough curiosity to stay, but Mary wanted him home. Stearns explained to Bird that she "suffered not so much from loneliness" as from a nagging "fear that something dreadful might happen to him."[10]

Exhausted but happy, Stearns greeted Mary at The Evergreens. He said Kansas's fertile plains offered "a great opportunity for struggling humanity," black and white alike. Stearns told her he was confident Kansas would be free and "a place for the 'panting fugitive,'" and that done, Missouri, Arkansas, and the Indian Territory [could] be cleared of slaves." At the suggestion of Lawrence, he gave an account of the trip to the Emigrant Aid Company directors and the "impressions he received as to its future from what he witnessed there." Emerson was curious about Stearns's impressions. When told that Kansas was "a very beautiful country," Emerson interrupted, "It is not a

130

beautiful country; for that you must have woods and mountains, and there are none in Kansas."[11]

Stearns had more on his mind than Kansas geography. Word arrived in Boston announcing Abraham Lincoln's nomination. Stearns said his only objection was that the Illinois lawyer supported the Fugitive Slave Law. Resigned to the selection, Stearns added, "He. may do . . . as well as another." That evening Wasson and Stearns discussed this relatively unknown presidential contender. Wasson claimed he had identified Lincoln more than two years earlier when the Midwesterner stated that "although our forefathers never suggested men were equal in all respects they ought to be equal before the law." Finally, the two men reached agreement, concluding that had the Republican hopeful been born in "New England or Ohio he would have been a good Free-Soiler." Regardless of his views on the Republican candidate, Stearns knew full well that the split in the Democratic party meant victory for the principles on which the Republican party stood.[12]

One person whose opinions and advice Stearns took to heart was Samuel Howe. At the end of June, Howe visited Stearns at the counting room. After exchanging pleasantries, the doctor suggested that they take the boys (Howe had one son, Henry) to see the new mammoth Stearnship the *Great Eastern*, berthed in New York after its first Atlantic crossing. Stearns agreed and, several days later, with his sons Frank and Harry in tow, arrived in Manhattan. The group settled in at the Fifth Avenue, the city's newest and finest hotel. The next morning, Howe and his son joined them to go see the steamer. With waves gently lapping at its black hull, the *Great Eastern* lay at a pier on the Hudson River. Much more enthusiastic than their boys, Stearns and Howe spent most of the day examining the ship from stem to stem. After having thanked the ship's officers, the party took a carriage across town to Broadway and visited an "ice-cream saloon," where Howe assured the boys they could get the "real article." When they were all cooled off by generous amounts of fresh ice cream, Howe swivelled around and asked, "Well, Stearns, what do you think of her?" Stearns had what many must have found an irritating way of seeing everything in business terms, for in a much too serious vein, he responded, "I think she is much too big. If a man is going to increase his business he should do it gradually and not at such a long jump." Reflecting a moment, he added, "I have known a number of failures from that cause."[13]

That summer Stearns apparently took additional time off from involvement in causes and politics, and he and his family may have visited the

White Mountains again to escape Medford's summer heat. But, in September, he was once again eager to be involved in public affairs, this time the Massachusetts Republican State Convention. The party, "full of the energy of youth and inspired by reformative ardor," according to one observer, became a magnet to progressive Northerners. Stearns wanted to represent Medford at the state convention in Worcester, but, unfortunately, even Medford Republicans remained antiabolitionist. Republican party leaders found him a seat as a delegate from a town in western Massachusetts. Frank Bird and his friends were pushing for the nomination of Stearns's lawyer, John A. Andrew, for governor. The businessman quickly joined them, contributing to the election fund. While not a good speaker, he was moved by the spirit of the moment, and his arguments for Andrew influenced many business acquaintances. For example, the Stearns and Company millhands saw to the election of an Andrew delegate in one of the Charlestown wards. Because the men who assisted in Kansas relief were likely to favor Andrew's election, he returned to his state network. Stearns contacted people personally and by letter with more satisfactory results.[14]

Stearns and the Bird Club did their work well, and Andrew received the nomination. Stearns remarked that it was the spirit of old John Brown that nominated the next governor of the Bay State. During the six weeks following the convention, Stearns was busy drumming up support for Andrew. The Beacon Street aristocracy attempted to block the Republican candidate, and the entire community was tense as the election drew near. Henry Wilson, campaigning alongside Stearns, wrote to Lincoln that "the people are disposed to listen and to go many miles to attend meetings." Like Stearns, Wilson sought to bypass the traditional approach and to go into the school districts and out-of-the-way places to solicit votes. Lawrence was the candidate for the Constitutional Union party, one of the Democratic party splinter groups. Lawrence had the support of aristocratic Beacon Street, which saw Andrew as "a person of no social consequences, a mere ranting abolitionist," one of their number remarked. While Wide Awakes, a paramilitary group of young Republicans, marched, Constitutional Unionists would shout:

> Tell John Andrew
> Tell John Andrew
> Tell John Andrew
> John Brown's dead![15]

132

After Stearns returned home from dining at the Bird Club on the Saturday before the November elections, one of the boys ran to get him. A long procession of bobbing torches was heading toward The Evergreens. The torchbearers' faces glowed in the flickering light as they filed into the front yard and overflowed into the field beyond. Suddenly, three cheers for Stearns filled the night air. Stearns stepped out and thanked them for the compliment. A Republican candidate for state senator invited him to join the procession. The marchers formed a hollow square in their midst, and Stearns, along with Frank and Harry, joined them as they proceeded a short distance to Ship Street.[16]

In an open field, hot coffee and Medford crackers awaited the marchers. The candidates spoke to the crowd and then called on Stearns. He mounted a wooden box and stood there, his long beard moving with the gentle night breeze. Surrounded by the "flaring torches, his face full of earnestness and determination," Frank recalled, Stearns declared, "I consider this to be the most important election that has ever taken place in our country." The crowd stirred as Stearns, pointing toward the Bunker Hill monument, explained that the election would decide whether "we are a nation of free men, or to be ruled by an oligarchy of slaveholders, as we have been for the past twenty-five years." His ruddy face lighting up, Stearns said, "Now, I have good news. . . . I was with Senator Wilson this afternoon and he assured me there could be no question but that Lincoln and Hamlin would be elected." Shouts and applause greeted Stearns, and he broke into a rare smile while waiting for the crowd to allow him to continue. He told them of his great confidence in Wilson because he was a very clever man and one who did not like to be found in the wrong, a statement that drew several chuckles from the audience. Stearns continued, "We are going to have the best governor that has ever sat in the statehouse at Boston, and," he paused, "I do not except Hancock and Adams." After a few more remarks, Stearns stepped down as applause and shouts filled the night.[17]

The following Tuesday was election night. Stearns stayed in Boston, as the telegraph chattered out the returns. Mary and the two older boys waited for George's arrival. Finally, after eleven o'clock, they heard his carriage clatter up the drive. Stearns burst into the mansion with a youthful stride and said, "Abraham Lincoln is elected president." The key states, Pennsylvania, Indiana, and Illinois, had Republican majorities. Wilson, at the last minute, panicked in regard to New York, but after twenty minutes of pacing, he learned that the Republicans had finally carried the populous state by a large majority. Stearns's face darkened when he said, "The only funeral is that Burlingame has been

133

defeated." A business acquaintance of Stearns, Anson Burlingame ran as a Republican for Congress in Boston. The following morning, the inhabitants of The Evergreens, including the servants, were in gay spirits. Stearns's somber personality, however, put a damper on the holiday mood. He gathered the household around and told them that, although they were pleased about the Republican victory, there would be thousands of federal officeholders who would lose their patronage jobs. Perhaps thinking back to his lead speculation, Stearns knew "what it meant for a man to have his bread taken away from him."[18]

But Lincoln had yet to be installed in office, and Stearns worried about Republicans' resolve. John Andrew shared the same doubts. The governor-elect wanted to keep in step with his party and to ascertain the actual state of affairs, especially regarding reports that the Buchanan administration was wavering in the face of Southern secession threats. In early December, the new Massachusetts governor invited Stearns to accompany him to Washington. However, the trip was postponed because Andrew had developed a nosebleed that, Stearns humorously remarked, needed to be "plugged." On December 20, 1860, the two men set off. After a short stop in New York, where Stearns met with both political and business acquaintances, they reached Philadelphia at three in the morning. The two travelers refreshed themselves at the Continental Hotel and then "went out in search of adventure," as one of them put it.[19]

It was hardly adventure at first. They talked to Horace Binny, whom Stearns described as "a splendid man 80 years old." A prominent lawyer and head of the Philadelphia Bar, Binny discussed the recent political events. Stearns agreed with the elderly gentleman, who declared himself "opposed to all compromises," and in favor of the maintenance of the Union "at all hazards." Binny told them that he had no wish to shorten his life, but he wished the next two months were past and he was able to see Lincoln. Their next stop promised a bit more excitement. They called on William H. Furness, a Unitarian pastor and outspoken abolitionist. Furness had just left his home after receiving word that a mob planned to disrupt a lecture by another abolitionist, Henry Ward Beecher. The two followed him to Beecher's meeting. Fortunately, Stearns said, "it went off without any attempt at disturbance." After a brisk walk, they returned to Furness's home, where the abolitionist speculated on the future. Later, Stearns and Andrew left for Washington.[20]

In Washington, the men visited several Republican luminaries: Charles Sumner, William Fessenden, Montgomery Blair, Lewis Cass, and others. Writing Mary to express his pleasure at accompanying Andrew, Stearns said, "He puts much in my way that is valuable and will be of future interest." What Stearns learned convinced him that the political situation was quickly passing into chaos and that no one in government seemed willing or able to prevent the consequences. Lincoln would, he believed, "have the encouragement of a full Union." Republicans he spoke to "would stand firm not yielding an inch" to the Southerners, whose leaders had, according to Stearns, "lost the control of the movement," which was now "obviously in the hands of a mob." In the Senate, the Republicans turned down Virginia's Senator John J. Crittenden's compromise package. One of the compromises, Stearns learned, was strengthening the odious Fugitive Slave Law. Republican Senator Benjamin Wade told the Southerners that because they planned to secede from the Union, they did not need to vote, for "it would then die of itself." Stearns told his friend that if this antagonism continued, it would mean the "immediate abolition of slavery, even if it requires an ocean of blood [and if] war with the Cotton States comes, I am sure of it." Stearns admitted that he was very glad to be present during what he considered "the great time of this century."[21]

On their return, Andrew discussed what would be his first moves as governor. Stearns believed that he needed the support of the farmers and mechanics of Massachusetts against the "demoralized crowds of our cities." Stearns said that the "verdict of the people of the U.S. in November" settled the slavery issue and made the uninformed masses aware of it. Urging Andrew to place Massachusetts on a war footing, Stearns said, "Events will justify your action. Be prepared."[22]

After Stearns returned to Massachusetts, he reflected on the scene in Washington to a fellow merchant. Southern secession, according to Stearns, was an attempt to destroy the North by creating a panic which would "break our banks, paralyze our industry, fail our merchants and starve our operatives." Stearns saw compromise measures as failed bribes, for there could be no compromise because neither side had faith in the other. "No act of Congress," he declared, "or resolution of a convention could be of any avail." He believed more firmly than ever that the issue was in the "hands of the Lord."[23]

Still, the issue of compromise would not die. When a call came for a Crittenden-sponsored peace conference, Stearns was shocked to learn that

Andrew contemplated sending commissioners. He and other members of the Bird Club expected the governor to uphold their radical views. Blooded by events in Kansas and at Harpers Ferry, Stearns could not understand Andrew's reluctance to force a civil war. Stearns also heard, incorrectly, that his political hero, Sumner, favored sending delegates to a peace conference. Stearns wrote to ask whether this rumor were true. Sumner responded vehemently, first by telegram and then by letter, that he was against sending a delegation: "No possible compromise or concession will be of the least avail." Andrew did eventually send commissioners, but to no purpose other than straining his relationship with the Bird Club and Stearns.[24]

Stearns believed the Republican party would stand firm and, when Lincoln took the oath of office, "Constitution, Union and the Enforcement of the Laws" would be their "Watchword and it {would} be responded to North, East and West." Secession, Stearns remarked, could be "put down in fourteen days, at least so General Scott says and he ought to know." As for Southerners, Stearns declared that not even coercion could "save them from the fury of the storm." He feared the collapse of order in the South and the obligation of the government to "send Northern troops to protect the {slave} holder and his slaves from white men maddened with hunger and bruted by whiskey." Stearns could not understand why Southerners had chosen this year to act. He had heard reports that in some cities in South Carolina, Georgia, Alabama, and Mississippi, "food {was} today selling at famine prices." Stearns saw this state of affairs in the South the work of the Lord as punishment for "African Slavery." He told Sumner, "Cotton was their God, and they demanded that the whole world should fall down and worship him." Stearns believed the issue would be settled by the "Eternal Laws of God, and, as he directs, Man will obey." Stearns meant not only those laws found within the covers of the Bible, but also the "unenacted Laws of Trade as his {God's} laws as well as those that uphold the Universe. They are against the South and will crush them." To his friends, Stearns recalled his Harpers Ferry testimony during which he indicated that the freeing of America would begin with John Brown and asked, "Have I not reason to reaffirm it today ?"[25]

Stearns also reaffirmed his commitment to Kansas. The drought he had encountered was creating new hardships. Clothing in the initial New England Aid Committee shipments to the territory was of such poor quality that it was not worth the transportation expense to distribute it. Stearns advised agents to give it away near Lawrence. New clothing was on the way and if they did not get enough in the way of donations, he would use his own money, up to $500 or $1,000, to buy new clothing. The committee shipped at least thirteen boxes of goods in early February. As for charging the settlers for donated clothing, Stearns suggested agents be "liberal, for many come in freely." He was also worried about the safety of Lawrence, for reports from James Montgomery mentioned continuing proslavery outrages. He suggested his agent George W. Collamore move from Lawrence to a safer location such as Atchison or Leavenworth.[26]

II

With Lincoln's inauguration in March, Stearns turned to business matters. Although he condemned patronage, if political favors were to be had, he wanted them to go to friends. In the third week of March, Stearns visited Sumner, who he believed was "slow and conscientious in making his decision" to award federal positions to party faithful. To Summer Stearns advocated that a fellow businessman, George Goodrich, who had been ruined in the Panic of 1857, be appointed collector of the port of Boston and old Free Soiler John G. Palfrey become Boston's postmaster. Stearns also recommended a number of men for minor positions in the customs house and Charlestown Navy Yard. Satisfied, he returned to Boston after a brief stop in New York.[27]

During his travels, Stearns's chief clerk wrote to him on a daily basis, and he, in turn, replied with instructions by telegraph. During his visits to New York, he attended to business matters. This particular New York stop included a visit to a firm managed by a Mr. Perkins and a Mr. Schmidt, wholesalers of lead ingots. When he called on them, they asked whether there was to be war. Stearns replied, "I think it will be war." Attempting to joke about the lucrative position they and Stearns would find themselves in if war came, Perkins laughingly said, "Bullets are made of lead, Mr. Stearns."[28]

Perkins had Fort Sumter, a federal installation in the harbor of Charleston, South Carolina, on his mind when he spoke of war. Writing to Sumner about his conversation with the wholesalers, Stearns said he told them in response to their question of whether the fort was to be surrendered that the position it occupied was of little importance. The lead pipe manufacturer, however, was shrewd enough to realize that it was, he wrote Sumner, "of the greatest interest that the Government should take a firm stand on some thing" and that it might as well be the fort. Stearns thought Lincoln should ask Congress for

100,000 men and $50 million, for such a request would, he said, "tone the North up to the crisis and receive the support of the Masses, both Republicans and Democrats." Writing to Sanborn about his work, Stearns remarked, "What Glorious Times these are. They will show that our Republic is worth saving."[29]

In April1861, these "Glorious Times" turned into civil war as Southern forces fired on Fort Sumter in Charleston Harbor. The next month, James Montgomery, the Kansas Jayhawker, told Stearns that Free Soilers in the territory were "in a perilous position" and would not be able to make a respectable fight against invading Missourians. Stearns feared for the safety of Kansas and decided to return to Washington to help lobby for its defense. He also wrote to Montgomery, who was now a colonel on the territorial governor's staff, to draw on him for $500, if necessary, for the defense of Bourbon and Linn counties on the Missouri border. Apparently, Montgomery was attempting to follow in John Brown's footsteps, at least in regard to obtaining financial support from Stearns. Because the Kansas territory did not have the authority to raise troops, a delegation petitioned the federal government for authority to raise troops at Fort Leavenworth and to receive arms for them.[30]

On May 6, Stearns started out for Washington with his son Frank. First, they went to Albany to talk with Governor E. D. Morgan. Stearns met Morgan at the Republican Convention and thought that the governor might share his concerns. Stearns did not find much satisfaction in the meeting, however, and later wrote to Mary, "I could not help thinking of Bottom with the ass's head as he broke over me in conversation." Morgan was, Stearns told her, one of the "heavy web order." After the meeting, George and Frank left Albany that night on the Hudson River Railroad in a sleeping-car. The next day, they had lunch in New York's famous Demonic's with John Hopper. During the meal, Hopper discussed the secessionists: "I tell you, Stearns, it would be better to let those devils go . . . . As it is, we must either crush them out, or be crushed ourselves." After lunch with Hopper, the Stearnses hurried to catch a train for Philadelphia, where they stayed the night. Writing to Mary that evening, he told her Frank was well but found the trip dull: "All cars [trains] and no fun, but he is very good company for me." He ended the letter to Mary with "Love and Kisses to Harry and Carl also as many as you can take for yourself." The next day they left Philadelphia on a train carrying a field artillery battery. Unfortunately, the weight was too much for a grade in Delaware and for several hours they waited until another engine was brought

138

down the line to help. When the Stearnses arrived in Washington at two in the morning, they found a portion of Willards Hotel ablaze and Fire Zouaves performing "wonderful gymnastics," Frank recalled, while extinguishing the flames. Stearns told the desk clerk, "There is no rest for me here," and went to another hotel. The next day, he returned to Willards and met with the Kansas delegation, among whom were James H. Lane and George W. Collamore.[31]

Stearns astutely realized that their only hope of obtaining aid was to appeal to the cabinet. As Stearns reported, however, official Washington was "all excitement and confusion," and he had a difficult time getting to see any cabinet member. Stearns convinced Frank P. Blair to appeal to his son, Postmaster-General Montgomery Blair, who granted Stearns an interview. Stearns had a long talk with Blair. In addition to discussing the question of Kansas regiments, Stearns told the postmaster-general he wanted to begin to lobby for emancipation. Blair said that the war "must, in the end, emancipate the slaves," but he urged Stearns to hold off: "At this time it would be injurious to hasten matters by any special movement." Blair told Stearns pointedly that "the Government would be against it" and that the idea would also be "derided in the North." Blair, however, promised the members of the Kansas delegation that they would receive authority to raise two infantry regiments. Tired but with his work completed and feeling that he was making himself useful, Stearns returned to Boston.[32]

A month later, Stearns left Boston again for Washington, to see what was causing the delay in granting permission for the Kansas regiments. For this trip, he had armed himself with a letter of introduction from Sumner to Secretary of the Treasury Salmon P. Chase. The interview with the secretary went well and Chase persuaded the War Department to issue the necessary orders. Stearns reported to Mary on June 17, "Today I have obtained . . . an order from the Secretary of War for three Kansas regiments including all their supplies."[33]

Although Stearns was pleased with this support for the Kansas regiments, he was not as happy about another decision from Washington. Martin Conway told Stearns that Secretary Chase had recently proposed a duty on imported lead to protect the miners of Illinois and his own state of Ohio. Although willing to lobby on behalf of others, Stearns accepted the information without any attempt to halt the legislation that could hurt his own business. According to Frank, Stearns did not "believe in the theory that the public welfare is best served by every man's pushing his own personal interest," apparently not aware of his father's efforts, in the 1840s, on behalf of linseed oil manufacturers. Frank claimed his father adopted the Roman maxim "A great nation can only be supported by great personal sacrifices."[34]

Stearns was not the only person to make sacrifices that summer of 1861. Ninety-day northern volunteers flooded the federal city, straining the government's resources. Public clamor grew to advance on Richmond, the Confederacy's newly established capital. In July came news of Bull Run, the war's first major engagement. Stearns called the Union defeat "the first step toward emancipation." Rationalizing the setback, Stearns believed that, if the North had won and the southern states returned to the Union with slavery intact, the abolitionists "should have all our work to do over again."[35]

Stearns also had much to say about a growing disenchantment with the Lincoln administration's unwillingness to work toward emancipation. Boston newspapers reported that Union generals in Virginia and elsewhere were returning slaves who crossed the lines to their owners. "How strange it is," he wrote to a gentleman who protested in a newspaper article, "that Slavery, the accumulation of all wrongs, should be so held in esteem by Northern men." Stearns thought it was absurd to return anything or anyone to the other side during a war, for civil war was placing a burden on northern personal holdings, such as ships, stocks, lands, and merchandise. Because Southerners regarded their slaves as property, Stearns thought they should accept any loss of slaves just as they would accept other material losses as the fortunes of war. Stearns sarcastically pointed out that "slave property, so says Lincoln, must be respected."[36]

Stearns had no intention of respecting the administration views on slave property and began to solidify plans he had discussed with other antislavery advocates. He wanted to build a broad spectrum of support and even wrote to John Greenleaf Whittier, requesting him to exert his "poetic genius" for the cause of emancipation. Whittier agreed with Stearns about the need for "striking more directly at the real cause of the war." The poet said that, if the present struggle did not involve emancipation, it would be "at once a most wicked and the most ludicrous war ever waged." Stearns could not agree more with these sentiments. The war was about slavery, and he intended to ensure that the Lincoln administration made emancipation a policy. Stearns's strategy also included an attempt to build a new political antislavery society made up of such Boston men as Wendell Phillips, Frank Bird, Frank Sanborn, and Samuel G. Howe. The purpose of the organization was to lobby to make total emancipation a Lincoln administration war policy. However, a number of prospective members seemed to think that the public mood did not favor such an organization, at least for the present, because most Northerners believed that the sole purpose for waging war was to preserve the Union and had nothing to do with emancipation. Therefore, Stearns wrote to J. Miller McKim, a longtime abolitionist, "We do not yet wish the movement to be made public."[37]

In the fall of 1861, the antislavery men recruited by Stearns formed an executive committee "to take such measures as they should deem best adapted to promote the object." Initially, the men circulated emancipation literature. Stearns composed a letter to Lincoln, stressing the need to emancipate African-Americans to assist in the Union's war effort. Sanborn contributed to the committee's public awareness campaign, and Stearns, whose patience was wearing thin, said that if Sanborn's articles were attacked, it would help in the discussion. Stearns also drafted a confidential letter to send to writers known to hold antislavery views. In fact, he had one clerk devote all his time that year to writing and circulating letters regarding emancipation. He told the recipients that the times were "propitious for the extensive reception of correct views" on emancipation. Stearns said that, if a broad-based organization could disseminate "truths" to the public, the people would decide that an "emancipation policy [would be] a necessity for bringing the war to a close." According to Stearns, without emancipation, the people could have "no reasonable hope of a speedy restoration of peace." Stearns wrote that although the committee could not compensate authors, those writers who contributed would have the "satisfaction of aiding in a good cause." Stearns also sent out copies of Charles Sumner's speeches and articles by editor Elizur Wright to influential citizens. He also tried to obtain funds to publish a book by Martin E. Conway on the subject. Despite these and other efforts, the administration resisted entreaties to order emancipation.[38]

Regardless of Stearns's interest in shaping public policy, he still had a business to manage and family responsibilities. Mr. Perkins's prediction that the war would require great quantities of lead proved to be correct, and, undoubtedly, Stearns received a great many contracts from both the state and federal governments. Business was decidedly good. However, the Lincoln administration's suspension of specie worried the conservative Stearns. When the Boston and Lowell Railroad superintendent asked Stearns how he was managing his finances in such uncertain times, he replied that he kept a close eye on his inventories and then bought "gold equal to the material on hand." The cautious businessman explained, "[In this way] I secure myself against both good and evil."[39]

Despite spending more time at work, Stearns maintained a close relationship with his sons but found, as all parents eventually discover, that when children grow older, their lives no longer revolve entirely around the family. Frank and Harry still boarded at Sanborn's school in Concord. That busy October, Harry wrote that he would not return home for the weekend because of a picnic planned at the Esterbrook Farm but that, if it rained, he would "come down at noon." In this letter, Harry also assured his father that he had been "a good boy this week and had good lessons. I have not 'cut up rough' but have been a good boy." Stearns must have smiled at the note, perhaps remembering that he had once remarked that a man could never be a man unless he was a boy first.[40]

That fall, Stearns also spent time with Mary. On Sundays he took her to the Boston Music Hall to listen to speakers discuss politics and "Negro philanthropy." Honored with seats on stage, the Stearnses usually invited the speakers and friends to supper at The Evergreens. The couple also attended antislavery gatherings, usually with Lydia Maria Child. Aunt Maria invited Mary to one such function in December. "If it amounts to nothing more," she wrote, "it will be a pleasant meeting with some whom it is always agreeable to meet." Aunt Maria also wrote that she was upset at news from Port Royal, on the coast of South Carolina, where "contrabands" were being returned to southern lines. She thought that, if the northern forces had welcomed the slaves, set them to work in the fields, and stimulated them with wages, they could have gathered and sent to New York millions of dollars of cotton. As it was, however, the rebels burned it in the fields. Aunt Maria speculated that perhaps a "wizard paralyzed our government and commanders by an evil spell." She also shared the Stearnses' disappointment with the president and his policies: "Lincoln says we must let things *drift*." Stearns surely chuckled as he read her next sentence, "What else could we expect from King Log?"[41]

By December, however, Stearns had had enough of "King Log." He decided the time had come for the committee to take action. The Emancipation League Declaration was made public; it stated that the object of the organization was to "urge upon the People and the Government EMANCIPATION OF THE SLAVES as a measure of justice, and as a military necessity." The league also declared that emancipation was the "shortest, cheapest, and least bloody path to permanent peace, and the only method of maintaining the integrity of the nation." More than a hundred people signed the league's declaration, including John Andrew, A. Bronson Alcott, Samuel Sewall, Richard P. Hallowell, and the Childses, as well as many who were not considered radical abolitionists. The Emancipation League elected officers during a public meeting in January 1862. Stearns became treasurer and provided most of the funds for the league's campaign. His patience, however, was apparently wearing thin with people who had pledged financial support and then refused to contribute. At this point, he also must have thought that people were taking him for granted as merely a banker for the plans of others, for after receiving a bill for another publication, he wrote to Frank Sanborn, "I did not understand that I was to pay for the printing . . . . [But] if I gave you to understand that I expected to pay for [the pamphlets] I will." In a postscript, he added, "Emancipation has been hard on my purse."[42]

The Union's troubles were also causing difficulties for others. Lincoln agonized over slavery until he was certain that the necessities of war weakened resistance to black emancipation. Moncure D. Conway, an antislavery minister from Virginia, reported to Stearns that during a visit with Lincoln, the president had told him it appeared that the great masses of this country cared comparatively little about the Negro and were eager only for military success. Disgusted with Lincoln and his administration, Stearns wrote Sumner that he "could hope for nothing good from the imbecility in Washington." Stearns believed only the Emancipation League was making progress in convincing the masses that freeing the slaves was a military necessity, playing down prewar abolitionist rhetoric that slavery was morally wrong. Stearns's next step was to encourage Lincoln to suggest a practical measure for emancipation, some type of definite legislation. Stearns rejected direct slaveholder compensation, believing that it would open the treasury to "unlimited pillage" and that an act of emancipation, when passed, should guarantee to each state a fixed sum and allow the authorities the "power of distribution." Stearns told Sumner that he thought "one to two hundred Millions should suffice." If the government offered such an option to the border states now, according to Stearns, they would accept the offer, for they were certain to be "anxious to finger the money." Stearns did, on occasion, have a sense of humor, and in closing, he related to Sumner the news that James Mason, now a Confederate emissary to England, had been seated in the Parliament gallery next to the "Haitian

Minister who is represented as of pure blood." Stearns said, "I think he must have dreamed that night of Ole Virginny."[43]

Howe was in "Ole Virginny" with the U.S. Sanitary Commission, the forerunner to the American Red Cross. He gave another view of Lincoln, writing to Frank Bird that the "President has been long on the anxious seat." Lincoln, he believed, considered slavery a "great stumbling block in the way of human progress." Howe asked a rhetorical question, "Why doesn't he speak out in meeting? Why it's because of his fatal habit of procrastinating." Stearns read the letter, but his active mind was seeking another avenue to promote emancipation.[44]

Less than a year earlier in Worcester, Stearns heard Sumner advocate the use of black troops. Sumner said that there was no need to "carry the war into Africa," that it would be enough to "carry Africa into the War, in any form, any quantity, any way." Stearns believed that, now that white men were reluctant to step forward to enlist, the "Worcester egg [had] hatched" and the idea of using black troops was "fairly standing on its legs." Medford, for example, was having difficulty meeting its enlistment quota. Although at a town meeting groans and hisses silenced Stearns's suggestion of enlisting African-Americans, he was certain that the lack of enlistments would necessitate total emancipation to obtain the necessary manpower to prosecute the war. Stearns wrote to Collamore in Kansas, asking him what people in the territory would think about black soldiers. Collamore responded that the feeling in the West concerning the enlistment of "persons of African descent" met with almost unanimous favor. If Kansas chose to raise black regiments, he was confident the federal government would accept them.[45]

The lead pipe manufacturer also received another letter from Collamore, but not about black regiments or emancipation. In July 1860, Stearns had lent a Kansas emigrant mortgage money at ten percent per annum. man, John B. Stuart, was delinquent in repayment, and Stearns wanted his money. Stuart had been paying the interest and part of the principal and told Collamore he had given Stearns to understand that he did not expect to be able to pay the principal until he could afford to and then only in installments. Stuart told Collamore that he had "no more to pay at this time" and that if Stearns were determined to take his home from him by taking advantage of his present circumstances, so be it. Collamore reported the situation to Stearns and advised him against foreclosure because of the legal fees of $150 were excessive and because the court would appraise the land at less than two-thirds of its actual value. Stearns instructed Collamore to accept Stuart's proposal.[46]

Stearns had another proposal on his mind, but this one political. He was having difficulty getting Sumner's speeches and others' articles on emancipation published. He decided that control of a newspaper could solve the problem and brought up the idea at a Bird Club dinner. There he found support. The best way to obtain a newspaper appeared to resurrect *The Commonwealth*, an old radical publication that had died in 1854 primarily because of its antislavery articles. Stearns asked Moncure Conway to edit the journal, for which Stearns was "ready to furnish the means for the present publication of a weekly newspaper." He wanted the publication to "fearlessly tell the truth about this war." On September 6, 1862, the newspaper was launched, as Conway's editorial said, "on unknown seas by the money and faith of Mr. Stearns . . . for liberty, justice and the Commonwealth of the United States." It also became an organ of John Andrew. In addition to articles on emancipation policies and the war, it paid attention to literature, and several writers made their debut on its pages, including Louisa May Alcott with her "Hospital Sketches." Others, Julia Ward Howe for one, also contributed.[47]

The same month that Stearns launched the newspaper, Union forces commanded by General George B. McClellan turned back an invading Confederate army led by General Robert E. Lee at Antietam Creek, Maryland. Although many people considered the engagement at best a draw, Lincoln used it as a platform to issue a preliminary emancipation proclamation, which declared, That on the first day of January in the year of our Lord, one thousand eight hundred and sixty-three, all persons held as slaves within any state, or designated part of a state, the people whereof shall then be in rebellion against the United States shall be then thence forward, and forever free. Stearns saw Lincoln's action as "a thunderbolt clearing the sky . . . [of] mists and dubious specters." The question whether to arm blacks, however, remained unclear, and Stearns thought that enlisting them was essential to guarantee emancipation.[48]

The fall and early winter of 1862, while antislavery activists waited for Lincoln's formal emancipation proclamation planned for January, Stearns took time out for personal matters involving the family of the man who had helped to move the nation to civil war. The Browns had asked him to invest money donated to the Haitian John Brown Fund, and, in thanks for his help, John Brown, Jr., had sent Stearns a box of Catawba grapes from his newly purchased farm on Put-in-Bay, near Sandusky, Ohio. The Stearnses invited the Emersons to visit The Evergreens to share the grapes. Responding to Mary's invitation, the Concord sage proposed leaving his wife with them: "Mrs. Emerson is well pleased with the hope of passing Thursday afternoon and Night." He said he would have liked to join them were it not for a speaking engagement in Salem. After the lecture Emerson planned to stay in Boston and to meet his wife the following morning at The Evergreens to enjoy the grapes.[49]

The Stearnses were also making plans for another reception. On January 1, 1863, a jubilee concert at the Boston Music Hall was scheduled to celebrate the news that the president's proclamation was "actually on the wires of the telegraph." When the message reached Boston, prayers of Thanksgiving and speeches of congratulations filled the music hall. According to participants Emerson read his "Boston Hymn," Wendell Phillips spoke, and at the end "the whole audience broke into tumultuous applause," followed by "rousing cheers for Lincoln and Garrison." A longtime abolitionist and friend of Lincoln wrote to the president that, in all his "antislavery life," he had "never witnessed such intense, intelligent and devoted 'Thanksgiving.'" He said it was like "the solemn joy of an old Jewish Passover."[50]

That evening, after the jubilee concert, George and Mary hosted a party, catered by J. B. Smith, an African-American, to unveil the bust of John Brown. William Lloyd Garrison, Samuel Sewall, Wendell Phillips, Bronson Alcott, Julia Ward Howe, Samuel Longfellow, Frank Sanborn, and many other antislavery advocates thronged to The Evergreens. Wendell Phillips unveiled the bust with a speech "so graceful, exquisite and timely" that, to Frank Stearns, it was more a poem than an address. Emerson read his "Boston Hymn" again, and Julia Ward Howe moved the hushed crowd by reciting in a "weird penetrating voice," according to Frank, her "Battle Hymn of the Republic." Now African-Americans would sing that battle hymn wearing the Union blue, for Lincoln had specifically stated that they would "be received into the armed service of the United States to garrison forts, positions, stations, and other places, and to man vessels of all sorts in said service." The bust of Brown in white marble stood on the landing of the curving staircase, its whiteness standing out from the contrasting black walnut wainscoting. One of the visitors, Elizabeth Powell Bond, said that she thought the bust had been placed in "what may well be designated a 'House Beautiful.'"[51]

Encouraged by its success in lobbying the administration to proclaim emancipation, the Emancipation League formed a committee to press Lincoln to appoint John C. Fremont as the military governor of the area of North

Carolina under Union control. The delegation, consisting of Phillips, Howe, Bird, Stearns, Moncure Conway, and three others, arrived on January 23 and stayed four to a room at Willards. Congressman Oakes Ames arranged for a meeting with President Lincoln and Secretary of War Edwin M. Stanton.[52]

On Sunday, January 25, the delegation, along with Henry Wilson, entered the White House. Lincoln jokingly commented on the dogs and cats wandering through the place by explaining that the White House was in a prolific state. At first Stearns and the others were annoyed at the president's gaiety at such a terrible time, but then they saw the pathetic change in his face. Wilson started to introduce the men, but Lincoln said he knew perfectly well who they were. Phillips expressed their joy at the proclamation. Leading up to the purpose of their meeting, he said that Northerners in general were now antislavery and upset that many government officials and military men were not adhering to the proclamation. Lincoln responded that his impression was that the masses were more dissatisfied at the lack of military successes. Phillips said he knew a way to give Lincoln's administration "another four years of power" and raised the issue of Fremont's governorship. Lincoln told them that, although he had a great respect for Fremont, the "pioneer in any movement [was] not generally the best man to carry that movement to a successful issue." After all, Lincoln reminded his visitors, Moses freed the Jews but "didn't take Israel to the Promised Land." Lincoln asked, "Suppose I should put in the South these antislavery generals and governors, what would they do with the slaves that would come to them?" Stearns had a ready answer: "We would make Union soldiers of all who were capable of bearing arms." All Lincoln could say to that suggestion was that his action in issuing the proclamation had "knocked the bottom out of slavery." Conway suggested that, if the military situation did not improve, the bottom would be put in again. Silence. Phillips took the hint and thanked the president for the audience. Lincoln bowed and told them he was pleased to meet "gentlemen known to him by their distinguished service." Their objective not reached, the delegation left the White House and returned to Willards.[53]

Stearns decided to host a supper at Willards for the Massachusetts congressional delegation and other antislavery members of Congress. He also invited the New York *Times* representative and several other journalists. He hoped to obtain some important expressions of opinion from the politicians at the dinner, but all that came forth were optimistic predictions for the future. The naive Stearns did not persuade Sumner to attend the dinner and, after the supper, finally began to understand why, for what politicians say in private is not necessarily what they repeat in public. Sumner reminded Stearns of what Dr. Samuel Johnson had once said about a dinner, "a good enough dinner but not a dinner to invite a man to."[54]

The dejected committee returned to Boston, where the men reviewed their trip. Conway said it was obvious that Lincoln was not competent to grapple with the horrendous combinations of issues before him, and Bird accused Lincoln of a great defect in character exhibited by ignoring moral forces. Stearns told them it was useless to "disparage his ability," for they had had their opportunity to present arguments, and the president simply bested them. Thinking that Lincoln might be open to another line of reasoning, Stearns wrote to Emerson to ask the sage to visit the president and explain that the "morality, intelligence and patriotism of New England" sustained the administration and that the section would continue to support Lincoln as long as it retained "confidence in the vigor and ability of the Government" to prosecute the war. Stearns said that Wendell Phillips should go along to make a political statement while Emerson concentrated on the moral and intellectual impressions.[55]

Stearns continued to look for ways to further the cause of the Union beyond emancipation. He said that government efforts to raise money for the prosecution of the war "disturbed the values of all commodities, tempted the wildest speculation and was rolling up an enormous debt." Gold now stood at $170 an ounce, and the business situation was growing serious. On February 5, 1863, Stearns sent an open letter to United States Sub-Treasurer John J. Cisco, in New York, suggesting ways to finance the war: "The labor of the country has paid its share of the debt in blood and toil. The Wealth must pay its share of the debt in money . . . . When Abraham Lincoln calls on the people to stand by their Government woe to the man who falters." Convinced the government was using "very expensive methods to obtain funds," Stearns advocated a simple plan: issue legal tender notes payable in gold or silver specie. Lacking hard money to back this issue, the government would have to negotiate foreign loans, but such loans would give the United States the advantages of having more currency in circulation and controlling gold's world market price because of the amount it borrowed. All the government need do to cause the price of gold to rise was draw on the loan money from the London exchange. It was a good financial program, and Cisco responded favorably to it. Writing to Secretary of the Treasury Salmon P. Chase about Stearns's plan,

Cisco said, "Whatever may be thought of the views advanced by him it must be conceded that his letter is written with marked ability." Although the administration eventually issued legal tender notes, it never negotiated foreign loans.[56]

III

Stearns next sought to assist in the war effort and at the same time ensure emancipation would eventually be extended to all slaves, not just those in the Confederacy, by raising black regiments. Governor Andrew was enthusiastic, especially since white recruiting was falling off. He thought African-Americans would seize the opportunity to "vindicate their manhood, and to strike a telling blow for their own race, and the freedom of all their posterity." When he was in Washington with the Massachusetts delegation, he spoke to Lincoln and Stanton. He discovered Rhode Island's governor had recently made a similar request to raise a regiment of "volunteers of African descent." The War Department gave its approval. Upon returning to Boston, Andrew received similar authorization' to raise volunteer companies of artillery and infantry that could "include persons of African descent."[57]

Unfortunately, Andrew failed to take into account two facts that would affect recruiting in Massachusetts. First, according to the 1860 census, Massachusetts had only 1,973 male blacks of military age. Superintendent of the Census Joseph Kennedy told the governor that, if blacks volunteered in the same ratio that whites did, the Commonwealth might muster 394 soldiers, not even half the size of a full-strength regiment. As a consequence, Andrew asked Stanton for permission to recruit in southern areas under Union control with large African-American populations. Stanton responded negatively. The second part of Andrew's recruiting problem was that African-American community leaders refused to assist the governor because he could not guarantee that competent black men, after a reason able period of training and experience, would be eligible for promotion to officer ranks.[58]

Facing failure before recruiting began, Andrew sent for Stearns and asked, "What is to be done?" The businessman replied that, if funds could be obtained, he personally would recruit a regiment of African-American men from the North and from Canada. Andrew placed the entire matter in Stearns's hands. Stearns first organized a committee, later called the "Black Committee," that included Amos A. Lawrence, James M. Forbes, Richard Hallowell, and several other businessmen. As chairman of the committee, Stearns published a subscription paper to raise funds to recruit "a model Regiment in all respects." The paper included statements from Alexander Hamilton and Andrew Jackson extolling the virtues and fighting ability of blacks in the American Revolution and in the War of 1812. Higginson, now a commander of black troops on South Carolina's Sea Islands, praised the quality of his First South Carolina Volunteers. Stearns listed several reasons for the need to recruit African- Americans: the black recruits trained now could eventually become well-trained noncommissioned officers for Southern regiments; blacks would fare better than white Northerners in the southern climate; and recruiting blacks would eventually take manpower away from the South. Stearns put himself down for $500, as did Forbes, Lawrence, Hallowell, and Gerrit Smith. When Smith sent his money, Stearns thanked him for his aid "to make this a true John Brown Corps."[59]

Stearns's enthusiasm and references to old John Brown caused the conservative Lawrence to remind him that the use of African-Americans, although extremely important, was also a very delicate matter. To maintain state support, Lawrence wanted the blacks encamped and drilled out of state. The plan's success, he told Stearns, "should not be thwarted or endangered by such a course of management as shall excite the animosity of the high and low whites." Stearns passed this information on to Andrew, who questioned the newly appointed commander, Boston patrician and veteran Robert Gould Shaw, about a separate training site. To his credit, Shaw refused to consider any location other than Readville where all Massachusetts regiments trained.[60]

With Frank and a Boston physician, Stearns set out at the end of February for Rochester, the home of noted free black newspaper editor Frederick Douglass. Stearns needed Douglass to help recruit and to publicize the recruiting throughout the northern African-American community in his newspaper, *The North Star*. Stearns made Douglass a recruiter, enlisted the former slave's two sons, and set up his headquarters in Buffalo. Then he crossed over to Canada to find recruits. In Toronto, he worked quietly because secession sympathy was strong there. While dining at the Clifton House in Niagara, Stearns shared a table with Southerners. When they discovered he was from Boston, the two Southerners spoke in loud voices to one another about "cowardly Yankees" and "nigger abolitionists." Stearns withstood the insults as long as he could and then, in a voice loud enough to be heard across the room, declared to a dining companion, "I consider it the proudest act of my life that I gave good old John Brown every pike and rifle he carried to Harpers Ferry."[61]

Stearns returned to Buffalo, "having already one hundred promises and twenty to leave this place." He was encouraged by the reception at both locations and returned to Boston to raise $20,000 for recruiting in New York and Canada. He wrote to Gerrit Smith to ask whether he had, as Stearns requested, talked with New York Governor Horatio Seymour about allowing Massachusetts to recruit African-Americans in his state. In Rochester, Frederick Douglass was "making our work public," Stearns said, and if Seymour opposed them, then Douglass "ought to keep his work out of sight." Stearns asked whether Smith would release his pledge of $3,000 to New York for recruiting expenses for use by Massachusetts, if Seymour did not wish to raise African-American regiments. Stearns eventually obtained Smith's pledge, because Seymour, a war Democrat, resisted abolitionist entreaties to raise troops in New York.[62]

While Stearns established his network to recruit for the newly designated Fifty-fourth Massachusetts Infantry, Mary was busy managing The Evergreens, distributing the fall harvest of Russet apples and finding fault with her hired man, who did not always sort the apples according to her "idea of what No. 7's should be." Mary was also suffering from severe headaches that must be, she told friends, the "work of a proslavery Secesh spirit." Still she found time to contact the Garrisons to tell them they would be receiving some fruit, trusting they would like receiving "half as well" as she liked sending. Mary asked the Garrisons to tell their son Wendell that Frank was in Concord but would respond to his note when he returned.[63]

George Stearns returned to find everything in order both at home and in the Black committee. The subscription fund was full, with more than the $20,000 required. Stearns's newspaper, *The Commonwealth*, was doing well despite a change in editors. Moncure Conway had gone to England to drum up support for the antislavery cause. Since the war had had an adverse effect on enrollment in Sanborn's school, Stearns made him the editor. The businessman took several days to arrange for a prolonged absence and then returned to Buffalo.[64]

The evening following his return to Buffalo, Stearns called a meeting of African-Americans. Breaking out of his reticent self, he spoke to the audience about the advantages that would accrue to those still in bondage and to the future of their race if they enlisted. "When you have rifles in your hands," he told them, "your freedom will be secure." In answer to a question similar to that raised by the African-American community in Boston concerning officer commissions, Stearns confronted the issue by saying that public opinion changes, offering as an example that only three months earlier in a town meeting people had hissed at him for even suggesting enlisting blacks. Stearns said he did not doubt that in six months' time African-American soldiers would receive commissions. The audience applauded, and Stearns asked, "Now, who will volunteer?" Silence. Finally, one man rose to his feet and told the businessman he would enlist if his family would not "suffer for it." Stearns took the opportunity and promised to "see they want for nothing." Although he could not make this promise to everyone, twelve more men agreed to serve.[65]

As the work progressed, Stearns left the actual recruiting to his agents, whom he paid $2 for every recruit. Recruiters spread out over the Northwest, down the Mississippi, and as far west as St. Louis, Missouri. Within a few weeks recruits started to pour in and Stearns directed their movement by telegraph "as easily as pieces on a chess-board," according to Frank. On March 24, 1863, Stearns wrote to Douglass from Buffalo that Frank would be bringing recruits, "32 to be examined here today . . . 11 from Rochester . . . and 20 or more at Binghamton." Once the men passed their medical examinations, Stearns said, they boarded "the Erie because they [the people who ran the railroad] want to help and the others don't." He also preferred the Erie Railroad because the recruits could remain on the same train with no transfers except to the Long Island Sound boat. This almost nonstop trip reduced the fear of disturbance by whites, many of whom objected to blacks' having arms.[66]

Stearns reported the good news "The West is waking up." His arrival also woke Buffalo up to the fact that "the black man will hold a higher position of respect in .. . this war than the Copperhead." New Yorkers who had seemed skeptical at first were surprised at the quality and quantity of the black recruits. On April 9, the Buffalo *Express* noted, "Some forty or fifty more of those colored men who we have been assured would not volunteer left here last evening" to join the Massachusetts regiment. Frederick Douglass praised Stearns's efforts and said that the tide of men now "setting toward Massachusetts" was largely due to the "zeal, industry and efficiency of Mr. George L. Stearns. According to *The Commonwealth*, Emancipation, Black Soldiers , and the Major 149 he was "moving about amongst us noiselessly, unostentatiously reaching his men here and dropping his good word there," motivating men in "scores and fifties to fill up the Fifty-fourth Massachusetts Regiment."[67]

Stearns worked ten to eighteen hours a day, writing letters and articles and attending meetings. Within two months, he had filled the Fifty-fourth's muster rolls. Elated by the African-American community's response, the lead pipe manufacturer started enlisting men for a second unit. "Have two hundred men towards a Fifty-fifth," he telegraphed Andrew. "What shall I do with them?" Andrew hesitated to form a second regiment because he feared the Lincoln administration would reverse its decision to employ black soldiers. Andrew wrote to Stearns at the end of March, "We may be shut down upon by the Secretary of War at any moment." Only after Stearns promised the additional men within four weeks did the governor relent. To Andrew's concurrence, Stearns replied, "I thank God for your telegram . . . . You shall have the men." The Buffalo *Express*, on May 11, 1863, reported that 17 5 black recruits had passed through the city and that many were expected to enter the Fifty-fifth Massachusetts that week. According to the paper, "The conduct of these colored soldiers was such as to call forth commendation at all points where they stopped." Stearns's recruiting network was so extensive that, in reporting on his operations, the *National Intelligencer* jokingly observed, "His crimping sergeants will shortly turn up in Egypt competing with Napoleon for the next Cargo of Nubians."[68]

While Stearns was away, son Harry, now nineteen, shouldered responsibility for managing The Evergreens and for running the lead business. Spring was slowly appearing in Medford, and the place began to look quite green. Harry wrote to his father that the Stearnses' crocuses were in bloom and that the greenhouses were doing fine. Harry said the gardener, Mr. Johnson, put in "the early vegetables so we shall soon have green peas and so forth." Reporting on the Stearnses' business, Harry told his father they had received some large orders. The Charlestown Navy Yard requested "24 rolls, 5 lbs lead amounting in all to 16,000 lbs ." Sold at 12.5 cents, this order, Harry explained, would amount to $2,000. Other orders were, as Harry said, "not so large, but some of them will make a large figure." To manage his schedule better, Harry changed the dinner hour from 12:15 to 3:15 P.M., "thereby abolishing supper," he told his father, so that he would have a chance to get through his duties at the counting house and then eat. Harry also reported other news to his father. Lincoln, the local gossip declared, was not satisfied with the fleet operations during an attack on Charleston. Also, General Joseph Hooker's Army of the

Potomac had recently pushed forward and now occupied Gordonsville. Harry mentioned that he had read and liked General Thomas's speech to black soldiers. Reflecting on the speech, Harry said, "I think now that the Government is in sound earnest now about the negroes. It [the speech] also showed a kindly feeling for them which I like very much." Harry also kept his father posted on the family. He said that little Carl was a "dear good boy." That spring of 1863, Harry at first wrote to his father that both Carl and Mary were well, but later he mentioned that Mary had taken to her room with headaches. On May 8, Mary seemed better, and Harry reported that, although mother still suffered from headaches, she finally came downstairs about nine o'clock and stayed all day. Perhaps, Stearns thought as he read the letter, the time had come to return home. Fifty-four years old, Stearns was tired and, because of the miserable wet spring in Buffalo, was not well himself.[69]

Happy and satisfied with recruiting, Stearns made plans to complete his business in Buffalo and return to Massachusetts. Upon reflection the businessman believed he had taken over from his Kansas hero by raising two "John Brown" regiments. These African-American soldiers would not only help destroy the slave power, but in the process emancipate all of their race in the South and in the border states. They would ensure, through their sacrifice, equality under the Constitution. At first, Stearns found that most of the whites opposed recruiting blacks, but now, as he prepared to leave Buffalo, he saw that "[Even the] most inveterate Democrat favors and aids it." His efforts at first were secret and confined to blacks, but now all the white officials in large cities and their citizens approved and encouraged his work. Even authorities at Cairo, Illinois, offered aid if Stearns would send a recruiting agent there. Stearns was certain that the government would now "arm One Hundred Thousand with the approbation of the entire North."[70]

While Stearns was still in Buffalo, he heard that both Wilson and Sumner had urged and procured the confirmation of brigadier rank for a Colonel Stevenson, who had not been "heretofore favorable to the policy of using the negro in our army." Stearns told Sumner that he could not believe that either Sumner or Wilson would "countenance such conduct . . . or . . . consent to be a party to an act utterly subservice of the principles that have heretofore marked your public life." Stearns said that he and others were gradually gaining African-American's confidence and "exciting their enthusiasm for the war" but that he could not honestly tell them they were "safe in going south, if I know that such men as Stevenson Emancipation, Black Soldiers, and the

154

Major 151 are to be put in command over them," especially if antislavery men approved.[71]

IV

Although Stearns may have misjudged Stevenson, events were beginning to prove that he was correct in predicting the government would be more than willing to arm blacks. Stearns learned through Charles Sumner that the Lincoln administration was ready to pursue full-scale African-American recruitment. Still, after years of struggling to persuade the government to accept his views, Stearns must have received with surprise an invitation to Washington to discuss recruiting with Secretary of War Stanton. He must have been even more surprised at Stanton's proposal. The secretary told Stearns that he knew of his recruiting bureau and that the government was prepared to use it. Stanton said he would be the best man to run the machine he had constructed and offered to make him an assistant adjutant-general with the rank of major. The surprised businessman would have, according to Stanton, "authority to recruit colored regiments all over the country." Stearns thanked the secretary and told him that blacks' serving in the army would certainly help achieve freedom and equality for their race. The final decision on his acceptance of the commission would have to wait until he returned to Boston. Stearns should not have been surprised for his work was well known across the North. A letter published in the *Springfield Republican*, declared, "Mr Stearns is the man whose indomitable energy and great business capacity has been brought to bear on the organization of the Fifth-four {sic} and Fifth-fifth [sic] Regiments."[72]

Apparently suffering from migraine headaches, Mary wrote often to complain about his absence recruiting the Fifty-fourth and Fifty-fifth Regiments. Stearns loved Mary and was concerned for her health. He knew she was unhappy about his absences, but the gentle businessman told her he comforted himself in the belief that this recruiting was an appointed work that he had not sought but that had sought him. Stearns explained to Mary that the "Divine Spirit" within them impelled the work that was so contrary to all Mary's ideas of a happy life. They understood both each other and the work before them. "A sweet peace," Stearns told her, "has come to my soul, so sweet that I welcome the sadness that comes with it."[73]

Stearns arrived at The Evergreens in good spirits. Mary listened as he explained what was at stake. He must have told her that here was the

155

opportunity to fulfill John Brown's dream of an army of African-Americans liberating their brothers and sisters. Mary apparently needed no more argument than the mention of her hero's name, for she gave her consent to his accepting the commission. Next, Stearns visited his counting room. Generated by the war boom, profits were up. Lead had its uses in war from minie balls for muskets to lead bars for ship ballast. Finally, Stearns drove to Charlestown to inspect the mill, which he found in good order. Apparently, Stearns could afford to be absent from Massachusetts, and, just as important, Mary seemed, at least for now, supportive of his recruiting efforts. How could she be otherwise? To deny her husband this opportunity would make a mockery of her impassioned hero worship of John Brown.

Stearns always attempted to keep out of the public eye, and even now some of his own neighbors were ignorant of his recruiting efforts. Mrs. E. D. Cheney, president of a ladies' society that presented the Fifty-fourth Massachusetts one of its flags, stopped Stearns to ask where he had been, "I supposed you were going to help us organize the Colored regiment." Mrs. Cheney said he would be pleased to know it was "doing well." Stearns must have smiled inwardly, making no reply. He later told the family he "but bowed and passed on."[74]

With personal and business matters running smoothly, this loyal supporter of John Brown followed his hero's footsteps to gather an army of African-Americans to destroy slavery once and for all. Stearns wired his civilian recruiters instructions to route black volunteers to federal military installations. He then traveled to Washington. There orders from the War Department confined his operations to the seaboard states for the present and promised $5,000 in government funds. The orders told the major to report on a regular basis to give "prompt information in regard to the assembly of recruits." Several days later, on June 17, Stearns received his commission and title, "Recruiting Commissioner for the U.S. Colored Troops."[75]

Stearns was thrilled by a letter that caught up with him in Washington. Wendell Phillips wrote that on May 28, when the Fifty-fourth had marched through Boston to board a transport for South Carolina, citizens crowded every square foot of sidewalk, and even conservative "State Street roared with cheers." He asked Stearns, "Is not that triumph?" Phillips reported that the regiment looked remarkably well and that Frank had been there in his parlor to see them march by. Phillips told Stearns that they owed it all to his "energy, sagacity, and unfailing hope." Phillips said that Stearns was indeed the "Buffalo king," in reference to his recruiting in that city, and that at a recent rally people in "Tremont Temple had cheered briskly. "[76]

Stearns, however, soon had less agreeable news. In May, Robert E. Lee's Army of Northern Virginia again crossed the Maryland border heading toward Pennsylvania. The telegraph wires hummed with requests from Union army commanders for more troops. Aware of the critical situation and headquartered in Philadelphia, Stearns offered Major General Darius Couch, Pennsylvania Military District commander, black soldiers. Couch refused his offer. Annoyed, Stearns telegraphed Stanton, "General Couch declined to receive colored troops . . . . Two companies here are ready to go for the emergency." Stanton's reply came swiftly. He informed Couch "that he was authorized to receive troops without regard to color." But Stanton also did not wish to create discord over the issue. He told Stearns, "If there is likely to be any dispute about the matter, it will be better to send no more. It is well to avoid all controversy." The secretary's attitude irritated Stearns.[77]

Stearns was even more irritated when he returned to Boston for a brief visit. Or.. July 12, the first names of men to be conscripted were posted in Boston. Arriving in the city the following morning, Stearns found the North End of Boston completely under the control of a mob of Irish workingmen infuriated at a draft to fight "for the niggers." Apparently not terribly concerned, Stearns breakfasted at the Parker House and then stopped at the State House to see Andrew. Andrew's office was in turmoil. When the governor looked up and saw the major, he called, "Stearns, you are just the man I want." Andrew explained that the wires were down and that he needed to contact a "first-rate militia company in Woburn." Andrew asked Stearns whether he would take his order to the unit's captain. Stearns agreed and, with a team of fast horses, reached Woburn and mobilized the company. Stearns thought that the disturbance was a "rebellion (not riot), organized by Jeff. Davis." Stearns later said, "Fortunately for Boston and all New England, a dose of canister . . . fired into a dense crowd . . . settled the affair." The riots terrified Mary who claimed her Irish cook, whose brother worked in Boston, said that a group of rioters planned to kill her husband and burn The Evergreens.[78]

The recruitment of African-Americans caused a different kind of problem in Philadelphia. Seeing Stearns's success, the Union League of that city attempted to recruit black regiments. Thomas Webster, head of the committee set up for that purpose, received permission from the War Department to recruit one regiment at a time. The League, however, had not been successful in raising a sufficient number of men. Help was on its way. Instructions from the War Department said that the government "expected and desired" that Webster "confer with Maj. Geo. L. Stearns . . . for the purpose of assisting in this work."[79]

Stearns had decided to set up his headquarters in Philadelphia. Quakers in Pennsylvania and elsewhere had long supported abolition, and many slaves over the decades had sought refuge in the City of Brotherly Love. From the large African-American population his agents had already secured several hundred of Philadelphia's blacks for the two Massachusetts regiments. Stearns opened an office at 1210 Chestnut Street and established a camp on Chelton Hill, on land donated by suffragist Lucretia Mott. Stearns called this camp-the largest established for black troops during the Civil War-William Penn. Telling Mary that the Quakers winced at the name, Stearns said, "But I tell them it is established on peace principles; that is, to conquer a lasting peace."[80]

Now that Stearns was in Philadelphia, government regulations, under which he now had to operate, held back his efforts. Stearns was eager to see as many African-Americans as possible in uniform as quickly as possible and considered it very inconvenient to muster men by company (one hundred men) . Instead of going by the regulation, he requested and received permission to muster by squad (ten men). Stearns also took issue with the regulation that required mustering regiments to full strength at Camp William Penn before sending them south. He said he was "anxious that the regiments raised here should be filled to 600 men only" and then sent south to be filled there to full strength with contrabands who could not reach the North. He also believed that the free blacks would inspire and assist the former slaves. When Lieutenant Colonel Louis Wagner protested his request, Stearns returned to Washington to see Stanton, who told the major that the regiments could be filled to the minimum. Unfortunately, Stearns's plan did not work out, for a year later, as he observed, it was "almost impossible to recruit for old regiments at the South."[81]

To speed up recruiting, Stearns worked not only at the federal level but at the local level. When the major spoke at a meeting of Philadelphia's Union League on June 8, 1863, he requested that it set up a supervisory committee to assist in recruiting. The committee was supposed to pass on all applications from whites who wished to command black troops. According to its bylaws, the committee would "determine the merits of each application" and then "immediately communicate to Major Stearns" the names of those recommended. The committee also appointed a general recruiting agent to act under Stearns's direction, because he had the final authority to recruit. In addition to recruiting African-Americans and selecting white officers, Stearns established the Free Military School for Applicants for the Command of Colored Troops. To defray recruiting expenses, Stearns also took steps to raise funds by subscription in large cities and received $50,000 in pledges from New England. One of the other recurring problems Stearns faced in recruiting blacks was the draft, not only because it occasionally caused rioting, but because one of its weaknesses was that a man could either pay for an exemption or hire a substitute to go in his stead. Stearns believed that this policy interfered with recruitment but that, when the draft was filled and African-Americans no longer had a chance to be paid as substitutes, recruiting would pick up again with spirit. Racial prejudice had been a problem, too, but, as a local paper observed, it had diminished because of the "laudably prompt" enlistments in Major Stearns's regiments.[82]

Stearns at this time was fearful that recruiting efforts would be hindered by the government's wavering attitude toward black troops. The refusal to commission African-American officers still dogged his efforts. Stanton consistently resisted all the entreaties from Stearns and other abolitionists, much to their dismay, to make this happen. Other disturbing news arrived from Washington. The government had decided to reduce the monthly pay of black soldiers from $13 to $10 and deduct $3 for uniforms. Also annoying and certainly not assisting the struggle for equality, the Fifty-fourth Massachusetts and other regiments recruited by Stearns often found themselves receiving an inordinate amount of fatigue duty. All of these issues weighed heavily on Stearns as he tried to persuade others to take up arms for his "John Brown Corps." He and the Philadelphia Committee decided to take up these issues with the Secretary of War.[83]

On July 19, 1863, Frank Stearns was in Washington with his father and Judge William D. Kelley, a member of the Philadelphia recruiting committee. After an hour of arguing with Stanton over the issues of black officers, fatigue duty, and unequal pay, to Stearns's "great disgust" the secretary refused to budge. Late that afternoon, Kelley returned to Willards Hotel with a newspaper. His eyes flashing, Kelley asked whether Stearns had heard the news. Without waiting for a reply, he told him that the Fifty-fourth had been repulsed at Fort Wagner, an installation guarding the sea approach to Charleston, South Carolina, and "cut to pieces." According to the newspaper, young Shaw and half of his officers were dead. Never before or after did Frank see his father so agitated. Stearns grasped the paper and sank into a chair.[84]

Several days after the Fifty-fourth's repulse, Stearns wrote a letter to Patrick Jackson. Stearns said he "sympathized very deeply" with him and "the rest of my friends who have relatives in the gallant 54th Massachusetts." The major reminded Jackson that he "had so much to do with the formation of it that all, both officers and men, hold the place of relatives in my affections." To Governor Andrew he wrote," My heart bleeds for our gallant officers and soldiers of the 54th. All did their duty nobly."[85]

Regardless of the news, recruiting continued in Philadelphia unabated. The members of the Union League appreciated his work and made him a member of the prestigious organization. Later that summer there were enough trained regiments at Camp William Penn to hold a review of the black troops. When these regiments finally moved south one observer noted, "people cheered them . . . and ladies of whose acquaintances any gentlemen might be proud bade them God speed . . . as the dusky volunteers with buoyant tread marched by."[86]

Unfortunately, those "dusky volunteers" and the others recruited by Stearns were in potential danger for word had come of Southern threats to enslave members of the Fifty-fourth Massachusetts captured at Fort Wagner. For those held prisoner by the rebels, Stearns told Patrick Jackson he would use all his "endeavors to protect them from the ferocity that is the natural result of slavery." He assured Jackson that he had spoken to Secretary of War Stanton about Southern threats to execute or to enslave African-American soldiers. Stearns reported Stanton delayed issuing a public proclamation, but had let the rebel government know that it would be held "accountable man for man and life for life." Stearns told Jackson that he would see that his letter of concern reached Washington. Stearns need not have troubled to forward the letter, however, for on July 20, 1863, Lincoln signed a proclamation which instructed that for every soldier of the United States "killed in violation of the laws of war a rebel soldier shall be executed" and that for every Union soldier enslaved a "rebel soldier shall be placed at hard labor."[87]

Stearns was still concerned over the Union's treatment of its own soldiers and urged Frederick Douglass to visit Washington to speak on behalf of blacks. Stearns was much taken with Douglass and believed him to be the right person to press the administration to modify its policies. Following Stearns's suggestion, Douglass managed to speak to Stanton, whose "manner was cold ... business like but earnest," Douglass later reported. Douglass tried to explain that an African-American was viewed at two extremes: "One claimed for him too much and the other too little." Douglass told him that the truth was that "he is simply a man." Stanton asked in what way the present conditions of "colored enlistments" conflicted with what Douglass had said. The noted free black replied in an instant, "Unequal pay, no incentives." The secretary blamed Congress and prejudice but said he was personally willing to give the same pay to black soldiers as to white and expressed his readiness to grant commissions for men recommended by their white officers "for their capacity for bravery." Stanton asked Douglass to assist General Lorenzo Thomas, in charge of African-American recruitment on the Mississippi. Douglass replied that he was already operating under the direction of Major Stearns. Later, explaining to Stearns that Stanton was "very imperative in his manner," Douglass said, "[I] felt myself stopped in regard to your own efficient services." Douglass rationalized his acquiescence to Stanton's request by telling Stearns that this offer echoed the Boston businessman's inquiry as to his "willingness to go south in this work."[88]

Douglass then visited President Lincoln and, he later said, "saw at a glance the justice of the popular Estimate of his qualities expressed in adding 'Honest' to the name of Abraham Lincoln." Douglass thanked Lincoln for his recent general order protecting African-American soldiers. According to Douglass, Lincoln "proceeded with an earnestness and fluency . . . to vindicate his policy respecting the whole slavery question." The president told the editor that the "bravery and general good conduct" of black fighting men were necessary for total emancipation, the same message Stearns conveyed to the African-American community. The interview, Douglass later told Stearns, assured him that "slavery would not survive the war."[89]

While waiting for Stanton to act-for Stearns found the War Department unable to meet his "rapid mode of working," he said-the restless businessman bombarded the department with telegrams and letters stating he was "ready to prosecute vigorously the work entrusted" to his care. A group called the Committee of Citizens of Boston, responding to Stearns's call for additional funds, raised $10,000 to pay extraordinary expenses for recruiting in southern states. The members promised an additional $50,000, and Stearns said he had "no doubt that New York and Philadelphia [would] respond as liberally to [his] appeal." Boston businessman John Murray Forbes chaired the committee. Forbes was in direct contact with Stanton, who wrote that he was looking for "some competent, organizing mind, earnestly devoted to the subject and willing to spend and be spent" recruiting black troops. What the secretary had in mind was a leader, perhaps a general officer. Though Stearns had the qualifications, his abolitionist background and demands for black equality must have grated on official Washington, for Stanton told Forbes that such a man had not yet manifested himself.[90]

Amos Lawrence, another committee member, put forth Stearns's name in a letter he wrote to Secretary Stanton in late August. Lawrence told the secretary that he had known Major Stearns in business many years and that, although he had some singularities, he was entirely reliable: "He is a man of property, very liberal and not ambitious of distinction: besides this he is cautious in making promises." If Stearns had told Stanton that with $50,000 he could get 50,000 men, Lawrence said that Stanton should believe him. Lawrence also told Stanton that the committee had $50,000 at Stearns's disposal and that the major could obtain the funds if he received Stanton's "support in the manner he expected." This statement indicated Stearns was not pleased with the War Department. After several months of recruiting, Stearns found himself, he said, "an applicant with many others" who could get "neither money, nor other aid" from "certain army officers."[91]

Still waiting for the War Department to act, Stearns made a few visits to drum up both support and customers for his recruiting network. He visited Colonel William Birney (son of the former Liberty party candidate), who was recruiting African-Americans in Baltimore and, as Stearns said, "sound to the core." Stearns gave Birney funds and the use of one of his agents, which led to an increase in recruits. On the same trip, Stearns spoke at Fort Monroe, Virginia, to Major General John Foster, who said he would gladly accept Stearns's help in recruiting. Foster also suggested that Stearns visit Brigadier General Henry Naglee at Norfolk. Unfortunately, less receptive to Stearns's ideas, the latter refused to cooperate, according to Stearns, "without a positive order." Stearns's temper rose when the general tried to advise him about recruiting, and he angrily told Naglee that it did not concern his department. Although Stearns found some support on this trip, his level of frustration at government ineptness grew. Not only did he have to wait for the War Department to act and to endure Naglee's reluctance, but also, while on this trip, Stearns noticed a goodly number of Union officers lounging and smoking on the piazza of the Hygeia Hotel at Fort Monroe. He later remarked to his son Frank that, if the government was so concerned about economizing, it would be better off reducing the number of officers than reducing the pay of black soldiers.[92]

Returning to his department headquarters in Philadelphia, Major Stearns found War Department orders. Stanton directed Stearns to report to Headquarters, Department of the Cumberland, commanded by Major General William S. Rosecrans. Stearns was to assist in recruiting and in organizing black troops in this department. According to the orders, Stearns was also to report by letter to Brigadier General Lorenzo Thomas (now at Vicksburg), who was responsible for "organizing colored troops in the Valley of the Mississippi." Stearns was to make frequent reports to Thomas and to act under his orders. Stearns wrote to Mary the news from Emancipation, Black Soldiers, and the Major 159 the War Department and said that Stanton had "waked up" and intended that he "plump [himself] down in Tennessee," the center of the "accursed institution." According to Stearns, Nashville was to the "South what Buffalo was to the West and East-a centre from which to radiate." The major declared that he was determined either to bum slavery out or be burnt by it.[93]

Just prior to leaving Philadelphia for his new assignment with the Department of the Cumberland, Stearns went to Boston for a brief visit to check on business and personal matters. George decided to foreclose on Stuart in Kansas. George Collamore, Stearns's Kansas agent handling the Stuart mortgage, thought the court's appraised value of the property, $2,000, was too high, a ploy to protect the mortgage holder. Collamore said the property was worth less now because "the fence rails [had] been sold . . . and the farm . . . run to weeds." Collamore told Stearns he would do his best for him, "let the condition be what it may." Stearns caught up on the rest of his affairs with Harry, who continued to manage the family business. The Monday he returned to Medford, Stearns drove Frank to Cambridge. Stopping his carriage outside the gate to Harvard Yard, Stearns told Frank, "Remember, not only while you are in College but all through life, that a man is known by the company he keeps."[94]

VI

On September 6, Stearns reported to General Rosecrans, who received him very kindly. Stearns spent from three in the afternoon till one in the morning with the General and came away with a favorable impression. Stearns later said that Rosecrans "was very free in his expressions of opinion" and was "heartily in favor of the employment of colored troops." Rosecrans asked several questions about the problems of recruiting in a slave state. Two questions, according to Stearns, seemed most' important: "Can slaves of loyal citizens of Tennessee be enlisted in the Army without the consent of their masters?" "Will all enlisted men become freedmen at the expiration of their terms of military service?" Because he could not answer Rosecrans's questions, Stearns wrote to Stanton and added a third, whether black noncommissioned officers received higher pay than privates and if so, how much?[95]

Rosecrans decided that Stearns could accomplish his mission best by establishing headquarters in Nashville. The general told Stearns he was to report any difficulties and to continue responding to instructions from the War Department. Rosecrans ordered the quartermaster to provide transportation for Stearns, for his assistants and for recruits. He also said Stearns could requisition clothing and rations, as well as other equipment, as necessary.[96]

Stearns met both with members of Rosecrans's staff and with local citizens. Cordial, but extremely busy, Brigadier General James A. Garfield promised to "give all the aid in his power," Stearns later recalled. The major also met with Captain Young, the commissary of musters, the man who would accept his regiments, with whom Stearns hoped to strike up a cordial relationship. Stearns reported to Stanton that he was very impressed with the department, for its "officers pride[d) themselves on the exact performance of their duties." The major also told Stanton that, in his encounters with local citizens, he found them in a "better state of preparation for the change" in recruiting blacks on a grand scale than anticipated. As for the African-Americans, Stearns said they appeared physically superior to others he had recruited and certainly as bright and intelligent. He also indicated, however, that most of them were former slaves without education and that Rosecrans suggested Stearns send north for blacks who could read and write to become noncommissioned officers, at least twenty for each of the regiments to be formed. Stearns took this advice and sent for literate northern blacks immediately upon his arrival in Nashville.[97]

While waiting in Nashville for Stanton's reply, Stearns reported to Andrew Johnson, military governor of Tennessee. The wily Johnson gave the abolitionist the impression that he was in complete agreement with Stearns's objectives. Also, Johnson appeared to have no desire to be subordinated to Rosecrans and, unknown to Stearns, believed that "political imperatives overrode military ones." He said that his primary concern was to transform Tennessee into a state loyal to the Union. That fall Johnson declared himself in favor of immediate emancipation, for he thought that now was the "time for settlement of the question."[98]

Stanton replied to the questions Stearns forwarded from Rosecrans. Slaves had to have their masters' permission to enlist and "all men who enlist [ed would], at the expiration of their term of service, be free." Stanton also wrote that if the army required it, Stearns could conscript slaves without their owner's consent. Owners would receive the bounty for those slaves enlisted in this manner, and these men would also be free at the end of their enlistment. Currently black noncommissioned officers were not authorized higher pay, but Stanton assured Stearns Congress would place them at parity with white soldiers of the same rank. Stanton also said that if General Rosecrans and Governor Johnson deemed conscription or the voluntary enlistment of loyal citizens' slaves without permission necessary, they could muster those men into the Army. The government would give the owners a list of persons so enlisted and compensate them in an amount not to exceed that authorized by law for volunteer bounties, but only if the owners provided emancipation papers. Men enlisted in this manner would then be free at the end of their initial term of service.[99]

Johnson received a copy of Stanton's response to Stearns. The governor balked at enforcing in Tennessee the policies Stanton worked out with Lincoln regarding enlisting slaves. According to Johnson, what the department really needed at the moment were more black laborers for the "prosecution of works" that were indispensable for sustaining the logistical support of Rosecrans's army. Johnson believed that all African-Americans would prefer to enlist so they could "go into [a training] camp and do nothing" rather than go to work on much needed projects, such as railroad construction.[100]

Surprised at hearing Johnson's stance secondhand, Stearns reported to Stanton that the governor objected to his plans to enlist all able bodied black men willing to serve. Quickly replying the same day, Stanton told Stearns not to "act contrary to the wishes of Governor Johnson." Johnson telegraphed Stanton as well. The governor was frank in stating his opinion that Major Stearns's mission, with his notions of black equality, would give "no aid in organizing negro regiments in Tennessee." Johnson urged caution in recruiting, lest it detract from Union support by loyal slaveholders in Tennessee. The governor then told Rosecrans he telegraphed Stanton about Major Stearns's mission in the department. Johnson explained that he and the commanding general of the department could organize blacks as either laborers or soldiers "as well without as with the aid of Major Stearns at this time."[101]

In reply to Johnson's telegram, Stanton telegraphed, "[Major Stearns is your] subordinate, bound to follow your direction, and may be relieved by you whenever his action is deemed by you prejudicial." Stanton also said that if Stearns were of no aid and his presence were obnoxious, he would be removed. To Stearns, Stanton sent a message that if a difference of opinion existed between Stearns and Johnson, because the latter was the state executive officer, the major should conform to the governor's wishes: "All dissention is to be avoided . . . and if there is any want of harmony . . . you had better leave Nashville and proceed to Cairo to await orders." Stanton informed Lincoln of the controversy. Lincoln telegraphed the distraught governor, urging him to do his utmost to see that he got every man "black and white under arms at the very earliest moment." Laborers were not as important, the president believed, as men under arms.[102]

Working against Stearns through Secretary of War Stanton, Johnson did not wish to confront the major with his complaints. Although Stearns suspected that the governor was both afraid of him and opposed to his work, their meetings were cordial, with Johnson sharing recent letters from Lincoln and Secretary Chase that were encouraging in regard to bringing Tennessee back into the Union. Working to bring Johnson, Stearns said, "over to the faith," he did not realize that his priorities were quite different from those of the harried war governor. Stearns believed he succeeded, but could not tell with absolute certainty. He said that if he had succeeded in winning the governor over, it would be a great gain. Johnson, on the other hand, knew that Stanton would support him against Stearns, if their feud ever escalated to the point that the secretary would have to step in to resolve differences of opinion. Resting secure in the knowledge of Stanton's support and heeding Lincoln's plea for more men under arms, Johnson allowed Stearns to stay in Nashville and begin recruiting.[103]

Almost ready to launch his recruiting drive, Stearns still had to find a suitable headquarters, for houses were scarce and rents high in Nashville. He wrote to Major C. W. Foster, Chief, Bureau of Colored Troops, that the shortage was due in part to the increased wartime population "but more to officers' occupying confiscated property having more room than they [could] use." Angry, Stearns also reported that these same officers showed an indisposition to aid him. Despite these setbacks, Stearns began recruiting on

September 24, 1863, from a room at the St. Cloud Hotel. The following month, he and his staff established a headquarters in an abandoned home on Nashville's outskirts. Shortly thereafter, Brigadier General Thomas contacted Stearns to request he forward all reports and rosters of black regiments to him at Vicksburg, except in such extreme cases as would require the immediate action of the War Department.[104]

Stearns had never been so close to the actual fighting as he was now. Confederate General Braxton Bragg's Army of Tennessee met the Army of the Cumberland on September 19 at Chickamauga. Because of a blunder, the rebels managed to exploit a gap in the federal center. On September 21, the Army of the Cumberland retired to Chattanooga. That evening, Stearns wrote to Mary that the news made for a "gloomy day in Nashville," for Rosecrans's army was in peril. He told his wife not to worry for his safety for Rosecrans was a brave commander, and, besides, he was a hundred miles from the "seat of war." In an earlier letter, Mary must have complained of his absence, for he reasoned, "If you could understand the nature of my work, you would say, 'stay and do it.' "[105]

Stearns told Mary that the African-American community in Nashville held him in esteem, probably because the blacks had heard of his support of John Brown. According to Stearns, these "poor people, saw him as their 'guardian.' They showed their thanks by offering "fruit and carriage rides and other demonstrations" that were gratifying. The community saw in his arrival the possibility of an end to the impressments that had been a part of life in Nashville since August 1862. Stearns arrived in the city during the largest impressment the blacks had experienced, which was due to Andrew Johnson's order to complete the Nashville and Northwestern Railroad. The conduct of the military authorities horrified Stearns. They would wait until Sunday church services to press African-Americans into service, even those black men who had passes, which the soldiers confiscated and burned. Observing all of this, Stearns said, "The colored men here are treated like brutes." On Sunday, September 20, he said "a large number were impressed and one was shot." The resister died three days later. Stearns protested to Stanton and asked for General Meigs, the Quartermaster General, to conduct an investigation. Although the major said that if Stanton ordered such an investigation, he would "get some light on the subject," Stearns really did not think military authorities would stop impressing blacks for forced labor. He decided to try a different tactic by holding a meeting of African-Americans and asking them to volunteer their services to gain respect from the authorities. On October 4, the Nashville *Dispatch* reported, "A number of negroes who have volunteered to work on the Northwestern Railroad paraded the streets yesterday." In one sense, Stearns believed that the irresponsible way impressments were being conducted would help him, as he said, "as soon as I establish a camp and show them they are safe inside of it." Once· enlisted, they "won't be likely to desert," Stearns said.[106]

So in Nashville, as in Philadelphia and in Buffalo, Stearns attracted African-Americans to the Union ranks. He was fortunate this time to receive the assistance of Captain Reuben D. Mussey, an energetic Regular detailed as a mustering officer. A Dartmouth College graduate, Mussey considered the recruitment of blacks "the sacred work of raising a fallen Race" and became the first Regular army officer to volunteer. Stearns started his recruiting work by first obtaining permission from Johnson to run an advertisement announcing the categories of blacks eligible to enlist, free and slave, and listing the establishment of recruiting stations at Nashville, Gallatin, and Murfreesborough. Of course, Stearns succeeded in Nashville for the same reason he had succeeded in Philadelphia and in Buffalo: he made detailed plans and implemented them through hard work. Edward J. Bartlett, an agent Stearns had taken with him from Philadelphia, said he "never saw a man who could dispatch so much business in a day as George L. Stearns."[107]

In order to expand recruiting, Stearns made extensive use of local African-Americans community leaders as agents. Also, the first companies formed went out on "scouting expeditions, to collect recruits for the regiment and men as laborers," Stearns explained. As recruits became scarce around Nashville, his agents went beyond the "Union picket line and generally reap[ed] a harvest of slaves." Some of Stearns's agents were not so meticulous as he in regard to recruiting techniques. A group of Davidson County citizens complained to the major that a black "having authority from Nashville," Jeff Baker, was enlisting their slaves "without any regard whatsoever to the published regulations." Stearns immediately sent another agent to find Baker and straighten out the matter.[108]

Stearns continued to demonstrate his humanitarian concern for African-Americans. He saw to it that new recruits received proper treatment during training. Realizing that in combat, units usually performed best if the commanding officers stayed with their men from enlistment on, Stearns urged that officers be assigned to his regiments early, if not at the beginning of training as the men enlisted. After initial training, Nashville's citizens "saw for the first time, a regiment of colored troops . . . recently recruited in this city by Major Starnes [Stearns]." The local papers thought the unit "attracted more attention than any body of troops that ever kept time to martial music" in Nashville. The Nashville *Daily Union* observed, "The colored people seem[ed] zealously enlisted against the rebellion."[109]

Adept at public relations before either journalism or the military had a word for it, Stearns was interested in these local attitudes not only on the use of black troops, but also on total emancipation. He directed two white agents to be "chiefly employed in influencing public opinion." Major Stearns also ordered his military secretary to write articles for the Nashville Daily Union reporting the positive aspects of black units. One account, for example, said, "Not a thing was touched on their [the black recruits'] route. The property of citizens was respected, and though they were five hours in Goodlettsville no depredations of any kind were committed." Stearns also made personal appeals, held public meetings, and used newspapers to encourage emancipation of the state's slaves who were not affected by President Lincoln's proclamation.[110]

On the evening of October 8, Stearns attended a meeting of slaveholders, who considered petitioning the president to act vigorously to enlist slaves. One of the attendees read a paper that advocated black recruitment and "Emancipation with compensation for the slaves of loyal owners." Stearns said that some of the slaveholders who did not desire compensation challenged the paper. One of them explained to Stearns that uncompensated emancipation would obtain the support of the "mass of the nonslaveholders" and that, if Union men were compensated, this support would be lost. The group eventually unanimously agreed to a draft resolution to the president, requesting him to continue black "enlistment vigorously, without compensation." Stearns marveled at the meeting, for there in the room with him were men he had sworn to destroy, men holding slave property of over one million dollars. He said that he had never met a "more sturdy set of men" and that in his life he had been "astonished before but never to the degree" he was that evening. Encouraged by the meeting, Stearns personally organized a group of slaveholders who owned $200,000 worth of slave property. This group petitioned Lincoln "to decree full, immediate, and uncompensated emancipation in Tennessee." Captain Mussey believed all of the major's efforts "had an effect and were to some extent instrumental in causing the great revolution in public opinion" in Tennessee.[111]

In addition to recruiting and public relations, Stearns worked to relieve the suffering of African-Americans displaced by the war. The army made no provisions either for the large numbers of refugees or for the families of those who enlisted. Stearns realized the morale of black soldiers would improve immeasurably if the men knew that their families were being cared for in their absence. He obtained access to a deserted building on the outskirts of Nashville and established a makeshift camp that provided shelter and army rations to women and children. Moved by Stearns's example, the army later set up a permanent camp in the city. Stearns also wanted African-American women to learn to become self-sufficient as part of their education for freedom in anticipation of emancipation, so he put notices in the local newspapers for "Persons desiring colored Female Servants."[112]

Seeing that freedom had a chance to become reality in Tennessee, Stearns sought to accomplish a number of goals, each contributing to his grand aim of "freeing and educating and enfranchizing the colored race, not as colored people, but as human beings." Aware of the freedmen's desire for education, Stearns believed schooling was an important step toward securing civil rights for blacks. His first effort in this direction was to create a school for "colored girls." The major also informed white chaplains of the units he organized to "make the instruction of the regiment a part and the principle [sic] part of their duty." Stearns believed more education and fewer prayers would lead to freedom and equality.[113]

On reflection, Stearns had reason to be satisfied with his accomplishments in Nashville. In just three months' time, he had built a substantial recruiting bureau and recruited more than six regiments, over six thousand men. With his organization running smoothly and a capable assistant in charge, he asked Stanton for leave. All his activities had tired the businessman, and he yearned to see his family. Harry had recently written to him, and the letter must have made Stearns long to return to Medford. The boy told his father that he had begun a "partial course at Tufts College," a school bordering The Evergreens, which included chemistry, French, and physiology. Harry said, "I suppose you will feel badly because I have left the store." He explained that he was not tired of the business and that he had not wanted to leave, but that his mother thought studies were important. Harry revealed his own desires, however: "I want to have an education as well as Frank." It was not only the family Stearns wanted to see but also his business. He had directed his lead pipe company by letters and telegrams through his chief clerk, William J. Bride, who now held a limited partnership. Now he needed to see how the business and Bride were faring.[114]

When Stanton did not reply to the request for leave, Stearns took matters into his own hands and went to Washington on December 17. Not exactly according to army regulations—but then Stearns always considered himself a free agent regardless of his commission—Stanton met with Stearns and agreed to allow him to go home and to take his own time returning to duty.[115]

After taking two weeks to settle his affairs and to enjoy Christmas with his family, Stearns returned to Washington. He arrived on January 8, his fifty-fifth birthday, and called on Stanton the following day. The secretary, however, was too busy to see him. For three days the major tried to see Stanton. Then the two men accidentally met at a reception. To Stearns's polite greeting, Stanton snapped, "When are you going to Tennessee?" Stearns replied, "As soon as I have had a conference with you." "Call on me tomorrow," Stanton said, "and I will try to find time to talk with you."[116]

Annoyed, hurt, and angered by Stanton's attitude, Stearns spent a restless night. As he lay awake at Willards, all of Stanton's "past roughness and want of consideration . . . [were] revived again and again," he recalled. Stearns told his wife that he did not "care for his haughty manner" and that he would not and could not "wait on a man whom decent society would not tolerate." Stearns said, "My sense of duty is satisfied; I have no desire to continue in public life." The following day he sent his resignation to Secretary of War Stanton, who immediately accepted it, explaining that he realized the pay was inadequate and the sacrifice so great that he had no right to insist on Stearns's remaining on active duty. In his note, Stanton also thanked Stearns for the aid he had given the cause.[117]

Unpleasant encounters with Stanton and his frustration over the sometimes ambiguous attitude of the federal government toward black soldiers were part of Stearns's decision to resign. In defense of his resignation, Stearns said, "The Government has not kept its faith with the colored man anywhere." He said that it refused in many cases to pay them an enlistment bounty, that their pay was less than that of whites, that they were used for an inordinate amount of fatigue duty, and that their families were "destitute of the necessaries of life." Stearns believed he could do as much good in a private way, a way much more suited to his comfort and to his satisfaction, than in military service.[118]

Sitting in his room at Willards, Stearns contemplated his next moves. After his run-in with Stanton and failure to understand President Lincoln's pragmatism, Stearns told Mary that he thought "men high in power were dancing over the graves of our slaughtered heroes." He said his depression was only temporary, for he believed God would watch over the nation as it passed through this crisis. He was certain that the Lord would "bring us out, tho' with much tribulation."[119]

So, weary to the point of exhaustion, but somewhat relieved at his decision not to remain in uniform, Stearns left Washington to settle affairs in Nashville. He had a great deal on his mind, and even though several months of rest would have been in order, it was not in his nature to remain inactive. The state of blacks, his family, and business all competed for his attention. Stearns had much to do. After a brief rest he was once again in fighting trim, planning the next move not only for emancipation but for establishment of full civil rights for blacks. Stearns would never give up, for, according to his friend Emerson, he was "a man for up-hill work, a soldier to bare the brunt; a man whom disasters, which dishearten other men, only stimulated to new courage and endeavor."[120]

NOTES

1. Stephen B. Oates, *Our Fiery Trial* (Amherst: University of Massachusetts Press, 1979), pp. 9-21.
2. Stearns, *Life*, p. 219.
3. David Lee Child to George L. Stearns, April 18, 1860, Stearns MSS, MHS.
4. David Lee Child to George L. Stearns, April 23, 1860, Stearns MSS, MHS.
5. Stearns, *Life*, pp. 221-222.
6. George L. Stearns to Frank and Harry Stearns, April 26, 1860, Stearns MSS, MHS.
7. George L. Stearns to Mary Stearns, May 1, 1860, quoted in Stearns, Life, p. 225.
8. Stearns, *Life*, p. 225; George L. Stearns to Mary Stearns, May 8, 1860, quoted in Stearns, *Life*, pp. 224-225; George L. Stearns to Charles Sumner, June 5, 1860, Sumner MSS, Houghton.
9. Allan Nevins, Prologue to Civil War, 1859-1862, vol. 4, of *The Emergence of Lincoln* (New York: Charles Scribner's Sons, 1950), pp. 247-251.
10. Ibid; Stearns, *Life*, p. 226.
11. George L. Stearns to Mary Stearns, May 17, 1860, quoted in Stearns, *Life*, pp. 225-226; "Minutes of the New England Emigrant Aid Society," May 29, 1860, Kansas State Historical Society, Topeka, Kansas; Stearns, *Life*, p. 225.
12. Stearns, *Life*, p. 227 and fn. 227.

13. Ibid., p. 230.
14. Nevins, *Prologue*, p. 299; Stearns, *Life*, pp. 231-232.
15. Henry Wilson to Abraham Lincoln, August 25, 1860, Robert Todd Lincoln Collection, Library of Congress, Washington, DC (hereafter cited as Robert Todd Lincoln Collection, LC); Pearson, *John Andrew*, 1:126.
16. Stearns, *Life*, p. 234.
17. Ibid.
18. Ibid., pp. 233-234.
19. Pearson, *John Andrew*, 1:133; Brooks, *Medford*, p. 465; George L. Stearns to Mary Stearns, December 22 and 23, 1860, Stearns Collection, KSHS.
20. George L. Stearns to Mary Stearns, December 22, 1860, Stearns Collection, KSHS.
21. George L. Stearns to Mary Stearns, December 22, 1860, Stearns Collection, KSHS; George L. Stearns to Samuel G. Howe, December 23, 1860, quoted in Stearns, *Life*, pp. 237-238.
22. Brooks and Usher, *Medford*, p. 465.
23. George L. Stearns to William L. Robinson, December 24, 1860, quoted in Stearns, *Life*, pp. 238-240; Stearns, *Cambridge Sketches*, p. 202.
24. Pearson, John Andrew, 2:156; Telegrams, George L. Stearns to Charles Sumner, January 31, 1861, and reply, Charles Sumner to George L. Stearns, January 31, 1861, The Magnetic Telegraph Company, Sumner MSS, Houghton; George L. Stearns to Charles Sumner, January 31, 1861, Sumner MSS, Houghton.
25. George L. Stearns to Charles Sumner, January 3, 1861, Sumner MSS, Houghton.
26. George L. Stearns to George W. Collamore, January 24 and February 9, 1861, Stearns MSS, MHS.
27. Stearns, *Life*, p. 244; George L. Stearns to Charles Sumner, March 14, 1861, Sumner MSS, Houghton.
28. Stearns, *Life*, p. 245.
29. George L. Stearns to Charles Sumner, March 16, 1861, Sumner MSS, Houghton; George L. Stearns to Franklin B. Sanborn, April 26, 1861, Sanborn MSS, Concord.
30. James Montgomery to George L. Stearns, May 8, 1861, James Montgomery Collection, Kansas State Historical Society, Topeka, Kansas (hereafter cited as Montgomery Collection, KSHS).
31. George L. Stearns to Mary Stearns, May 7, 1861, Charles Robinson Collection, Kansas State Historical Society, Topeka, Kansas (hereafter cited as Robinson Collection, KSHS); Stearns, *Life*, pp. 246-248.
32. George L. Stearns to Mary Stearns, May 10, 1861, quoted in Stearns, *Life*, p. 248; George L. Stearns to [?], May 14, 1861, Stearns Collection, KSHS.
33. George L. Stearns to Mary Stearns, June 17, 1861, quoted in Stearns, *Life*, p. 251.

34. Martin F. Conway to George L. Stearns, July 12, 1861, quoted in Stearns, *Life*, p. 253; Stearns, *Life*, pp. 253-254.

35. Stearns, *Life*, p. 254.

36. George L. Stearns to Horatio Woodman, September 19, 1861, Stearns MSS, MHS.

37. John G. Whittier to George L. Stearns, September 13, 1861, quoted in Stearns, *Life*, pp. 256-257; George L. Stearns to Franklin B. Sanborn, September 5, 1861, quoted in Sanborn, Howe, p. 283; George L. Stearns to J. Miller McKim, McKim Collection.

38. George L. Stearns to Lysander Spooner, October 1, 1861, Slavery Manuscripts, New York Historical Society, New York, New York (hereafter cited as Slavery MSS, NYHS); George L. Stearns to Franklin B. Sanborn, November 2, 1861, Sanborn MSS.

39. Stearns, *Life*, p. 259.

40. Harry L. Stearns to George L. Stearns, October 3, 1861, Stearns MSS, MHS.

41. Lydia Maria Child to Mary Stearns, December 1861, Child MSS.

42. Emancipation League, Declaration, November 19, 1861, Antislavery MSS, BPL; George L. Stearns to Franklin B. Sanborn, November 2, 1861, Sanborn MSS.

43. Moncure D. Conway, *Autobiography, Memories and Experiences of Moncure Daniel Conway*, 2 vols. (Boston: Houghton Mifflin, 1905), 1:346; George L. Stearns to Charles Sumner, February 1862, Sumner MSS, Houghton.

44. Samuel G. Howe to Frank Bird, March 5, 1862, quoted in Sanborn, Howe, p. 284.

45. Brooks, *Medford*, p. 466; George L. Stearns to Charles Sumner, February 10, 1862, Sumner MSS, Houghton.

46. John B. Stuart to George Collamore, July 27, 1862, and George L. Stearns, July 1, 1862, Stearns Collection, HSHS.

47. Harold Schwartz, *Samuel Gridley Howe: Social Reformer* (Cambridge, MA: Harvard University Press, 1956), p. 182; George L. Stearns to Moncure D, Conway, July 31, 1862, Moncure D. Conway Papers, Columbia University (hereafter cited as Conway Papers); Conway Autobiography, 1:369; Brooks, Medford, p. 466; The Boston *Commonwealth*, September 6, 1862.

48. Roy P. Basler, ed., *The Collected Works of Abraham Lincoln*, 9 vols. (New Brunswick, NJ: Rutgers University Press, 1955), 5:434, "Preliminary Emancipation Proclamation," September 22, 1892; Stearns, *Life*, p. 269.

49. John Brown, Jr., to George L. Stearns, October 27, and 31, 1862, Stearns Collection, KSHS; Mary Brown to Barry Clark, May 15, 1862, KSHS; Ralph Waldo Emerson to Mary Stearns, November 10 and 15, 1862, quoted in Rusk, *Emerson*, 5:294-296.

50. Mrs. J. Quincy to Mrs. President Lincoln, January 2, 1863, Robert Todd Lincoln Collection, LC; Nina Moore Tiffany, *Samuel E. Sewall; A Memoir* (Boston: Houghton Mifflin, 1898), p. ll5; Benjamin Rush Plumly to Abraham Lincoln, January 1, 1863, Robert Todd Lincoln Collection, LC.

51. Stearns, *Life*, pp. 275-276; Elizabeth Powell Bond to Oliver Johnson, extract of a private letter, n.d., Stutler Collection; Mary E. Burtis, Moncure Conway, 1832-1907 (New Brunswick, NJ: Rutgers Universiry Press, 1952), p. 91; Conway, *Autobiography*, pp. 379-381; Stearns, Life, p. 279; Basler, *The Collected Works of Abraham Lincoln*, 6:30.

52. Burtis, *Moncure Conway*, p. 91; Conway, *Autobiography*, pp. 379-381; Stearns, Life, p. 279.

53. Ibid.

54. Conway, *Autobiography*, p. 382; Stearns, Life, p. 279.

55. Conway, *Autobiography*, p. 383; Frank Bird to Moncure D. Conway, 1885, quoted in Conway, *Autobiography*, fn. p. 383; Stearns, *Life*, p. 280; George L. Stearns to Ralph Waldo Emerson, February 18, 1863, Ralph Waldo Emerson Collection, Houghton Library, Harvard University, Cambridge, Massachusetts (hereafter cited as Emerson Collection, HL).

56. George L. Stearns to John J. Cisco, February 6, 1863, open letter in the New York *Herald*,[?], 1863, and attached letter, John J. Cisco to Salmon P. Chase, February 7, 1863, miscellaneous letters received by the Secretary of the Treasury, National Archives, Washington, D.C.; Stearns, *Life*, p. 281.

57. William Schoular, *A History of Massachusetts in the Civil War* (Boston, 1868), p. 509, quoted in Richard H. Abbott, *Cotton and Capital* (Amherst: University of Massachusetts Press), p. 119.; L. Thomas to Governor of Rhode Island, January 15, 1863 and Edwin M. Stanton, January 26, 1863 in U.S. Government, *War of the Rebellion: Official Records of the Union and Confederate Armies* (Washington, DC: 1890) (hereafter cited as OR), ser. 3, vol. 3, p. 16, 20-21.

58. Dudley T. Cornish, *The Sable Arm: Negro Troops in the Union Army, 1861-1865* (New York: W. W. Norton, 1966), p. 107; Pearson, *John Andrew*, p. 70; Stearns, *Cambridge Sketches*, p. 264.

59. Stearns, *Cambridge Sketches*, p. 264; subscription paper for the Fifty-fourth Massachusetts Volunteers, February 13, 1863, Miscellaneous, MHS.

60. Subscription paper for the Fifty-fourth Massachusetts Volunteers, February 13, 1863, MHS; George L. Stearns to Gerrit Smith, February 15, 1863, Gerrit Smith Collection, Syracuse University Library, Syracuse, New York (hereafter cited as Smith Collection, SUL); Robert Gould Shaw, Letters, privately printed, (Cambridge, 1864), p. 260.

61. Mary Stearns to Mr. and Mrs, William Lloyd Garrison, March 4, 1863, William Lloyd Garrison Collection, Boston Public Library (hereafter cited as Garrison

Collection, BPL); Stearns, *Life*, pp. 288-289; John Brown, Jr., to Mary Stearns, February 12, 1889, Stearns Collection, KSHS.

62. George L. Stearns to Gerrit Smith, March 13, 1863, Smith Collection, SUL.

63. Mrs. Mary E. Stearns to Mr. and Mrs. William L. Garrison, March 1863, Garrison Collection, BPL.

64. Conway, *Autobiography*, 1:388-389.

65. Stearns, *Cambridge Sketches*, p. 265.

66. Stearns, *Life*, p. 289; George L. Stearns to Frederick Douglass, March 24, 1863, Frederick Douglass Papers, Frederick Douglass Memorial Home, National Park Service, Washington, D.C. (hereafter cited as Douglass Papers, NPS).

67. George L. Stearns to Frederick Douglass, March 24, 1863, Douglass Papers, NPS; Buffalo Express, March 24, and April 24, 1863; Boston *Commonwealth*, April 1 7, 1863.

68. George L. Stearns to Mary Stearns, May 7, 1863, quoted in Stearns, *Life*, p. 291; John Andrew to George L. Stearns, March 31, 1863, quoted in Pearson, *John Andrew*, 2:81-82; Buffalo *Express*, May 11, 1863; Washington *National Intelligencer*, March 16, 1863, quoted in Cornish, *The Sable Arm*, p. 108.

69. Harry Stearns to George L. Stearns, April 21, and May 8, 1863, Stearns MSS, MHS.

70. George L. Stearns to John Andrew, April 30, 1863, quoted in Pearson, *John Andrew*, 2:83-84; Stearns, *Cambridge Sketches*, p. 269.

71. George L. Stearns to Charles Sumner, May 21, 1863, Sumner MSS, Houghton.

72. Stearns, *Life*, p. 296; Letter to the Springfield Republican, date unknown, quoted in Brooks and Usher, *Medford*, p. 469.

73. George L. Stearns to Mary Stearns, May {?}, 1863, quoted in Stearns, *Life*, p. 293.

74. Stearns, *Cambridge Sketches*, p. 269.

75. C. W. Foster to George L. Stearns, June 15, 1863, OR, ser. 3, vol. 27, p. 361; General Order no. 178, June 17, 1863, ibid., p. 374.

76. Wendell Phillips to George L. Stearns, May 28, 1863, quoted in Brooks and Usher, *Medford*, p. 469.

77. George L. Stearns to Edwin M. Stanton, June 18, 1863, OR, ser. 3, vol. 27, pt. 3, p. 203; Edwin M. Stanton to Darius Couch, June 18, 1863, ibid.

78. Stearns, *Life*, pp. 297-298; George L. Stearns to Dr. W. J. Bauer, July 17, 1863, quoted in Stearns, *Life*, pp. 299-300.

79. C. W. Foster to George L. Stearns, June 22, 1862, OR, ser. 3, vol. 3, pp. 404-405.

80. George L. Stearns to Mary Stearns, July 12, 1863, quoted in Stearns, *Life*, p. 302.

81. George L. Stearns to Edwin M. Stanton, June 27, 1863, Bureau of Colored Troops, Record Group 94, National Archives, Washington, D.C. (hereafter cited as RG 94); Louis Wagner to C. W. Foster, January 10, 1864, ibid.

82. By-Laws of the Supervisory Committee for Recruiting Colored Regiments," n.d., Historical Society of Pennsylvania; Maxwell Whitman, *Gentlemen in Crisis: The First Century of the Union League of Philadelphia, 1862- 1962* (Philadelphia: The Union League, 1975), p. 49; Philadelphia North American and United States Gazette, July 1, 1863.

83. Stearns, *Life*, pp. 303-304.

84. Ibid., pp. 303-305.

85. George L. Stearns to Patrick Jackson, July 28, 1863, Antislavery Collection, New York Public Library, New York, New York (hereafter cited as Antislavery Collection, NYPL); George L. Stearns to John Andrew, July [?], 1863 quoted in Stearns, *Life*, pp. 305-306.

86. Whitman, Gentlemen in Crisis, p. 49; Philadelphia *North American and United States Gazette*, October 4, 1863.

87. George L. Stearns to Patrick Jackson, July 28, 1863, Antislavery Collection, NYPL; Luis Emilio, *A Brave Black Regiment* (Boston: Boston Book Company, 1894), pp. 96-97.

88. Frederick Douglass to George L. Stearns, August 1, 1863, an open letter in Rochester *Douglass' Monthly*, August 1, 1863; Frederick Douglass to George L. Stearns, August 12, 1863, Abolitionist Collection, Historical Society of Pennsylvania, Philadelphia, Pennsylvania (hereafter cited as Abolitionist Collection, HSP).

89. Ibid.

90. George L. Stearns to Salmon P. Chase, July 29, 1863, Salmon P. Chase Collection, Library of Congress, Washington, D.C. (hereafter cited as Chase Collection, LC); George L. Stearns to C. W. Foster, August 5, 1863, Bureau of Colored Troops, RG 94, LC; Edwin M. Stanton to John Murray Forbes, August 11, 1863, quoted in Hughes, *Forbes*, 2:69.

91. Amos A. Lawrence to Edwin M. Stanton, August 26, 1863, Bureau of Colored Troops, RG 94, LC.

92. George L. Stearns to Mary Stearns, July 26, 1863, quoted in Stearns, *Life*, pp. 306-307; George L. Stearns to Edwin M. Stanton, August 17, 1863, OR, ser. 3, vol. 3, pp. 683-684; Stearns, *Life*, p. 305.

93. C. W. Foster to George L. Stearns, August 13, 1863, OR, ser. 3, vol. 3, pp. 676-677; C. W. Foster to George L. Stearns, August 15, 1863, RG 94, LC; George L. Stearns to Mary Stearns, August 17, 1863, quoted in Stearns, *Life*, p. 308.

94. George Collamore to George L. Stearns, August 8, 1863, Stearns Collection, KSHS; Stearns, *Life*, p. 298.

95. George L. Stearns to Edwin M. Stanton, September 16, 1863, OR, ser. 3, vol. 3, p. 816.

96. Headquarters, Department of the Cumberland, Trenton, Georgia, Special Field Orders no. 243, Bureau of Colored Troops, RG 94, LC.

97. George L. Stearns to Edwin M. Stanton, September 11, 1863, Bureau of Colored Troops, RG 94, LC.

98. Peter Maslowski, *"Treason Must Be Made Odious": Military Occupation and Wartime Reconstruction in Nashville, Tennessee, 1862-1865*, Ph.D. dissertation, Ohio State University, 1972 (University Microfilms, Ann Arbor, MI, 1973), pp. 44, 176; Andrew Johnson to Abraham Lincoln, September 17, 1863, OR, ser. 3, vol. 3, p. 819.

99. George L. Stearns to Edwin M. Stanton, September II, I863, OR, ser. 3, vol. 3, pp. 785-786; Edwin M. Stanton to George L. Stearns, September I6, OR, ser.3, vol. 3, p. 8I6.

100. Andrew Johnson to Edwin M. Stanton, September 11, I863, OR, ser. 3, vol. 3, pp. 819-820; Andrew Johnson to William S. Rosecrans, September I7, I863, OR, ser. 3, vol. 3, p. 820.

101. Ibid.

102. George L. Stearns to Edwin M. Stanton, September I6, I863, OR, ser. 3, vol. 3, p. 8I6; Edwin M. Stanton to Andrew Johnson, September I8, I863, OR, ser. 3, vol. 3, p. 823; Edwin M. Stanton to George L. Stearns, September I8, I863, OR, ser. 3, vol. 3, p. 823; Abraham Lincoln to Andrew Johnson, September I8, I863, OR, ser. 3, vol. 3, p. 821.

103. George L. Stearns to Mary Stearns, September IO, I863, quoted in Life, p. 310. George L. Stearns to Edwin M. Stanton, September I6, I863, OR, ser. 3, vol. 3, p. 8I6; Edwin M. Stanton to Andrew Johnson, September I8, I863, OR, ser. 3, vol. 3, p. 823; Edwin M. Stanton to George L. Stearns, September I8, I863, OR, ser. 3, vol. 3, p. 82I; Abraham Lincoln to Andrew Johnson, September I8, I863, OR. ser. 3, vol. 3, p. 821.

104. George L. Stearns to C. W. Foster, September 24, I863, Bureau of Colored Troops, RG 94, LC; Lorenzo Thomas to George L. Stearns, October 8, I863, Records of the Adjutant General's Officer Commission Board, RG 94, LC.

105. George L. Stearns to Mary Stearns, September 2I, I863, quoted in Stearns, *Life*, p. 310.

106. Ibid.: Maslowski, *Treason*, p. 211; George L. Stearns to Mary Stearns, September 10, I863, quoted in Stearns, *Life*, p. 310; Brooks and Usher, Medford, p. 472; Nashville *Dispatch*, October 3, 1863; George L. Stearns to Edwin M. Stanton, September 25, I863, OR, ser. 3, vol. 3, p. 840

107. Maslowski, *Treason*, p. 217; Announcement, Headquarters, Commissioner for the Organization of U.S. Colored Troops, n.d., enclosure to letter, George L. Stearns to Edwin M. Stanton, September 25, 1863, OR, ser. 3, vol. 3, p. 840; Edward). Bartlett to [Frank P. Stearns?], n.d., quoted in Stearns, Cambridge Sketches, p. 276.

108. Nashville *Daily Union*, October 6, 1863; M. Parham to George L. Stearns, October 6, 1863, Johnson MSS, LC; John Bowen to George L. Stearns, October 8, 1863, Johnson MSS, LC.

109. Thomas Morgan to War Department, OR, ser. 1, vol. 35, pt. 1, p. 298; Nashville *Dispatch*, October 4, 1863; Nashville *Daily Union*, October 15, 1863.

110. Reuben D. Mussey to C. W. Foster, October 10, 1864, OR, ser. 3, vol. 4, p. 772; Nashville *Daily Union*, October 11, 1863.

111. [George L. Stearns to Charles Sumner], letter titled "For use not for publication," October 9, [1863], 10 P.M., Sumner MSS, Houghton; Reuben D. Mussey to C. W. Foster, October 10, 1864, OR, ser. 3, vol. 4, p. 772.

112. Reuben D. Mussey to C. W. Foster, October 10, 1864, OR, ser. 3, vol. 4, p. 770; Nashville *Daily Press*, December 3, 1863.

113. Reuben D. Mussey to C. W. Foster, October 10, 1864, OR, ser. 3, vol. 4, p. 771-772.

114. George L. Stearns to Amos A. Lawrence, November [?], 1864, quoted in Stearns, *Life*, p. 316; Harry Stearns to George L. Stearns, October 5, 1863, Stearns MSS, MHS.

115. George L. Stearns to Mary Stearns, December 18, 1864, quoted in Stearns, *Life*, pp. 318-319.

116. Stearns, *Life*, pp. 322-323.

117. George L. Stearns to Mary Stearns, January 13, 1864, quoted in Stearns, *Life*, p. 322; George L. Stearns to Edwin M. Stanton, January 13, 1864, quoted in Stearns, *Life*, p. 322; Edwin M. Stanton to George L. Stearns, January 13, 1863, quoted in Stearns, *Life*, pp. 322-323.

118. Extract of a statement published by George L. Stearns, n.d., quoted in Stearns, Life, pp. 324-325.

119. George L. Stearns to Mary Stearns, January 23, 1864, quoted in Stearns, *Life*, p. 326.

120. George L. Stearns to Samuel Johnson, January [?], 1864, quoted in Stearns, *Life*, p. 325; printed broadside, "Remarks on the Character of George L. Stearns at Medford, April 14, 1867, by R.W. Emerson," n.d., Stearns MSS, AAS.

7

The Right Way

For the Spirit of the Universe seems to say: "He has done well; is that not saying all?

– Ralph Waldo Emerson

The "Major," a title Stearns had little objection to his acquaintances' using, received word of the 300,000 man recruiting quota levied on the states. He immediately used this information to write to Andrew Johnson in January 1864, appealing this time not for blacks, but for southern whites. Knowing of Johnson's humble background and his concern for poor whites, Stearns laid out a plan to the governor that not only would help military authorities obtain recruits but also benefit poor whites and eventually restructure southern society. Stearns proposed Johnson allow northern recruiters to operate in Tennessee to fill their state quotas. The benefits would be numerous. Presently, northern bounties for enlistments were extremely high. Tennesseans' enlisting could, he explained, "relieve their families from destitution." The men recruited would join veteran northern regiments. This arrangement would be desirable not only from a military standpoint because the men would learn by example from veterans, but also as a socialization process for poor whites. In this way, Stearns explained, from their Yankee comrades they would "learn habits of thrift and industry and a union of sentiment and princip[le] far more powerful than any formed by legislation." As a manufacturer, Stearns also saw that by using Southern whites on the battlefields, the North could keep factories running with its skilled labor force intact. He asked Johnson to advise Stanton if the plan was acceptable. In the same letter, Stearns told Johnson he hoped to purchase abandoned plantations. Northerners he hired would then supervise free African-American laborers cultivating cotton. Stearns waited in Washington, but there was no response from Johnson. It is interesting to speculate on what the impact of his ideas might have been on the combat efficiency of the integrated veteran regiments, on postwar national unity, and on Tennessee's economy.[1]

Stearns's ideas were becoming increasingly directed toward a reconstruction of southern society on a northern model. He had prospered under a free labor system, and he believed Southerners, both black and white, could do the same. Because Stearns was impatient for social change, he had become increasingly hostile to the administration, especially since the December 1863 restoration policy for the states in rebellion. Lincoln planned to grant a full pardon to rebels who took a loyalty oath and agreed to obey all federal legislation regarding slavery. Prominent Confederate leaders were not eligible. When one tenth of the whites who voted in 1860 swore allegiance, they could establish state government. What bothered Stearns and other abolitionists was that Lincoln announced he would accept "a reasonable temporary arrangement in relation to the landless and homeless freed people, so that the two races could gradually live out of their old relationship to each other, and both come out better prepared for the new." Lincoln, still fighting a civil war, wanted to make reentry into the Union as attractive as possible. Stearns was too caught up in his plans for a reconstructed society to have any and had no faith in the current administration. Impatient, he contemplated a number of ways to change the ship of state's course. As a consequence, he became involved in several activities designed to realize a new Southern society.[2]

Now at the start of the new year, he reviewed the Washington scene and discussed options with Sumner and other congressmen. At Willards Hotel, he grew morose. Even a bright sunny January thaw, breaking the terrible cold that had gripped the city, failed to cheer Stearns. He wrote to Mary that the political situation was complicated: "No one knows where he is or who, or what statements to depend on . . . President, Cabinet, M.C.'s [members of

Congress], Senators, all are alike." Then, too, wartime Washington was much too gay for his somber mood. Stearns decided it was time to leave and to visit Nashville to wrap up recruiting affairs and promote his scheme to farm abandoned plantations.[3]

Stearns arrived in Nashville and soon found two abandoned cotton plantations near Murfreesboro, Tennessee. There he sought to hire free black males at wages of $15 a month plus room and board. Unfortunately, the previous year Stearns had recruited too well, enlisting more than six thousand able-bodied men for the Union army; now few males were available. Undaunted, Stearns hired women at $12 and children on a scale down to $3 for the youngest able to work. Stearns's farmhands planted five hundred acres of cotton that spring. In addition to cotton, the former slaves put in crops of corn and other grains. The blacks toiled heroically with a few improvised tools, because the plantation had been stripped of everything movable, to do the other work required, on farmland that had lain fallow for eighteen months.[4]

As Stearns later told a Tennessee slaveholder, his free labor "made a crop that paid handsomely for the outlay," and except for the interruption caused by marauding Confederates, "the profit would have been very large." According to Stearns, when he hired the blacks, he told them that any person who failed to work would be discharged. By the end of the 1864 growing season, one man was fired for breaking the farm rules, and one woman let go for laziness. "I can assure you," Stearns wrote to the slaveholder, "Northern laborers will not do better: for in the exigencies of the crop, when hard work was required, they worked with proportionate energy."[5]

Satisfied that the recruiting network was in good hands and his cotton farmers well on their way, Stearns visited General Ulysses S. Grant at his headquarters to ask him, as he told Mary, whether he would order that black troops receive treatment equal to that of whites. He later told Frank that Grant was direct and decisive. The general, he said, agreed and promised to do what he could to remedy the abuses Stearns mentioned. Satisfied with their meeting, Stearns returned to Boston. Yet, still discouraged by the administration's perceived indifference toward blacks, he sought to awaken the North to the need to ensure that African- Americans obtained rights of citizenship as well as freedom.[6]

I

While Stearns was away, the Massachusetts Anti-Slavery Society held its annual meeting in Boston. Wendell Phillips offered a motion criticizing Lincoln's restoration policy for it left the former slaves at the mercy of their onetime masters. Like Stearns, Phillips was impatient with the president's failure to acknowledge the need to secure for African-Americans all the tools of citizenship: employment, education, and suffrage. William Lloyd Garrison opposed Phillips's motion and voiced support for Lincoln, stressing his accomplishments. He explained that Lincoln continually showed a willingness to change for the good. Phillips responded that the unequal treatment of black soldiers proved his real indifference and failure to change. The society passed the motion criticizing the administration. The vote implied that Phillips and some, but not all, abolitionists would not support Lincoln's candidacy in 1864.[7]

Whom would they support if not Lincoln? George told Mary in a letter in January that a confrontation was drawing near between Lincoln and Secretary of the Treasury Salmon P. Chase. He was correct in his observation, for the secretary was actively seeking support for a presidential bid. The Bird Club supported the Chase movement. On February 20, however, when the secretary's possible candidacy became public, Republican leaders responded negatively. The Republican National Committee moved four to one to endorse Lincoln, and even Chase's state party leaders declared their support for the president. As a result, on March 5 the secretary issued a statement declaring he was not a candidate.[8]

Another challenger to Lincoln's renomination was Major General John C. Fremont, former Free Soil Party candidate. He appealed to many abolitionists, and because he was a military man, backers believed he would also draw the soldier's votes. While Phillips joined the Fremont movement, Stearns remained uncommitted, perhaps more for practical reasons than for any other. Stearns had been, except for occasional visits, away from his home and counting room for more than a year. Now he was devoting time to the family and business.

He returned home to face unexpected criticism and became embroiled in a minor skirmish with J. Miller McKim. A member of the Philadelphia Union League, McKim actively supported Stearns's recruiting efforts. McKim believed Stearns's resignation meant abandonment of the fight to see African-American soldiers receive equal pay and rights. At the end of March, the *National*

Anti-Slavery Standard published a letter McKim wrote attacking Stearns for resigning his commission. The letter began, "Am I not sorry that he has resigned?" The answer to this rhetorical question was no, because a staunch abolitionist, Captain R. D. Mussey, replaced Stearns in Nashville. McKim expressed dismay not only that Stearns resigned, but also that his friends gave the incivility of Secretary of War Stanton as a reason. McKim said that treatment of this nature was simply a "liability of shoulder-straps" and that "even two stars are not always sufficient to save a man from being snubbed." The friends McKim referred to in his letter did mention Stanton's behavior, but they explained that Stearns saw it as a reflection of Stanton's attitude toward black soldiers and did not take it personally. Indignant at the tone and the implications of McKim's letter, two days later Stearns wrote a rebuttal which was published in the *National Anti-Slavery Standard*. He explained that the secretary's incivility had not been the issue. The rudeness could have been borne if behind it there had been an indication that Stanton supported the use of black troops. As long as it had appeared that the government would, as Stearns explained, deal honestly with African-Americans, he remained in uniform. Now, however, more than a year after the Fifty-fourth and Fifty-fifth Massachusetts Infantry regiments had been mustered into federal service, the pay issue remained unresolved. Also, in contrast to whites, black soldiers in Nashville endured unfair treatment with excessive fatigue duty, poor rations, shoddy uniforms, and miserable quarters. Stearns believed many more African Americans would enlist if the government honored its pledges of equal pay and treatment.[9]

In closing his rebuttal to McKim Stearns attacked the Lincoln administration. As long as the border states were excluded from the Emancipation Proclamation, slaveholders would continue to believe the institution might revive, and masters would remain rebels. If slavery were totally eradicated from the Union, slaveholders would automatically become Union men. If, Stearns said, Stanton had allowed him to recruit in Kentucky, the state would now be loyal instead of a thorn in the Union army's side. The government, he declared, ordered the white farmers' sons to serve and taxed Northerners heavily, and Union men "cheerfully respond Amen." The governor of Kentucky refused to allow the federal recruitment of blacks, and Abraham Lincoln, ignoring the fact that more than 100,000 blacks were wearing the federal uniform, "says Amen."[10]

When the Emancipation League met in Boston the following month, Lincoln received a great deal of similar criticism. Stearns asked Emerson to address the gathering. The Concord literary figure begged off: "Much experience has taught me to be very cautious in making speeches in behalf of any cause to which I have good will." Wendell Phillips accepted the invitation and launched a vicious attack on Lincoln, in part echoing Stearns's recently published sentiments and adding his own. "Judged by three years experience," Phillips told his audience, the administration was a "military and civil failure." The Confederates, he declared, were "weaker, poorer and less numerous," yet the war continued because there was "no statesmanship in the White House and no generalship in the field." Lincoln, he claimed, "considered slavery as the only sacred thing in this country." Responding to hisses and groans from the audience, Phillips said that if the league members did not care for his views of the president, it was not his fault, but Lincoln's. Phillips announced he would do everything possible to prevent the president's reelection. After he stepped down, the league proceeded to elect officers for the coming year. Stearns became treasurer. His friends Samuel G. Howe and Frank W. Bird were among four men chosen as vice presidents.[11]

President Lincoln had little to fear from Phillips. On June 7 the Republican Convention, meeting in Baltimore, nominated him for a second term. Although Stearns remained impassive about Lincoln's candidacy, Andrew Johnson's nomination as Lincoln's running mate thrilled him. "If anything can reconcile one to the renomination of Abraham Lincoln," he told Johnson, "it is the association of your name on the same ticket." Stearns would have preferred Johnson as the presidential candidate because of what he saw as the war governor's "broad and sound views of public affairs." At a mass meeting, Johnson repeated sentiments Stearns had discussed in Nashville. Slavery, Johnson told the convention, was dead, and emancipation meant not only freedom, but also opportunity for African-Americans to receive an "equal chance in the race of life." Destroying the slavocracy, he believed, would free more whites than blacks. Stearns wrote to Johnson declaring that no serious opposition faced the Republicans. Stearns promised Johnson his cooperation and that of those working for him.[12]

Stearns was referring not only to the now defunct Chase movement but also to the recently announced Fremont candidacy. The Radical Democratic party meeting in Cleveland on May 31 had nominated Fremont for president. In addition to Phillips, several other friends of Stearns, Frederick Douglass, and

Moncure Conway supported the candidacy. A former supporter of Fremont's Free Soil bid, Stearns viewed the general's current office seeking with suspicion. Republicans leveled charges that Copperheads, northern Democrats who wished to make peace with the Confederacy, were encouraging the Radical Democratic party. Also, Fremont's running mate, Colonel John Cochrane, held a dubious track record of voting for Pierce, Buchanan, and the choice of many Southerners before the secession, John Breckenridge—all of whom Stearns heartily despised.[13]

That summer of 1864, Stearns followed the political maneuvering of Fremont and diehard Chase supporters. He also spent time with his family and in business pursuits consulting with his partner and foreman. At the end of July, John Hopper, whom Stearns had befriended many years earlier, died in New York. Stearns must have attended his friend's funeral, perhaps thinking of his own father's premature death and wondering about the future's uncertainty.

In August 1864, Stearns could remain inactive no longer. He arranged a meeting with Fremont, who was summering at Nahant, Massachusetts, and Wendell Phillips, Frank Bird, A. Bronson Alcott, and several other Emancipation League members. His purpose was to discuss and to clarify Fremont's candidacy and goals. Meeting at The Evergreens, Stearns and the others subjected Fremont to a barrage of questions. The general anticipated a split in the Democratic Party Convention between the Copperheads and the war Democrats. He predicted the latter would dominate the gathering and choose him on a radical platform. With the support of these men and the radical Republicans, favoring African-American equality and harsh treatment for the South, he was certain to defeat Lincoln. Stearns did not share Fremont's optimism. Phillips, on the other hand, was elated and wanted to organize New England radical Republicans in support of the general.[14]

Events on the battlefield, however, had a profound effect on Stearns's next step. Grant and George G. Meade's Army of the Potomac were held up before Petersburg, Virginia, in a siege that produced nothing more than long casualty lists. General William T. Sherman, commanding the Armies of the Ohio, the Tennessee, and the Cumberland, remained stymied before Atlanta. General Philip H. Sheridan's newly formed Army of the Shenandoah had yet to destroy the elusive Jubal Early, operating in the Great Valley of Virginia and posing an uncomfortable threat to Washington. The military situation appeared so bad that Lincoln himself believed he would not be reelected.[15]

The military situation, combined with Lincoln's pocket veto of a reconstruction bill proposed by Congressmen Henry W. Davis and Benjamin Wade, spawned yet another attempt to unseat the president. The Wade-Davis bill was an attempt to take restoration of the South to the Union out of the executive office. The bill also required that fifty percent of the South's 1860 voters, not Lincoln's ten percent, take the oath of loyalty prior to readmission, preventing all former rebel officeholders from voting and serving in office in any future government. By withholding suffrage, however, the bill would not allow freedmen to participate in the restoration of the Southern states. Senator Zachariah Chandler, Benjamin Wade, Charles Sumner, John Andrew, and Salmon P. Chase, who had resigned from the cabinet, joined Stearns and other abolitionists in opposing the administration.

The rift occurred not only because of the Wade-Davis bill, but because of many Republicans' belief that Lincoln was too weak. Sumner said that what the country needed was a president who could "make a plan and carry it out." All of these men supported the idea of convincing Lincoln and Fremont to withdraw from the race and scheduling a new Republican convention at the end of September. Although the group mentioned Chase, Grant, and General Benjamin Butler as people who could unite Republicans, Stearns probably had his eye on Andrew Johnson.[16]

Wasting no time Stearns, on August 21, wrote a letter to Fremont, advising him of what he called the "growing dissatisfaction in the Republican ranks" and the growth of a movement to call for a new convention. To assist in this patriotic effort, Stearns asked Fremont whether, if Lincoln withdrew, he would do the same to assist in what Stearns termed an "attempt to place the administration on a basis broad as the patriotism of the country and as it need[ed]." On August 25, Fremont responded favorably to Stearns's proposal, asking for an immediate understanding between his supporters and those of Lincoln.[17]

Again, events elsewhere in the nation caused Stearns and the Republican dissidents to change their plans to oust Lincoln. On September 2, 1864, Sherman wired that his forces occupied Atlanta. Then, six days later, Major General George B. McClellan accepted the Democratic nomination and disavowed the peace platform passed in Chicago. He insisted, however, that the southern states should be readmitted with all their former rights. Sherman's triumph and fear of a McClellan victory made it clear that Lincoln remained the strongest candidate for the Republican ticket. Stearns and the other dissidents allowed the call for a new convention to die. Fremont's candidacy, however, did not die so easily. Stearns was now concerned about a possible McClellan victory. Senator Wilson reported to Lincoln that the Democratic Convention results had his New England friends concerned. He expected that in a few weeks they would be hard at work for Lincoln's reelection to save, as William Lloyd Garrison expressed it, the "country from the shame and calamity of a copperhead triumph." On September 8, Stearns called another meeting with Fremont. He invited the same men who had convened in August, except Wendell Phillips, to meet at The Evergreens at noon on September 9. He assured Bronson Alcott that this meeting was not to be a "Fremont meeting, but rather a gathering of persons opposed to his present position." Over lunch, Stearns asked Fremont to attend a rally at Faneuil Hall to withdraw from the race and to declare his opposition to the "cowardly and treasonable" Chicago convention. He told the general he would make public the invitation. Although the rest of the details of the meeting are unclear, Fremont was now aware that his support was quickly eroding.[18]

Stearns remained under some criticism for his role in calling for a new convention. Several days after his meeting with Fremont, an article appeared in *The Liberator*, taken from the Boston *Daily Advertiser*, attacking Stearns as "indiscreet, discontented and ambitious," as well as disloyal and factious. Stearns did not see the letter until it appeared in *The Liberator*; Garrison had remained loyal to Lincoln throughout the controversy. Stearns would not have replied, but since Garrison reprinted the attack, he believed it necessary to respond. Stearns falsely claimed that he had only privately expressed his opinions, which were that "Mr. Lincoln [was] unfitted by nature and education to carry on the government for the next four years." He denied active involvement in the recent controversy and support for Fremont. Stearns claimed merely to endorse the comments of Republican leaders who, a week before the fall of Atlanta, thought Lincoln's reelection impossible. The fall of this Southern bastion, according to Stearns, crushed the call for a new convention. Stearns went on to say that he always supported those who "struck the hardest and most direct blows at the rebellion." This, he declared, was his idea of antislavery work.[19]

Stearns redeemed himself by following through on his public invitation to Fremont. He placed Fremont in an uncomfortable position, for given the current political and military situation, any attack on Lincoln would be viewed as treasonous. In declining to attend, the general restated his reasons for opposing Lincoln, but also declared his intention to stand aside in order that a united Republican party would be successful against the Democrats, whose platform meant permanent separation and the reestablishment of slavery.[20]

II

Stearns and other abolitionists, including Samuel G. Howe, Wendell Phillips, and Frederick Douglass, believed there remained a need to lobby for African-American liberty. On September 20, 1864, Stearns sent out letters that described in general terms a plan to create "a society, or League, of Radical Anti-Slavery men of the United States." Once the election was over in November, new issues and those still requiring attention, such as the passage and ratification of the Thirteenth Amendment, would surface. His plan now was to obtain two thousand names of interested people who would form the core of an organization and then decide a course of action. To compile a membership list, he proposed that interested members of Congress and eminent citizens of the states each send him fifteen names and addresses of those they believed to be assets to such an association. Stearns planned to print the list and to send each person named a copy, but not until after the election. He assured letter recipients that he would safeguard the list to prevent its use by any candidates.[21]

Stearns did, however, send a copy of the letter to one candidate, Andrew Johnson, hoping that he would approve and support a movement of this nature. Stearns explained that such an organization had long been needed but difficult to create. It seemed to Stearns that when an impartial group of informed citizens organized an association, it immediately became a "party machine, to be controlled by selfish leaders for their own purposes." His organization avoided this problem because, as he saw it, "every member of the League [would] enjoy the same opportunity for Communicating with the rest," thus preventing a bureaucratic filtering down of information. Another advantage to his organization, according to Stearns, was the ability to expand the membership by sending a request out to the original two thousand to add more people to the list in the same way they had entered the league.[22]

Now happily involved, Stearns kept clerks engaged compiling the list in the counting room on Milk Street while Mary was busy with social engagements now that her husband was home. In October she invited the Emersons to spend the day at The Evergreens, even offering to send her coachman to Concord to pick them up. Emerson accepted, but insisted on taking the Boston and Maine Railroad to Medford. At dinner, Emerson shared his hosts' happiness at Sheridan's recent string of victories in the Shenandoah Valley at Winchester, Cedar Creek, and Fisher's Hill. Emerson also delighted the Stearnses at a series of six Sunday evening lectures. The Stearnses' high spirits reflected rising morale throughout the North and the fact that, as the gloom was lifting, people were eager to attend such lectures.[23]

The following month, however, Boston's citizens sensed a rise in tensions because of the impending presidential election. On November 8, after casting his vote for Lincoln, Stearns and other Bird Club members gathered in Andrew's executive office to wait for the election returns. In Nashville, Captain R. D. Mussey wired Secretary of War Stanton that Lincoln was receiving the soldiers' votes: "The Western Army fights rebels equally well with ballots and bullets." The results were much the same in Boston. Although unable to give an entirely accurate count, Governor Andrew wired Lincoln that he had received 124,000 votes compared to McClellan's 830. When all the returns were counted for the nation, Lincoln had won fifty-five percent of the total and received 212 electoral votes; McClellan had garnered 12. While obviously relieved at McClellan's defeat, Stearns was ready to renew his efforts to see the war won in order to secure the full benefits of citizenship for African-Americans.[24]

In December, George and Mary Stearns decided to sponsor representative recruits as part of a program to induce men to enlist. Stearns's recruit was an Irishman, Patrick Galliger, and Mary sponsored Daniel Rakin. Both men were from Medford. The Stearnses were doing all they could as citizens to see that the war came to a successful conclusion, even enlist the help of Irish immigrants, a body of citizens not entirely sympathetic to emancipation.[25]

Stearns hoped the benefit of citizenship for both these groups would be reaping the fruits of their own labor. Stearns himself had a very financially successful year. When the Internal Revenue published personal incomes for 1864, Stearns was listed under Politicians "who have made their mark." The list for Massachusetts contained more than four hundred names. Stearns reported an income of $51,988, $4,000 more than Amos A. Lawrence. In fact, only fourteen other men in the Commonwealth of Massachusetts had incomes greater than Stearns's. His friend Samuel G. Howe showed earnings of $7,250, $600 less than John Andrew, and Frank Bird reported an income of $9,600.26. At the beginning of this profitable year, Stearns published a pamphlet, "A Few Facts Pertaining to Currency and Banking," which he dedicated to the new Congress in response to the issuing of paper currency as a wartime measure. Stearns believed that the previous Congress had erred in establishing a national bank as a means of creating additional currency to finance the war. Currency and banking, according to Stearns, were two separate financial issues. He believed people regarded finance as incomprehensible because they attempted to combine these two aspects of it instead of trying to understand each one separately. Stearns thought that understanding one issue at a time would be much simpler: bankers should stay out of the business of issuing paper notes and only conduct business by borrowing hard money, gold and silver, at low rates and lending it at higher rates; only the federal government should issue currency, backed with sufficient reserves of gold and silver specie. Stearns believed these measures would stabilize the economy and prevent such financial upheavals as those in 1837 and 1857, when redemption of bank-issued currency required calling in outstanding loans. Stearns thought that the government should base its currency issue on three principles: notes should be made in such a way that they could not be counterfeited; notes should be easily convertible into gold and silver specie; and a reserve of coins should be maintained to ensure immediate redemption. If the government established a national currency under these guidelines, Stearns said that citizens would view their paper money "like the constitution, sacred," and such a move "would do more than any thing else to cement the Union."[27]

Stearns was certain that, although the nation was now absorbed in a war, it would soon be "united for a common prosperity." According to him, now more than ever Congress needed to institute a strong financial system to enable the nation to pay off the national debt once peace was secured. The effect of Stearns's pamphlet is uncertain, for the issuance of greenback paper currency begun in 1863 continued without the safeguards Stearns proposed, and by the war's end, businessmen were clamoring for a resumption of gold and silver payments, showing their distrust of federal paper currency.[28]

While in the army, Stearns had not completely turned over all his business matters to others, and sometime in December he visited his lead wholesaler, Mr. Schmidt, in New York. Dining at the Brevoort House, Stearns became ill, so ill that Schmidt feared his guest would die before he could put him on the train to Boston. Stearns was in a stupor when he arrived in Massachusetts the following morning. A conductor put him into a carriage. Arriving at The

Evergreens, Stearns found his wallet missing and had to have the servants pay the coachman. Bracing himself in the doorway, Stearns murmured, "Home at last," and then collapsed. He did not utter a word for a week.[29]

The Stearnses' family doctor, Perry, who had treated Charles Sumner, had passed away, so during George's long absences, Mary had begun to use the services of a homeopathic doctor, a physician who treated the patient with a minute dose of a remedy that in a healthy person would produce symptoms of the disease. Frank Stearns was skeptical of this form of treatment and said it was appropriate enough for his mother's headaches, but not for a serious illness. In addition to her belief in homeopathic medicine, Mary was becoming eccentric in other ways. A relative recalled that, during the past year, Stearns had often arrived home to find "Madam Stearns secured in her bedroom, shades drawn, and in bed with the vapors." Though Stearns doted on her, the reverse was not always true, for apparently Mary neglected her husband during this illness. Still a student at Harvard, Frank had not heard from his mother for some time, so he walked from Cambridge to The Evergreens, where he found his father alone in the house, except for a chambermaid. When Frank entered the sick room, poor Stearns could only move his eyes. Frank recommended that his mother hire a nurse, but she would not hear of it. Fortunately, Stearns found enough strength to look after himself and slowly recovered. Within six weeks, he was again active in his campaign.[30]

Stearns directed his activity to yet another movement he described to Charles Sumner as the "friends of Radical Reconstruction," whose purpose was to see Lincoln place Governor John Andrew in the cabinet. This diverse group of friends included Bird Club members, Boston businessmen, nine members of the Massachusetts congressional delegation, a number of western congressmen, and a scattering of other influential men outside Massachusetts. Stearns began lobbying by firing off letters to a number of friends in Washington. He wrote to Andrew Johnson to ask for the vice president-elect's assistance, for not "political but antislavery motives." Andrew's presence in the cabinet would, Stearns said, "carry great antislavery strength to Mr. Lincoln's administration." Stearns explained Governor Andrew possessed other assets: a good legal background, a sound capacity for business, a willingness to cooperate, approachability, and a keen decision-making capability and willingness to follow through. All of these factors, Stearns said, made Andrew eminently "fit to control our national affairs." Stearns had his clerks working furiously, sending out the same letter to other influential people. Sumner received one, and so did Gerrit Smith, along with a host of other people throughout the North. Nothing came of Stearns's efforts, however. In fact, Sumner refused to support the governor's bid for a cabinet seat because he was eager to become secretary of state.[31]

Stearns took a moment from his lobby efforts to send a letter to the Bureau of Colored Troops, asking for a copy of War Department order 329, which authorized Stearns to recruit African-Americans in Maryland, Missouri, and Tennessee. Stearns asked whether the War Department had printed the order. Assistant Adjutant General Forbes, whom Stearns addressed as "My dear friend," could "spare the clerical force and I think I do not ask too much" to have the order copied. Stearns said he wanted the order for a historical collection of documents relating to the recruitment of African-Americans. Forbes relayed the request to Secretary of War Stanton, who told Forbes to deny it. On the draft response to Stearns, Forbes at first wrote that the document was not on file, but he must have had second thoughts about the lie because he told Stearns that the order had not been published and that he, therefore, could not comply with Stearns's request. Stearns apparently saw this bit of official spite for what it was and wisely let the matter drop.[32]

Mary was also involved in publishing, in this case a book she planned to title "Emerson." In December she entered into a conspiracy with Bronson Alcott to have him write the book and print it privately as a birthday present for Emerson. Alcott referred to the project as "our Surprise Book." He quoted Mary several prices for printing and, because he knew she wanted the best, recommended printing fewer copies in order to purchase the most expensive print/bind option, the one with an engraved medallion and calfskin binding for $3 a copy. Before deciding, Mary became ill again, this time for about three months. Writing to a friend on March 10, 1865, George remarked that Mary had dined with the family for the first time in months. Stronger now, Mary went ahead with her plans for the "Surprise Book." She decided on the more expensive binding and then complained about the price of the frontispiece, a photograph of Emerson. Alcott wrote Mary that the publisher could make the birth date, May 25, but that work must begin immediately. In his letter to Mary, Alcott said he hoped that "fair Spring days, birds, flowers, friends, and your own fresh heart, may speedily revive and restore [your health]."[33]

Despite his recurring ill health, which appeared to be primarily related to bronchial problems, Stearns was becoming increasingly involved in the growing controversy over whether antislavery societies, having accomplish-ed their objective, should now disband. Phillips and others believed the work should continue until African-Americans obtained all the implied rights of citizenship. Garrison, having waged a thirty-year crusade for emancipation, considered the single most important issue settled. Although Stearns never joined the American Antislavery Society, he viewed with apprehension the suggestion that both state and national societies should disband. Through the Boston *Commonwealth*, Stearns urged the members of the societies to remain united until African-Americans received all the rights of citizenship.[34]

To ensure that Garrison would not accomplish his objective of dissolving the American Antislavery Society, Stearns agreed to join Wendell Phillips and attend the annual meeting at the Cooper Union in New York City. In the crowded hall, Garrison introduced a resolution to abolish the society because it had accomplished its sole objective, the end of slavery. Garrison said the time had come to work outside the society for whatever needed to be done to aid the freemen. Phillips rose among cheers, hisses, and groans to challenge Garrison. Phillips's support came partly from black abolitionists like Charles L. Remond and Frederick Douglass. Douglass said that slavery in the South would continue as long as African-Americans were denied the ballot. Also at the meeting, Senator Wilson pleaded on behalf of Radical Republicans that the society still had a purpose.[35]

On the convention's second day, a vote was called on Garrison's proposal, which was defeated 148 to 118. Garrison then refused the organization's presidency and resigned. Garrisonians followed his example. As a result, Stearns finally joined the society. Phillips assumed the presidency, Gerrit Smith and Concord poet John G. Whittier became vice presidents, and Stearns joined the executive committee. He returning to Medford after the convention was a jubilant Wendell Phillips, who remarked to Mary, "It was the Major that did it." Unfortunately, in taking such a stand with those viewed as radicals, Stearns was again ostracized by his society's conservative segment.[36]

Stearns cared little about the snubs he received on the streets of Boston after the New York meeting of the Antislavery Society. He told Moncure Conway, with emancipation achieved, he and others could now "advocate Negro Suffrage with as much zeal and confidence too that we shall obtain it as we did emancipation last year." Men like Garrison, Lincoln, and even Phillips, he explained, were "straws on the current carried along by the gravity that propelled events." For example, Louisiana, whose readmission the president sought under his restoration plan, Stearns remarked, was "kept out in spite of

Mr. Lincoln." The new chief justice, Salmon P. Chase, decided that the readmission of the state in what he referred to, according to Stearns, as "her present rebellious and chaotic condition" was unconstitutional. Justice would prevail, Stearns said, regardless of men who resisted.[37]

Stearns was concerned that a moderating mood might infect the attitude of the north toward the resisting rebel states as the string of Union victories lengthened and the Confederacy's fall loomed. On March 25, the Boston *Commonwealth* announced that "a complete exposition of the questions before the country in this epoch" would be presented in a pamphlet by Major Stearns, who pledged to circulate copies to all who wanted them. The following month, just prior to General Robert E. Lee's surrender, Stearns fell ill again, delaying the project. Before he could recover and circulate a single copy, the nation was stunned at the moment of victory by the assassination of Lincoln. No doubt Stearns was shocked and saddened by the event, but he was a man with a purpose and his direction was clear. On April 7, 1865, three days after the president's death, Stearns sent out ten thousand copies of a collection of speeches and articles by radical Congressman William D. Kelley of Pennsylvania, Wendell Phillips, Frederick Douglass, and old Liberty party man and Bird Club member Elizur Wright. The collection also included a letter written to Stearns by a New Jersey man, William Heighton, commenting on Stearns's letter seeking to organize a new society of antislavery men.[38]

Kelley's speech, Stearns said, showed that in the nation's early days, African-Americans were allowed to vote in most states. After Kelley's came Douglass's and Phillips's speeches, which, Stearns claimed, called attention to the necessity and justice of African-Americans' obtaining the vote. Words by Wright and Heighton, on the other hand, illustrated the "political and economic consideration that should induce us to grant it." In a cover letter, Stearns told the recipients that if they sent a contribution he would forward an additional twenty copies for $1 or one hundred copies for $4, which, he noted, was less than cost. Or, instead, Stearns would mail copies directly to anyone whose address was forwarded. Still, Stearns was not satisfied that he and others were doing everything they could to educate the public.[39]

III

Stearns had long had in his mind the publication of a journal, one that, Frank said, would "take elevated views of political subjects, and especially advocate liberal and unprejudiced legislation for the benefit of the freemen." For some time Stearns maintained contact with Charles Eliot Norton, editor of the literary journal *North American Review*, and J. Miller McKim, the Philadelphia abolitionist, with whom he had made peace. McKim solicited funds from numerous freedmen aid societies for a publication similar to the one Stearns had in mind. The three men now believed they had enough capital, $100,000, $90,000 of which had come from the sale of stock, to launch a new publication. Stearns contributed $10,000, a "much larger amount .. . than anyone else," he said. To finalize arrangements, Stearns went to New York to meet with Norton. Writing from the Brevoort House, Stearns told Sumner that Norton and he planned to establish "a weekly Newspaper to advocate advanced opinions . . . . And we expect to secure some of the best Editorial Talent of the Country." Earlier Stearns had asked, in turn, George William Curtis and Whitelaw Reid to become editor in chief. Both men responded negatively. Norton then recommended Edwin L. Godkin, a young correspondent for the London *Daily Times*. Garrison's son, Wendell, was the choice for associate editor responsible for issues relating to the freedmen.[40]

In May 1865, Stearns, his son Frank, and Phillips met *The Nation's* potential editor in chief, Edwin L. Godkin. Over dinner at the Brevoort House, the men discussed the periodical's editorial policy. Stearns wanted the journal to maintain democratic principles and to support legislation that would promote equal distribution of the "fruits of progress and civilization." Also, he thought the publication should keep before the country the condition of African-Americans in the South with a view toward their gaining all the rights of citizenship. Stearns wanted the issues of importance to the nation, such as public education and legal, economic, and constitutional issues, discussed with, as he said, "greater honesty, accuracy and moderation than are now to be found in the daily press." National issues and policies were the primary object, but Stearns also wanted, he declared, reasonable criticism of literature and art to take the place of the "extravagant, untrustworthy and often venal puffery" now in most criticism. Above all, *The Nation* would not represent any one point of view but would impartially and factually discuss political and social issues facing the country. Stearns then told Godkin that the periodical was not, as he might expect, to represent the "interest of New England Manufacturers, Pennsylvania Miners or New York Free Traders, but broadly in the interest of the people of our whole country." Godkin replied that he was glad to hear Stearns take this position; for a moment, he said, "I was afraid you intended to ask me to advocate the interest of New England Manufacturers." Most of the four hour conversation, however, revolved around reconstruction of the Southern states and the condition of African-Americans. With the first issue of *The Nation* scheduled to appear in July, Frank later recalled that it had been a "most harmonious meeting."[41]

In May, at the meeting of the reorganized American Antislavery Society, Andrew Johnson's name was on everyone's lips. Phillips told the audience that he believed in Johnson and that the new president would support their goal of achieving African-American suffrage. Stearns was euphoric. "How grandly Andrew Johnson looms," Stearns exclaimed to Sumner. "All he has said in public I heard from him in private in Nashville." Sumner, however, was not as optimistic and told Stearns that while Johnson supported suffrage for African-Americans, his conversations with the president had indicated that he was in doubt as to how to achieve it.[42]

On May 17, 1865, Stearns wrote a lengthy letter to Johnson to warn him of the danger the nation was in from "Southern Aristocrats and their allies in the late Democratic Party." Stearns told Johnson that a revolution had placed him in the presidency. He asked whether Johnson would be true to the "Democratic principle of Government or [whether he would] like all his predecessors ally himself with capital and continue the war against labor." Stearns said that now was the time for the chief executive to carry out the principles set forth in the Declaration of Independence. Stearns told Johnson that, because all men are created equal before God, he must assure the nation he would use his "utmost endeavor to make them so before the law." Johnson, Stearns said, must use his power to secure for all men "equal right and privileges," for, if not, "oceans of blood" were shed in vain. Stearns was confident that the president would support these aims and told Sumner, "With Abraham Lincoln Whiggery died and today the Union Party is Democratic under the lead of Andrew Johnson."[43]

Sumner, however, continued to be concerned about the president's course of action regarding African-American suffrage. With Congress adjourned, public opinion must continue to be brought around to support black suffrage, Sumner said. It would be much better to organize reconstruction under the federal government and, if possible, by act of Congress, than to mold it to support the president's plan for local action, especially regarding suffrage. Sumner wrote to Stearns suggesting that it would be best to continue the public dialogue on reconstruction. The senator said that "any discussion which can postpone this till Congress meets, will help negro suffrage. Without such postponement the course is endangered."[44]

Although certain in his own mind of Johnson's course, Stearns had no intention of letting up on the campaign to influence public opinion. The pamphlet released in April drew such favorable response in words of encouragement and donations that he decided to issue a second, "Universal Suffrage and Complete Equality in Citizenship." Stearns wanted a million copies circulated and offered fifty copies for $1 or three hundred for $5. For the pamphlet, he selected a sermon by the Reverend Henry Ward Beecher on the rights of African-Americans, highlights of Andrew Johnson's speech on his nomination for the vice presidency recorded by a reporter from the New York *Times*, and a speech given by Wendell Phillips, "The Lesson of President Lincoln's Death." In a cover letter, Stearns claimed, "We have full evidence in this pamphlet that justice requires, and the President of the United States favors, the claim of all men to democratic equality which is their birthright." He also asked how the United States could dishonor "our Revolutionary fathers," who had declared that all men were born " 'free and equal' under the law, by refusing to grant this right to a portion of our citizens because they differ in color."[45]

Stearns believed the nation had gone through another revolution, beginning with the firing on Fort Sumter and culminating in Lincoln's death. Stearns declared, "[What Lincoln] refused us while living, his death has given to the country. It in one week doubled the antislavery strength of the North and made justice to the black loyalist a necessity." With his "friend" Johnson in office, he was certain that this goal, the goal of the martyred John Brown, could be achieved. Even with deteriorating health, Stearns moved from one enterprise to the next, using his wealth and managerial skills to accomplish the goal of a nation where all men were equal before God, the law, and their fellow citizens.[46]

IV

On May 29, 1865, Andrew Johnson and reconstruction were very much on the minds of the men attending the Emancipation League's annual meeting at the Tremont Temple in Boston. That same day, Johnson issued two proclamations regarding reconstruction. One granted amnesty to those Southerners who would take an oath of allegiance. Just as Lincoln had proposed, he exempted certain categories of Confederate government officials, officers above the rank of colonel or commander, former members of the U.S. Congress, federal judges, or officers who resigned and then served the Confederacy, Confederate state governors, those who committed war crimes, and those who owned taxable property in excess of $20,000. The next proclamation named a provisional governor for North Carolina and called for an election to name delegates to attend a constitutional convention. He specifically stated that only white men who had taken the oath could participate. Samuel G. Sewall, Emancipation League president, could not be present, and Stearns presided over the assembly. Congressman William Kelley, whom Stearns invited, addressed the gathering, telling the audience that "all men must be made free and equal before the law." It was Congress, their representatives, he said, who would require the treasonous states to enact "just and righteous rules in regard to the status of the colored population." The league's members then offered nominations for officers for the next year and elected Stearns, the former treasurer, as one of four vice presidents. Samuel G. Howe received enough votes to become another vice president, and Frank Bird took Stearns's place as treasurer.[47]

Following the election of officers, a number of resolutions were passed. Most dwelt on enfranchising African-Americans in the southern states, and one stated that "since the denial of rights to black men was the cause of the disruption of the Union, their enfranchisement and full equality before the law must be the cornerstone of its reconstruction." Wendell Phillips spoke, and then former governor of Massachusetts George S. Boutwell addressed the league. Of all the speakers at the meeting, only Boutwell brought the audience to their feet when he told them that not a single rebel state should be readmitted "until its Constitution secured in the strongest manner possible a vote for the negro." After many attempts, Stearns quieted the hall only to have Charles Slack, the Boston *Commonwealth's* new editor, ask the crowd for three cheers for the sentiments just expressed. Finally, Stearns called for adjournment.[48]

The following month, Stearns lessened his hectic pace. With Bronson Alcott's help, Mary managed to see that Emerson received his gift. Although she asked to remain anonymous, Mary still wanted to know whether Alcott had any indication of Emerson's reaction to the "Surprise Book." After seeing the Emersons, Alcott's daughter May reported that they had "escaped the displeasure of the Divinity, and won his forbearance if not good will." The following day another note appeared at The Evergreens. Alcott wrote that Emerson had stopped by to thank him. Alcott reported that, although he was complimentary, Emerson hinted that, should any other copies be printed, he would prefer his name not appear on the cover. Emerson was, Alcott put it, eager to learn the name of "the lady whose taste had touched the leaves with so much beauty." The following day, Mary had George drive them to Concord to reveal her role in Emerson's gift. Stearns used the visit to ask Emerson's assistance in writing and speaking for African-American suffrage. The meeting was pleasant, the Stearnses were well received, and Emerson seemed supportive. Stearns, however, sensed an unexplained difference in his host's manner, an "aristocratic reserve." As soon as he was able to, Stearns disengaged Mary and left for the more comfortable surroundings of the Alcotts'.[49]

The friendship between the Alcotts and the Stearnses seemed to grow as the contacts between the Stearnses and the Emersons lessened. The Emersons must have introduced the couples in the late 1850s, for the earliest correspondence between Mary and Alcott was just after John Brown's execution. Alcott received a copy of the autobiography Brown wrote for Harry Stearns, "a piece of work," Alcott told Mary, "done in a style of English unsurpassed." That praise of Brown alone was enough to win Mary's friendship. With three sons, Mary apparently doted on at least one of the Alcotts' four daughters. Louisa Alcott sent Mary some verses with the hope to know her better so that, as Alcott told Mary, she "may thank the friend who bestows her kindness on one near and dear to her." Louisa referred to Mary's gifts of flowers to her sister May. Also taken with May's art, Mary offered, in 1864, to pay for her study with the German artist and anatomist Dr. Rimmer of Boston. Louisa, whose works were being published regularly in Stearns's *Commonwealth*, remarked privately, with sisterly pique, that May "is a fortunate girl and always finds someone to help her .... Wish I could do the same."[50]

When the Stearnses arrived at the Alcotts', a group of youngsters were playing a new lawn game, croquet. Fascinated by the play, Stearns watched for several minutes. Curiosity satisfied, he joined. Alcott in the garden to discuss African-American suffrage and, as he had earlier proposed to Emerson, to ask for his support. Alcott not only was receptive but also seemed eager to discuss recent political events and to put forward his own ideas concerning the opportunity that awaited the nation. As Stearns drove the carriage back to

Medford, he commented that Emerson had finished his work and "little more [was] to be expected from him." Bronson Alcott, on the other hand, apparently was eager to seek out new endeavors, and Stearns believed his most productive days were still to come.[51]

Later that June, Stearns attended a social gathering in Cambridge connected with *The Nation*. He met James Russell Lowell, whose literary work championed Lincoln. Stearns found his hero worship of the martyred president grating, for Frank said his father thought Lowell "surprisingly ill-informed concerning public affairs." What saved the evening was a chance introduction to a sixty-year-old law professor at Harvard Law School, Theophilus Parsons, the son of a former Massachusetts chief justice. Thought by many to be a conservative, Parsons had what Frank called a "growing mind" and was a man "with a heart in him." Stearns had a brief, but stimulating conversation with the professor. Parsons shared his thoughts on reconstruction of the southern states and invited Stearns to
visit him in Cambridge.[52]

Stearns wasted no time in accepting the offer. Parsons laid out to the businessman an alternative reconstruction plan. Stearns was excited, for what this learned legal expert had in mind was close to his own ideas. Stearns urged Parsons to expand his thoughts and to publish them, for such fresh ideas were sorely needed. When Parsons asked where he should make the plan public, Stearns, realizing that the professor's conservatism would add weight to his own ideas, suggested a public meeting of influential people to endorse the plan. Stearns told Parsons to have the speech ready to deliver at a meeting at Faneuil Hall where Parsons would be voted president. Stearns also promised to secure the support of fifty notable men as vice presidents and then took a draft of Parson's plan to several prominent Boston merchants, among them John Murray Forbes, Alpheus Hardy, and Henry Lee. For a long time after his involvement with John Brown became known, Hardy and Lee had refused to talk to Stearns. But now that time had passed their participation would be helpful because they held conservative views. Stearns made certain that no prominent abolitionists appeared on the list of people calling the meeting. Stearns also invited Emerson to speak at the meeting, but as he expected the Concord sage declined.[53]

On June 21, Professor Parsons addressed a crowded Faneuil Hall. Frank said his father thought the address was at least equal to Daniel Webster's orations, with clear thoughts, cogent reasoning, and an emphatic delivery.

Parsons reviewed the effects slavery had had on Southerners, eventually leading them to espouse states rights in order to support the "peculiar institution." He then pointed to the danger inherent in allowing the states to be readmitted with their slavery laws intact. Even if slavery were abolished, the masters would attempt to reestablish themselves and subjugate their former chattels. They certainly would not tax themselves to educate freemen or allow Northern philanthropic agencies to operate in their states. To avoid these pitfalls, Parsons said, African-Americans must have the full rights conferred by citizenship and be able to protect those rights through the ballot box. When the professor finished, Faneuil Hall rang with applause. A committee of seven, including Stearns, Whittier, and Richard H. Dana, was appointed to have the address printed for circulation. Stearns agreed to send a copy to Johnson.[54]

Stearns's efforts were arousing not only sentiments of support for African-American suffrage, but also some criticism. Democratic and conservative Republican newspapers complained heartily of all the attention blacks were receiving in the media, in churches, and at public meetings. Concerned that the president would form the wrong impression of Stearns's activity, Lawrence wrote to assure Johnson that the meeting at Faneuil Hall was not "called by men of extreme views to create an opposition to yourself and your administration." He explained the opposite was true and some of the best legal authorities in Massachusetts carried on the discussion with propriety. All those involved understood the president's position, the difficulties he faced, and wanted to support him. Stearns sent a similar letter and a petition inviting Johnson to Massachusetts to speak on reconstruction.[55]

That same month Stearns eagerly awaited the first issue of *The Nation* and the realization of his hope for a truly progressive journal supporting radical reconstructionist views. Unfortunately, that first issue, on July 6, 1865, shattered his dreams. One can only speculate on Stearns's reaction when he glanced at the second item in the first column titled "The Week." "The objectionable paragraph," as Garrison called it, read:

> The negro's success in assuming a prominent position in the political arena seems to be in the inverse ratio of the earnestness with which it is sought to suppress him and put him out of sight. Everybody is heartily tired of discussing his condition and his rights, and yet little else is talked about, and none talk about him so much as those who are most convinced of his insignificance.[56]

Stearns immediately wrote to Norton and Godkin, for, his son said, he was "not the man to endure this with impunity." Godkin ignored Stearns's letter, and several more issues appeared with articles that indirectly disparaged the work of Stearns, Phillips, and others. Stearns also heard that Godkin made a statement deriding him personally. Stearns was furious . Apparently Godkin's own agenda for *The Nation* was to duplicate English journals in reviewing politics and literature at a level that would appeal to an elite audience-hardly what Stearns and the other radical backers had in mind. Godkin made some changes, but later issues dealt with the suffrage question in a conservative, low-key tone, not in the strident call to action Stearns wanted. Then, too, other articles in *The Nation*, such as one written by a former proslavery Harvard professor on the rights of belligerents, appeared to defend the rebel states. Also, Godkin rejected a free trade manuscript because he was afraid of offending Philadelphia stockholders. Writing to Stearns in August, Sumner asked him to suspend publication of *The Nation* because "it did more hurt than good." Sumner rhetorically asked Stearns whether there was anyone whom the publication "inspired, strengthened or instructed in the good cause. Not one."[57]

Sumner's letter moved Stearns to act. On August 14, 1865, he circulated to the stockholders an open letter to Charles Eliot Norton. Stearns claimed Godkin had misled the stockholders and had no intention of upholding the objectives he and the other backers had in mind. Stearns reminded Norton that many stockholders subscribed because they knew the idea for its creation was, as he said, "projected by me." Further, Stearns reminded Norton that he held a significant block of stock. The reason he had invested so much was to "secure its foundation on a broad basis." In the preliminary discussions with Godkin, Stearns told Norton, he had specifically stated that *The Nation* was to be edited with the "broadest principles of justice, and for the public good, excluding party and individual interest." Now, Stearns said, in addition to disparaging civil rights for African-Americans, Godkin refused to publish an informal article concerning free trade so as not to offend a special interest group. If Godkin were as honest with him, Stearns declared to Norton, "as I was with him, I should have saved $10,000." Stearns appended to his circular a letter to Samuel G. Ward, a New York financier and author, stating, "Either Mr. Godkin must cease to be the editor, or I must cease to be a Stockholder."[58]

Godkin wasted little time in responding to Stearns's attack. On August 23, he published an open letter denying the free trade article charges. The fight was beginning to have almost comical overtones, if it were not for Stearns's frustration at seeing his $10,000 tied up in a venture that was doing more harm than good. The issue also alienated one of Stearns's acquaintances, Samuel G. Ward. When Ward saw a private letter to him attached to the broadside attacking Godkin, he wrote to Stearns that he had no right to publish their private correspondence. Stearns responded that he did have the right to publish his own words, but it was discourteous of him not to ensure Ward received the letter before its publication. Stearns told Ward he would "not willingly hurt your feelings or those of any man."[59]

Stearns was, however, willing to use any means to rid his publication of Godkin, including smear tactics. On September 4, he wrote to Norton that Godkin had been introduced to him as an Englishman. Now Stearns said, "Common report / too discrete it would seem to be false / says he is an Irishman." The irate stockholder now wanted Norton to reveal Godkin's nationality. Norton responded that Stearns was in error to think he had misrepresented Godkin's nationality at their first meeting, because Godkin was of Irish birth, as his father had resided in Dublin. Stearns would not let the matter drop and immediately wrote to Norton that he was not in error: "My memory is perfectly clear on this point"; besides, the information he had received about Godkin came from Norton. Stearns was, therefore, "surprised to find his Nationality was on the other side of the Channel."[60]

Stearns fought this correspondence battle with Godkin and Norton until May 1866, when he and a majority of his Boston associates instituted legal proceedings to force Norton and other supporters of Godkin to purchase their shares in *The Nation*. The plan failed and Stearns gave up the battle. He consoled himself by claiming that, even if Godkin had followed Stearns's program for the journal, his lack of editing talent would have made for a small circulation and matching political influence.[61]

Although distracted by the controversy over *The Nation*, Stearns that August invited the new chief justice of the Supreme Court, Salmon P. Chase, to lunch at The Evergreens. Stearns wanted Chase to meet with Professor Parsons; Wendell Phillips; Alcott who declined; and four other men to discuss reconstruction. Promptly at 10 A.M., Chase arrived, and the men sat down to talk. Chase had read Parson's Faneuil Hall speech and was pleased with the points raised. The professor responded that he was especially concerned that, in addition to suffrage, there was a need for large plantations to be broken up to provide land for African-Americans. Chase agreed that blacks should own land, but told the group that such land reform was impossible in this country.

The chief justice viewed this type of "agrarian law as a very dangerous precedent, as dangerous as monarchy itself." Presiding over the luncheon, Mary said, "Those who till the soil come to own the soil." Chase said that this type of arrangement should be true but that, in most instances, it was not. The subject of Lincoln's Emancipation Proclamation also came up during the discussion. Phillips criticized its length and said that freedom should be declared "in one grand sentence." Chase responded that it was a legal document and such papers are always lengthy. Mary told Chase that she especially liked Lincoln's phrase "By doing justice to the black race, we insure freedom for the white." Chase told Mary he had written that passage of the proclamation and described the circumstances. Then the chief justice turned to Stearns and asked him about his experiences in Tennessee. Stearns briefly recounted his observations while in the border state and said he had found the "peculiar institution" even more vile than he believed possible. At 4 P.M. the chief justice departed, leaving a satisfied George and a glowing Mary at the door of the mansion.[62]

Professor Parson's address at Faneuil Hall arrived from the printer, and Stearns adroitly used the text to put forward some of his ideas to President Johnson. Stearns explained that the address had no political significance, that a noted jurist from Massachusetts had merely carefully prepared and thoughtfully expressed his opinions. Stearns also asked Johnson to note that "our most eminent lawyers, our most influential and wealthy bankers, our leading merchants and manufacturers" signed the address. Given enough time, he said, all of the prominent citizens in Massachusetts would have placed their signatures on the document. Stearns asked Johnson to have Parson's plan for reconstruction made into law for the best interest of the nation. Closing his letter, Stearns said, "In offering these views for your consideration, we beg leave to express our confidence in your judgement, your firmness and your fidelity."[63]

Reflecting on his letter to Johnson, Stearns wrote to Sumner. Initially convinced, as Stearns had been, that Johnson would reconstruct the South on the basis of African-American suffrage, Sumner was increasingly alarmed at Johnson's course. What first changed Sumner's opinion of the president's direction was the latter's approval of the call of North Carolina's provisional governor for an election by loyal white voters of a state constitutional convention. At first, Sumner thought the president was having a "strange hallucination." After conferring with other Radical Republicans, however, the senator realized that Johnson harbored no intention of allowing African-

American suffrage. Stearns, on the other hand, was still not convinced, and in fact, he saw the North Carolina issue differently. He told Sumner that he was glad that Johnson did not appoint a Northerner as a military governor and that there was no objection to the exclusion of African-American suffrage in the state's primary convention If Johnson had authorized both of these arrangements, Stearns believed, Copperhead sentiment would have "arisen in the North and the failure of reconstruction, which is inevitable, would have been charged to the Negro, falsely to be sure, but with great effect." Stearns was not certain of the president's direction, for Johnson's actions appeared contradictory to the ideas expressed to Stearns in Nashville. At present, however, Stearns said he was not worried and told Sumner that they would have to continue to wage the campaign to achieve their goals. Two points were clear to Stearns: they must not quarrel with the president, and they must use every means possible to delay the admission of the rebel states. Fully confident, Stearns told Sumner, "We have justice, the Constitution and examples of the founders of our Govt. on our side." Stearns was certain they would prevail, if "we work patiently and wisely."[64]

For the moment, Stearns remained content. To relax, he made frequent visits to the Alcotts' home. On September 8, he left his Boston counting room for Concord, where Mary was to meet him for dinner at the Alcotts'. Stearns waited for Mary until, as Alcott later told her, "it was plain you had declined setting out." May Alcott was the most disappointed, for her mother was away and, as her father later said to Mary, she had put the meal together, a "plain repast, and only wanted your presence to make it all she had wished" for her benefactor. Bearing a basket of peaches from his orchard and political information to discuss with Alcott, George enjoyed the stay. He also finalized a loan for an addition to the Alcotts' home. In their conversation, Stearns expressed a desire to visit his wartime friend to clarify in his mind the president's position and, if necessary, to persuade Johnson of the need to reconstruct the rebel states on the basis of African-American suffrage.[65]

V

Soon after his visit to Concord, Stearns visited Washington. At ten in the morning on October 3, he was ushered in to see the president. After exchanging pleasantries, Stearns told Johnson Northerners were concerned about the direction his reconstruction policies were taking. They and Stearns wanted to support him but were confused over conflicting reports. For example, Stearns explained, rumors were circulating that Johnson was going over to the Democratic party. At this, the president laughed and asked Stearns whether he had ever known a man who disagreed with him and then, when finally catching up, said the position had been his own all along. Stearns said yes, and Johnson responded that was the case of the Democrats. He would freely discuss the present state of affairs. Johnson explained that the Union had crushed the rebellion and that now it was time to rebuild the states' governments, but the rebuilding would not go quickly: "It is better to let them reconstruct themselves than to force them to do it." After all, Johnson said, the federal government could then correct any misguided course. As for African-American suffrage, that was a question, Johnson reminded Stearns, no one could even have raised in the North just seven years earlier. Now many expected the federal government to push the South to move even further than the North. If the chief executive determined voting eligibility in the South, Johnson explained, he might equally do so for Pennsylvania. He said that what might have been his position as governor of Tennessee could not be policy in the White House. "It will not do to let the negroes have universal suffrage now," he told Stearns, for "it would breed a war of races." If the African-Americans received the vote, Johnson declared, they would, for self-protection, vote with their former masters and not with the mass of whites who had never held slaves and hated blacks. The apportionment of Congress was fixed until 1872, and by that time, Johnson said, "enlightened public judgement [both North and South] . . . without regard to color, might extend the elective franchise to all who possessed certain mental, moral, or such other qualifications."[66]

Stearns's interview with the president lasted about an hour. Johnson was obviously no fool and understood the political advantage of satisfying Stearns. Earlier he had attempted to mislead Radicals in much the same way. On August 15, Johnson had advised Provisional Governor William L. Sharkey of Mississippi that if his constitutional convention allowed literate African-Americans who possessed a minimum of $250 to vote, he would "completely disarm the adversary . . . . As a consequence, the radicals, who are wild upon negro franchise, will be completely foiled." It was increasingly apparent to everyone except Stearns that Johnson was simply not interested in African-American suffrage. However, Stearns was so pleased with what transpired that he rushed back to Willards Hotel to record the conversation.

207

He noted that Johnson was as cordial and his conversation as free as they had been in wartime Nashville. Stearns set out for Medford and went over his interview with the president. He sent a copy of the transcript of their conversation to Johnson and shared his thoughts with him. After Johnson reviewed and returned it, Stearns told him, it would "go far to promote a good understanding between you and our leading men," whether he limited its circulation or published it. But, as Stearns said, the "whole tenor of your words led me to believe it was not intended to be kept private." (The wily Johnson must have chuckled at that statement.) Stearns went on to tell Johnson that the publication of his thoughts on restoration of the states with the rationale for the way he was proceeding would "inspire our whole Northern people with confidence in your administration."[67]

Stearns quizzed friends as to whether he should make the president's remarks public. Some advised against it, and others encouraged him to do so. Telling Moncure Conway that his past dealings with Johnson had taught him to respect the man's honesty, sincerity, and ability, Stearns said, "I shall trust him until he for the *first time* deceives me." Earlier Stearns had told the president that he "did not associate to any great degree with politicians but rather with those who, representing the advanced moral sense of the country, earnestly labor for the good of our people." Stearns believed that Johnson's views placed him on a higher moral plane than many other Republicans because, even in Massachusetts, party leaders did not place African-American suffrage on their platform. Even some Republicans believed the issue settled, and Radicals had, he said, allowed the "summer to pass without action on their part, and now some whine, and others grumble." Stearns believed that, as usual, party leaders were timid and not up to what he understood to be northern sentiment. Stearns now planned to pin the president to the position he had taken in the interview and then to convince the chief executive that the Constitution contained a "warrant for Negro Suffrage in those states where the exclusion of the Colored people from the franchise would place the State Governments in the hands of one-third to one-half of their citizens."[68]

Stearns ignored the Radicals' criticism that followed the interview's publication. Interestingly, most Republican newspapers either praised its content or remained neutral. Theodore Tilton, editor of the radical, crusading New York *Independent*, attacked Johnson's fear of a race war, calling it the old proslavery argument against emancipation. The *National Anti-Slavery Standard*, so critical of Stearns's resignation, also found fault with Johnson's logic in the interview. An editorial said that it was absurd for the president to say he could not interfere with the Southern states' authority to govern voting requirements when he had used that authority to appoint provisional governors and had repudiated the rebel states' debts. The *Standard* also challenged Stearns's efforts to reconcile Johnson with the Radical Republicans. The paper assured "Mr. Stearns that the Radicals mean[t] to smash the reconstruction policy of the president [if the] true friends of the Negro will stand by them."[69]

Possessed by a desire to educate the public on the question of African-American suffrage further, Stearns ignored the controversy that arose from the interview's publication. When passing through Philadelphia and New York to visit Johnson, he secured promises to help raise money to publish a new publication to advocate the position he had once had in mind for *The Nation*. Although Stearns probably did not receive any large sums of money from these pledges, he decided to launch a weekly newspaper anyway, with his own funds. He called it *The Right Way*, deriving the name from an antislavery monograph by Lydia Maria Child. Stearns initially decided to distribute the paper free of charge throughout the nation. His purpose was to provide, he said in the first issue, "the fullest information, combined with the soundest argument, on the questions now before the country, which are, for the most part, not well understood." Stearns hoped that the public so informed would pressure congressional delegates and the president to ensure that African-American suffrage became part of any reconstruction policy. Stearns hired William Wilde Thayer, a young abolitionist and journalist, as publisher and made Professor Alpheus Crosby of Salem, Massachusetts, his editor. Crosby had a good reputation as a constitutional lawyer and as a writer. William Lloyd Garrison, who had ended *The Liberator*'s publication, allowed Stearns the use of his offices on Washington Street in Boston. Stearns also hired twenty young women to mail out thirty thousand to fifty thousand copies of The Right Way each week. In the first issue and for the next several months, Stearns asked that readers form clubs to receive *The Right Way* and other pamphlets. He also requested contributions to extend the circulation. Stearns mentioned that Major General Oliver 0. Howard, the Freedmen's Bureau chief, had agreed to distribute the newspaper through the agency.[70]

In October, still not satisfied that events were moving as they wished, Stearns and some New York businessmen finalized plans to revitalize the South on a Kansas Emigrant Aid model. On the pattern of his 1864 success with his two Murfreesboro cotton plantations, Stearns helped organize and purchased stock in the American Land Company, an agency whose purpose was to bring plantation owners together with emigration societies and individual northern farmers and mechanics "desirous of transferring their labor and skill to the South." The company would be a clearinghouse for those who might "on grounds of pecuniary profit, of business enterprise, of patriotism or philanthropy desire to contribute through the organization of industry, to the material means by which the South [could] be restored." Stearns saw that John Andrew, who had chosen not to run again for governor, became the company's president. Its main offices were in New York, with a branch in Boston. In November, Andrew wrote to the officer in charge of the Freedmen's Bureau Commissary Department that he expected large and small capitalists either to invest in cotton lands or to make loans to freemen, poor whites, or immigrants interested in purchasing small freeholds cut up from large plantations. If this venture succeeded, in addition to bringing a profitable ten percent return, it could, Andrew and Stearns thought, make emancipation "an early and visible success."[71]

VI

In early November, however, Stearns became ill. All of his efforts to promote suffrage were taking a toll on his health. The American Land Company had scheduled a meeting for November 16 in New York, and because Stearns desperately wanted this venture to succeed just as the Massachusetts Emigrant Aid Company, he wrote Andrew that he would be at the American Land Company office at 57 Broadway in New York for the meeting, if "my health permits, and I have no doubt it will."[72]

The following month, the twenty-seventh state, Oregon, ratified the Thirteenth Amendment, and one week later Secretary of State William Seward declared it in effect. Although Stearns never doubted its ratification, George and Mary had no celebration at The Evergreens as they had for Lincoln's Emancipation Proclamation. Stearns did not allow time to recover from his November bout with bronchial problems. Now his relapse, as he explained to Andrew Johnson had caused him to "suspend all mental as well as physical labor." Stearns's friends became alarmed at his condition. Howe wrote Mary, with, he said, "much concern, that your husband has been and is, quite ill." Knowing Mary's distaste for nursing, he offered to go out to The Evergreens. Mary replied that George was better and had resumed his correspondence, but was still resting. Howe and Phillips visited Stearns and found him tired yet ready to renew the struggle, having just completed another letter to the president.[73]

While resting at The Evergreens, Stearns read articles in the Boston newspapers indicating that the rift between Johnson and Congress was widening. In December, while still exercising his powers over the states in regard to reconstruction, the president continued to maintain, as he had in the State of the Union address, that he lacked the authority to require the former rebel states to accept African-American suffrage. Ignoring the apparent contradiction in Johnson's arguments, Stearns continued to plead with Johnson. Why did Stearns persist when the situation looked so bleak? First, he thought he had a mutually respectful, personal relationship with Johnson. After all, he had discussed these issues with the man on a number of occasions. Although, while in Tennessee, Johnson had certainly shared some of Stearns's beliefs concerning emancipation, it is unlikely he was willing to go as far in the area of civil rights. Johnson, it was said, had a trait of listening without comment to people with whom he disagreed. So while giving Stearns the opportunity to speak without argument, he complained to Stanton about the major's radical ideas. Obviously Stearns took Johnson's silence as agreement, just as Charles Sumner had before realizing that the silence did not mean approval. Stearns persisted because he really had not taken the full measure of the man in the White House and believed that the public pressure he was attempting to generate would lead Johnson to ensure suffrage and civil rights as it had led Lincoln to emancipation.[74]

In December, Stearns wrote to Johnson. He told the president that the "Southern people [did] not at all appreciate their new position." The defeated slaveholders were still clinging to what he referred to as "aristocratic prejudices." Knowing Johnson's desire to want to destroy this class, Stearns said that apparently the southern ruling class was rapidly attempting to establish the "old order of affairs and to subjugate the laboring classes, both white and black." Blacks would suffer, he believed, but whites would suffer more. Stearns asked Johnson what the answer was to correct the present state of affairs. Remembering their most recent interview, Stearns now advocated that laws regarding civil rights for African-Americans apply equally North and South. Stearns appealed to Johnson's vanity, telling him he was, because of his background, best fitted to "lead in this transformation of our legislation." African-American suffrage, Stearns reminded Johnson, was neither a new nor a radical concept, for when the Constitution was adopted, only New Jersey and South Carolina had denied blacks the ballot. Now the nation had the opportunity to restore those rights. He understood that it could not be done instantly, but that African-Americans must be protected until the entire nation could be persuaded to grant civil rights to all its citizens. Stearns told the president that he saw this step as the "true policy of Reconstruction." In closing, Stearns declared, "That God will give you wisdom and strength, in proportion to the responsibility he has laid on you, is the daily prayer of-Your friend ."[75]

The new year brought both dismay and hope in regard to Johnson's attitude. The President shocked abolitionists when he addressed a delegation of African-Americans headed by Frederick Douglass. Johnson dismissed their request for the ballot by telling the delegation it would create a race war. The only solution he offered was for their race to leave the South. After the delegates left, Johnson remarked to his secretary, "Those damn sons of bitches thought they had me in a trap, I know that damned Douglass; he's just like any nigger, and he would sooner cut a white man's throat than not." Here Johnson revealed his true "poor white" feelings toward African-Americans, feelings he kept hidden from Stearns. Then in February, rumors of a compromise between the president and Congress surfaced. Apparently, the rumor went, Johnson would approve the Freedmen's Bill and Congress, in turn, would see to the early readmission of Tennessee.[76]

Recovered from his illness, but still weak, Stearns decided to go to Washington with Frank. His intent was to influence Johnson in regard to the pending legislation. Stopping in New York, he met J. Miller McKim, who asked about a reconciliation between him and Godkin. Not in the best of moods, Stearns became angry and shouted that no compromise was possible for Godkin was a disappointment and must resign. McKim was overwhelmed at the harshness Stearns displayed and meekly left. Arriving in the capital, Stearns was invigorated by the Washington weather, which felt "like April, clear and warm," he reported, "all windows open. Sidewalks dry and the whole outside inviting to a walk or ride." He telegraphed Mary, for he did not want her to be anxious about his health. On February 19, Johnson shocked Congress and abolitionists by vetoing the Freedmen's Bill. Just prior to this Stearns had reported to his son Harry that he had not seen the president and had "a disposition at present to stay away." The veto finally convinced him that Johnson would not support civil rights, and from that time forward, Stearns joined the ranks of those opposed to the president and his reconstruction policies. Stearns was optimistic about the future. Congress, he said, "will stand up to the work it has before it and the country will support [it]." Stearns believed his role was clear, for he had arrived, in "the 'Nick of Time.' Just when I am most wanted and of course incur attention." Frank said that while they were in Washington, their room in Willards became a rendezvous place for senators and congressmen. They returned time and again, even though Stearns gave no dinners and rarely passed out cigars, the normal bait used by lobbyists. Introduced on the floor of the Senate, Stearns held a caucus with Henry Wilson and several other senators for more than two hours while the proceedings continued.[77]

According to Frank, his father's stay in Washington was a "triumphal procession." At a reception given by John W. Forney, publisher of the influential Philadelphia *Press*, Stearns conversed with Thaddeus Stevens, the Radical congressman from Pennsylvania. The congressman and fellow manufacturer eyed Stearns and, referring to his interview with Johnson in October, said gruffly, "The note is protested, Major, and comes back to the endorser." Stearns took the rebuff in stride and laughingly responded, "Well, the endorser is good." Chief Justice Chase overheard the conversation and came to Stearns's rescue, saying that, at least it seemed to him, that Johnson at the time was fence-sitting and that now "he has tumbled over into a ditch on the wrong side." Chase believed Johnson to be a fool, but one too dangerous to laugh at. The conversation turned to speculation as to the next election. Thinking of Chase's unsuccessful 1864 bid, Stearns advised the chief justice in a fatherly way "to think as little about that as you can. The nomination of a president is like a thunderbolt: no one can foresee where it will strike."[78]

Although Stearns never saw Johnson again, he did have contact with a cabinet member, Secretary of the Treasury Hugh McCulloch, with whom he discussed the resumption of gold and silver specie payments. Disenchanted with McCulloch's idea to bring down the price of gold by constricting the circulation of currency, Stearns believed that the secretary had no practical experience and that he had not reasoned out the consequences of such a policy. Stearns warned him that such a course of action would shake the business world's confidence, causing gold to rise in price rather than to drop. McCulloch ignored Stearns's advice, and to the consternation of businessmen Stearns's prediction was fulfilled.[79]

VII

Satisfied he had exercised a strong influence on Washington's policymakers, Stearns returned home in March. Frank was relieved, for his father seemed physically depleted and nervous. Meeting Stearns, the Reverend Samuel Johnson confirmed Frank's opinion, expressing surprise at how fatigued his friend appeared. He pointedly told Stearns to take a vacation, perhaps to Switzerland, but Stearns would not hear of it, for he faced too many pressing issues to leave now.[80]

On his return Stearns did, indeed, face some financial issues. He finally sold the stock in *The Nation* at fifty percent below par, hoping that the purchaser would gain a controlling interest in the journal and thereby change its policy. Then Stearns went to New York to see whether he could end a lead price war begun by his old competition from the 1850s, the New York Lead Company. Prompted by declining war profits, the firm had again begun to cut prices and to invade its competitors' territories. Calling on the firms competing with New York Lead, Stearns attempted to reconcile differences and to stabilize prices. He failed. The price war had created such bitterness that all the firms were determined not to yield an inch. He returned to Boston and reduced his profit margin to stay competitive.[81]

The Right Way was also in financial difficulty. Stearns had spent considerable sums for Kansas relief, John Brown, emancipation, recruitment of African-American soldiers, and pressure for civil rights and suffrage. He informed readers that the weekly cost to him personally was $1,000, less postage, and that the return of donations had averaged only $150 a week. The businessman also received some contributions from wealthy friends, but the amount was insignificant. Therefore, he could no longer continue free circulation. Subscribers would have to send forty cents for a six-month subscription plus fifty cents for prepaid postage. If the paper received a sufficient number of subscriptions, it would continue. His appeal was successful and sufficient fees arrived at *The Right Way* offices. The newspaper continued its operations for almost another year. Stearns now vowed that the purpose of *The Right Way* was "to oppose the policy of reconstruction adopted by the President as dangerous to the peace of the country and subversive of good government." In the months that followed this declaration, article after article attacked Johnson's program. Its editor, William W. Thayer, said that the paper enraged Johnson so much that he issued an order forbidding the military in the South to circulate it.[82]

VIII

On March 17, 1866, *The Right Way* announced a call for a meeting to form the Impartial Suffrage Association. This new organization would realize the culmination of Stearns's efforts during the past year to form an organization to replace the Emancipation League. Stearns had in mind an organization that could lobby Congress in much the same way the league had. He wanted the association to influence Congress in regard to the readmission of only those states that guaranteed full and complete suffrage for all their citizens. The association met on March 27 in the Boston Board of Trade room, formed committees, and drafted a constitution, stating its central objectives to "secure to all citizens throughout our entire country the full enjoyment of EQUAL CIVIL AND POLITICAL RIGHTS without regard to race and color."[83]

On April 30, the Joint Committee on Reconstruction offered to Congress a constitutional amendment prohibiting states from denying citizens their civil rights or equal protection under the law. The proposed amendment also called for the reduction of a state's congressional delegation if it denied suffrage to any male citizen. It also sought to disqualify from holding office former leaders of the Confederacy. Among the abolitionists, reaction was mixed. Stearns wrote to Sumner, "I am not willing to accept as a finality any thing less than Impartial Suffrage." In regard to the present legislation, he believed it was the best Congress could do at present and "better the members should pass it rather than have no policy." He wanted Massachusetts to take the lead in impartial suffrage; he saw no harm in the state's congressional delegation's supporting the amendment and then "asking all we need at a future time." While Phillips lobbied against the proposed Fourteenth Amendment, Stearns supported its passage and held out for African-American suffrage either in the legislation readmitting southern states to the Union or in another amendment. To support the amendment's passage, Stearns organized a meeting to be called at the invitation of the Impartial Suffrage Association at Faneuil Hall on May 31. Speakers offered support for the recent moves by Congress, and the group passed several resolutions. Former governor and now congressman George S. Boutwell concluded the meeting by saying that he would never vote for readmission of any state unless it "previously guarantee[d] enfranchisement to the Colored citizen."[84]

In the midst of the furor over the amendment, Frank's activities at Harvard distracted his father. Frank and two other members of the class of 1867 had established the first newspaper at the institution. The paper criticized college customs and satirized faculty members. As a consequence, the three editors of *The Collegian* had received notification in May that if another issue appeared they would be suspended. Stearns allowed the young men to use the offices of *The Right Way* to continue their paper, but under a different name, while they appealed to the Board of Overseers. Freedom of the press won out, and Stearns helped the student editors defray the expenses of their paper's first issue, which they now called *Advocate*.[85]

With Congress adjourned that July, after having passed a civil rights bill on April 9 and a revised Freedmen's Bureau bill, both over a presidential veto, Stearns's activity slackened. Mary was ailing more now than at any time previously, remaining in her darkened room for weeks at a time. Frank observed that the illness probably had more to do with her homeopathic doctor than any disease. Still, Stearns was concerned. On one sultry July morning, he sent her fresh fruit from Boston and promised to return early that afternoon. Although it caused him pain, Stearns even sent little Carl to stay with relatives. However, the doting father knew this was necessary, for the youngest son, Frank said, was a "perpetual teaser." Stearns should have seen to his own health, for it was still not the best. Frank Bird wanted him to go to the Adirondacks for fishing, but Mary would not hear of it. Unfortunately, Stearns, his son said, was of a class of people who would not admit to being ill until they were on their deathbeds.[86]

The summer of 1866 passed quickly for Stearns and with it some of his former ability to handle so many projects simultaneously. In early September he received an invitation to speak to a convention of Southern Unionists in Philadelphia. He declined because of pressing personal and business matters, but sent a letter criticizing the president while acknowledging his good works in wartime Nashville. Stearns went so far as to blame Johnson for the brutal July 30 attack by a New Orleans mob on a convention of radical whites and blacks meeting in that city. About the same time, Stearns was considered as a candidate for Congress. The *Boston Commonwealth* ranked him second in popularity among the contenders. He declined. Although not a candidate, Stearns managed to be active in the 1866 congressional elections and went to

Democratic-controlled New York to assist Republicans there. He wrote Mary that Connecticut had gone to the "bow-wows" and voted Democratic. He was elated, however, that enough Republicans were elected to ensure a solid two-thirds majority in both houses of Congress.[87]

In that fall of 1866, Stearns faced a financial crisis almost as serious as the one he had experienced in attempting to comer the lead market in the 1850s. First, the drop in gold prices cost him $10,000. Then some small investments made in friends' businesses were lost. Also, the American Land Company was in dire straits, due to cotton crop failures for two consecutive years. This organization tottered for several months and then, in late 1866, announced the suspension of business. Stearns and others, including John Andrew, lost their entire investment. For the first time, a haggard Stearns turned to his two older sons, Frank and Harry, for help. After discussing the family's financial condition, the three men agreed that they should sell The Evergreens so that the family could live more economically for the next few years.[88]

Mary was so vehement in her opposition to their plan that Stearns had no choice but to drop the matter. He took Harry out of school and told him to run the estate in a stringent manner and to make their greenhouses tum a profit. The supporter of Kansas freedom, John Brown, and African American emancipation and civil rights tried to withdraw from political activity. He opposed the agitation Phillips initiated to impeach Andrew Johnson. Then in January Phillips's and Johnson's actions finally persuaded Stearns that the president's removal by impeachment was essential to realizing civil rights for blacks in the South. But. Stearns did nothing to assist in the movement.[89]

Still, in January 1867, Stearns was distracted by another friend arid another cause. Howe formed a committee to raise $20,000 for the Cretans in rebellion against their Turkish rulers. He asked Stearns to assist in the fund-raising and then travel to Crete to, as the Boston Commonwealth declared, "dispense the bounty." Stearns grasped the opportunity, Frank later said, in "a kind of desperation in the precarious condition of his affairs," both financial and medical. This time Mary agreed with her husband's plans. Perhaps the romance of the expedition appealed to her. Howe thought they would make a strong team. Both men visited New York and came away with sufficient donations for the trip. They made plans to travel to the island of Crete that spring.[90]

In early February, however, Stearns changed his plans when he received samples of a new type of pipe from a former employee of his rival, the New

York Lead Company. A young clerk by the name of Shaw had invented a process for lining lead pipe by placing a chilled tin cylinder inside the tubing. In this process, the two metals would combine to form a satisfactory tin-lined pipe. Stearns was excited by the new invention and believed the product would revolutionize the industry. This process eliminated the danger of lead poisoning, and lead pipe lined with tin would withstand greater pressure than the current product. Stearns saw the new process as a way to reestablish his wealth. The ecstatic manufacturer told Howe that, under the circumstances, he would be unable to make the trip. Stearns hurried to New York to consult Shaw. Other manufacturers, such as the Tathams, were skeptical, but Stearns was not discouraged. He agreed with Shaw to form a company to issue stock in all the large cities in the country. Stearns spent a great deal of time in New York through February and March, testing the new product and drawing up plans for its eventual production and distribution.[91]

In his attempt to reestablish the financial base that had allowed him to work for African-American freedom, Stearns for the moment was leaving Southern reconstruction and overseas adventures to others. On March 2, 1867, he ceased publication of *The Right Way*. The final issue called for military rule of the South and for establishment of provisional state governments in the region. Although the work he had begun in Kansas many years before was still not finished, Stearns finally lost the base from which he had conducted his personal crusade. Emancipation had, indeed, been hard on his purse.[92]

In April 1867, Stearns was in New York again testing the new pipe. On the morning of April 4, he became ill. Mr. Shaw immediately called a carriage and got Stearns to his room at the Brevoort House. Stearns requested a physician, but before one arrived, he lost his speech. Mr. Shaw consulted with the doctor, who diagnosed the case as pneumonia and wired Mary. The message indicated that her husband's condition was serious. That evening, Mary boarded the train for New York with her Boston homeopath, Dr. Payne. Stearns rallied slightly by the time his wife arrived, and he greeted her with a few words. To reassure her, Stearns belittled his condition and complained not at all. Mary's doctor soon fell into an argument with the attending physician, whom Mary dismissed. Not believing his condition serious, Payne found an elderly local homeopath, Dr. Bayard, to treat Stearns and then returned to Boston. Other than visit once a day to administer a tasteless and harmless medicine, Dr. Bayard did little. Unlike in his previous illnesses, when she had been reluctant to be with him, Mary remained at his bedside constantly, perhaps sensing that her husband's strength was ebbing. Even in a deteriorating condition, Stearns was attentive to Mary. Seeing the rays of the strong spring sun move across his bed, he begged Mary to enjoy a walk in nearby Washington Square. His thoughtfulness may have given Mary hope that he was recovering. Unfortunately, Stearns's condition worsened, and breathing became more difficult. On April 9, at five in the afternoon, without uttering a word, George Luther Stearns died.[93]

Mary made arrangements to return to Medford with her husband's body. Funeral services were held at The Evergreens. More than fifty friends attended the simple Unitarian ceremony. Mary asked Emerson to speak. He accepted but during his address began to belittle Stearns, referring to his romantic generosity, and saying that it was fortunate he had died before old age overtook him because he "would not live to see his sons waiting to occupy his shoes." Seeing the pain in the mourners' eyes, the following speaker, Theophilus Parsons, attempted to counter Emerson's remarks. The major's life and his character, he said, were refreshing, for too often public services were linked with personal ambition. In Stearns's case Parsons found "a man who wanted absolutely nothing for himself," not even praise. "In him," Parsons said, "I have lost my truest friend and America her best patriot." With these words, the service ended, and a procession followed Stearns's body to its resting place in Mount Auburn Cemetery near Cambridge. At the grave site, the services were simple but impressive. At the end, Mary and her sons placed flowers on the grave. Parsons turned to Bronson Alcott and said, "Death is the one universal fact." Alcott responded, "Except life."[94]

The following Sunday, April 14, in Medford's Unitarian Church a memorial service was held for Stearns. Again invited to speak, Emerson this time did justice to Stearns. He began by saying, "We do not know how to praise good men until they depart." We think, he said, of how when they lived their services were taken for granted. Emerson recounted Stearns's career, his Kansas work, his support of John Brown, and his constant efforts to free and elevate African-Americans to their rightful place in the nation. "Be not too proud in your grief," Emerson told the assembly, "when you remember that there is not a town in the remote State of Kansas that will not weep with you as at the loss of its founder; not a Southern State in which the freedmen will not learn today from their preacher that one of their most efficient benefactors has departed." Emerson went on to acknowledge that there was "hardly a man in this country worth knowing who does not hold his name in honor . . . . For the Spirit of the Universe seems to say: 'He has done well; is not that saying all?'"[95]

The May 1867 issue of *Atlantic Monthly* carried a tribute to George Luther Stearns by one of his friends. Poet John Greenleaf Whittier wrote of the man's generosity and industriousness and observed

> Ah, well!—the world is discreet; There are plenty
> to pause and wait; But here was a man who set
> his feet sometimes in advance of fate.[96]

NOTES

1. Stearns, *Life*, p. 329; George L. Stearns to Andrew Johnson, January 2, 1864, Johnson MSS, LC.
2. Stephen B. Oates, *With Malice toward None* (New York: Harper & Row, 1977), pp. 371, 380, quote from p. 367, source unknown; President Abraham Lincoln, "Proclamation of Amnesty and Reconstruction," December 8, 1863, Basler, *The Collected Works of Abraham Lincoln*, 7:53-56.
3. George L. Stearns to Mary Stearns, January 23, 1864, quoted in Stearns, *Life*, p. 326.
4. George L. Stearns to Andrew Johnson, January 23, 1864, Johnson MSS, LC; George L. Stearns to E. C. Cabell, September 29, 1865, printed in *The Right Way*, November 25, 1865. Frank Stearns claims the date the venture began was March 1863, but this is in error for his father was in New York state that month recruiting the Fifty-fourth and Fifty-fifth Massachusetts Infantry.
5. Ibid.
6. George L. Stearns to Mary Stearns, March 4, 1864, quoted in Stearns, Life, p. 328. Actually General Grant was and had been very supportive of recruiting blacks for combat and not just labor units. Oates, *With Malice toward None*, pp. 371, 389.
7. James M. McPherson, *The Struggle for Equality* (Princeton, NJ: Princeton University Press, 1964), pp. 260-261; Oates, *With Malice toward None*, p. 355.
8. George L. Stearns to Mary Stearns, January 23, 1864, quoted in Stearns, *Life*, p. 326; McPherson, *The Struggle for Equality*, pp. 263-264; Salmon P. Chase to James C. Hall, March 5, 1864, printed in *The Liberator*, March 18, 1864.
9. J. Miller McKim to the editor of the New York National Anti-Slavery Standard, March 20, 1864; The Liberator, February 12, 1864; George L. Stearns to the editor of the National Anti-Slavery Standard, quoted in the *Boston Commonwealth*, April 8, 1864.
10. Ibid.
11. Ralph Waldo Emerson to George L. Stearns, May 7, 1864, quoted in Rusk, Emerson, 5:375; *The Liberator*, May 13, 1863.
12. George L. Stearns to Andrew Johnson, June 9, 1864, Johnson MSS, LC; *The Liberator*, June 24, 1864.
13. Oates, *With Malice toward None*, p. 389; McPherson, *The Struggle for Equality*, p. 270.

14. *The Liberator*, July 29, 1864; George L. Stearns to A. Bronson Alcott, August 8, 1864, A. Bronson Alcott Collection, Concord Free Public Library, Concord, Massachusetts (hereafter cited as Alcott Collection).

15. Abraham Lincoln, memorandum concerning his probable failure of reelection, August 23, 1864, quoted in Basler, *Collected Works*, 7:514; Oates, *With Malice toward None*, p. 395.

16. Allan Nevins, *The Organized War to Victory*, 1864-1865, vol. 8 of *War for the Union*, pp. 83-84; Oates, *With Malice toward None*, p. 393, source of quote unknown; McPherson, *The Struggle for Equality*, pp. 280-281.

17. George L. Stearns et al. to John C. Fremont, August 21, 1864, printed in the Boston *Commonwealth*, August 26, 1864.

18. Henry Wilson to Abraham Lincoln, September 5, 1864, Robert Todd Lincoln Collection, LC; William L. Garrison to Samuel J. May, September 6, 1864, Antislavery MSS, BPL; George L. Stearns to A. Bronson Alcott, September 8, 1864, Alcott Collection; George L. Stearns et al. to John C. Fremont, September 9, 1864, printed in *The Liberator*, September 30, 1864.

19. George L. Stearns to the editor of *The Liberator*, September 12, 1864, printed in *The Liberator*, September 16, 1864; Oates, *With Malice toward None*, p. 396.

20. John C. Fremont to George L. Stearns and "Others," September 17, 1864, and John C. Fremont to[?], September 17, 1864, both printed in the Boston *Daily Evening Transcript*, September 22, 1864. In his father's biography Frank Stearns *The Right Way* 215 ignores the incident, mentioning nothing about his father's activities from February until late fall 1864.

21. George L. Stearns to [blank on copy of the letter], September 20, 1864, Smith Collection, SUL.

22. George L. Stearns to Andrew Johnson, September 26, 1864, Johnson MSS, LC.

23. Ralph Waldo Emerson to Mary Stearns, October 3, 1864, quoted in Rusk, Emerson, 5:383; A. Bronson Alcott to Mary E. Stearns, November 27, 1864, quoted in Herrenstadt, *Letters of Alcott*, pp. 359-360.

24. Stearns, *Life*, p. 339; Reuben D. Mussey to Edwin M. Stanton, November 9, 1864, Robert Todd Lincoln Collection, LC; E. B. Long with Barbara Long, *The Civil War Day by Day* (Garden City, NY: Doubleday, 1971), p. 594.

25. "Lists of Persons Who Put in Representative Recruits, and Names of Recruits," OR, ser. 3 vol. 5, p. 921.

26. Boston *Commonwealth*, September 2, 1865.

27. George L. Stearns, *A Few Facts Pertaining to Currency and Banking; Adapted to the Present Position of Our Finances* (Washington, D.C., 1864), p. 11.

28. Ibid.

29. Stearns, *Life*, p. 339.

30. Ibid; George Lindsey Stearns to the author, July 31, 1973.

31. Donald, *The Rights of Man*, p. 209; George L. Stearns to Andrew Johnson, January 16, 1865, Johnson MSS, LC; George L. Stearns to Charles Sumner, January 16, 1865, Sumner MSS, Houghton; George L. Stearns to Gerrit Smith, January 16, 1865, Smith Collection, SUL; Donald, *The Rights of Man*, pp. 209-212.

32. George L. Stearns to C. W. Foster, February 1, 1865, Bureau of Colored Troops, RG 94.

33. A. Bronson Alcott to Mary E. Stearns, December 17, 1864, quoted in Herrenstadt, *Letters of Alcott*, p. 361 ; George L. Stearns to Moncure D. Conway, March 10, 1865, Conway Papers.

34. Boston, *Commonwealth*, April29, 1865.

35. *The Liberator*, May 26, 1865, and June 2, 1865; McPherson, *The Struggle of Equality*, pp. 304-305; Stearns, Life, pp. 352-353.

36. George L. Stearns to Moncure D. Conway, March 1, 1865, Conway Papers; Stearns, *Life*, p. 353.

37. Ibid.

38. Boston, *Commonwealth*, March 25, 1865; George L. Stearns, ed. [?], "Equality of All Men before the Law," pamphlet dated April17, 1865, copy found in the Tennessee State Library, Nashville, Tennessee.

39. Ibid.

40. Stearns, *Life*, p. 333; George L. Stearns, circular addressed to Charles Eliot Norton, August 14, 1865, Charles Eliot Norton Collection, Houghton Library, Harvard University, Cambridge, Massachusetts (hereafter cited as Norton Collection); George L. Stearns to Charles Sumner, April 30, 1865, Sumner MSS, Houghton; McPherson, *The Struggle for Equality*, pp. 323-324.

41. Stearns's circular to Norton, August 14, 1865; Stearns, Life, p. 335; McPherson, *The Struggle for Equality*, pp. 323-324.

42. *The Liberator*, June 2, 1865; George L. Stearns to Charles Sumner, April 30, 1865, Sumner MSS, Houghton; Charles Sumner to George L. Stearns, May 4, 1865, quoted in Stearns, *Life*, p. 344.

43. George L. Stearns to Andrew Johnson, May 17, 1865, Johnson MSS, LC; George L. Stearns to Charles Sumner, April30, 1865, Sumner MSS, Houghton.

44. Charles Sumner to George L. Stearns, May 4, 1865, and May 11, 1865, quoted in Stearns, *Life*, p. 344.

45. George L. Stearns, ed., *Universal Suffrage and Complete Equality in Citizenship* (Boston: Press of George C. Rand and Avery, May 25, 1865.)

46. George L. Stearns to Andrew Johnson, May 17, 1865, Johnson MSS, LC; George L. Stearns to Charles Sumner, May 8, 1865, Sumner MSS, Houghton.

47. James M. McPherson, *Ordeal by Fire* (New York: Alfred A. Knopf, 1982), pp. 498-499; *The Liberator*, June 2, 1865.

48. Ibid.

49. A. Bronson Alcott to Mary E. Stearns, May 30, 1865, and May 31, 1865, quoted in Herrenstadt, *Letters of Alcott*, pp. 369, 370; Stearns, *Life*, pp. 344-345.

50. A. Bronson Alcott to Mary E. Stearns, January 13, 1860, in Herrenstadt, *Letters of Alcott*, p. 309; Martha Saxton, Louisa May (Boston: Houghton Mifflin, 1977), p. 263.

51. Stearns, *Life*, p. 345.

52. Ibid.

53. Stearns, Life, pp. 348-350; Ralph Waldo Emerson to George L. Stearns. June [?]1865, in Rusk, Emerson, 5:418. The same letter appears in Stearns, Life, p. 347, but is not dated.

54. Ibid.

55. Amos A. Lawrence to Andrew Johnson, July 1, 1865, Johnson MSS, LC.

56. *The Nation*, vol. 1, no. 1, July 6, 1865, p. 1.

57. Stearns, Life, pp. 336-337; McPherson, *The Struggle for Equality*, pp. 324-325; Edwin L. Godkin to Edward Atkinson, July 17, 1865, quoted in broadside, George L. Stearns to Charles Norton, August 14, 1865, Norton Collection; Charles Sumner to George L. Stearns, August [?]1865, quoted in Stearns, *Life*, p. 337.

58. Broadside, George L. Stearns to Charles E. Norton, August 14, 1865, Norton Collection; George L. Stearns to Samuel G. Ward, July 26, 1865, Stearns Collection, Houghton Library, Harvard University, Cambridge, Massachusetts (hereafter cited as Stearns Collection, HLHU).

59. George L. Stearns to *The Nation* shareholders, September 3, 1865, in a broadside, George L. Stearns to Charles E. Norton, Norton Collection; George L. Stearns to Samuel G. Ward, August 15, 1865, Stearns Collection, HLHU.

60. George L. Stearns to Charles E. Norton, September 4, 1865, Norton Collection; Charles E. Norton to George L. Stearns, n.d., but on reverse of above letter, Norton Collection; George L. Stearns to Charles E. Norton, September 9, 1865, Norton Collection.

61. Stearns, *Life*, pp. 337-338.

62. A. Bronson Alcott to George L. Stearns, August 4, 1865, in Herrenstadt, Letters of Alcott, p. 373; George L. Stearns to A. Bronson Alcott, August 3, 1865, Alcott Collection; Stearns, *Life*, pp. 353-355.

63. George L. Stearns to Andrew Johnson, August 16, 1865, Johnson MSS, LC.

64. Donald, *The Rights of Man*, p. 223; George L. Stearns to Charles Sumner, August 16, 1865, Johnson MSS, LC.

65. A. Bronson Alcott to Mary E. Stearns, September 8 and 11, 1865, in Herrenstadt, *Letters of Alcott*, pp. 374-375, 375-376.

66. *The Right Way*, November 18, 1865.

67. Ibid.; George L. Stearns to Andrew Johnson, October 8, 1865, Johnson MSS, LC, quoted in McPherson, *Ordeal By Fire*, p. 500.

68. George L. Stearns to Moncure D. Conway, October 23, 1865, Conway Papers.

69. New York *Tribune*, October 23, 1865; New York *Independent*, October 26, and November 9, 1865, *National Anti-Slavery Standard*, October 28, 1865, all quoted in McPherson, *The Struggle for Equality*, p. 337.

70. George L. Stearns to Charles Sumner, October 11, 1865, Sumner MSS; William Wilde Thayer, "Autobiographical Sketch," unpublished typescript by Laura Conwell Thayer, November 1, 1892, William Wilde Thayer Manuscripts, Library of Congress, pp. 24-25.

71. *Boston Commonwealth*, October 14, 1865, and February 10, 1866; John Andrew to "Officer in Charge," Commissary Department, Freedman's Bureau, November[?], 1865, quoted in Pearson, John Andrew, 2:269.

72. George L. Stearns to John Andrew, November 14, 1865, John Andrew Collection, Massachusetts Historical Society, Boston, Massachusetts (hereafter cited as Andrew Collection).

73. George L. Stearns to Andrew Johnson, December 14, 1865, Johnson MSS, LC; Samuel G. Howe to Mary Stearns, December 12, 1865, Stutler Collection; Stearns, *Life*, p. 364.

74. Andrew Johnson to Edwin M. Stanton, December 17, 1863 and Andrew Johnson to Major General William S. Rosecrans, September 17, 1863, in OR, ser. 3, vol. 3, pp. 819-820; Donald, *The Rights of Man*, p. 224.

75. George L. Stearns to Andrew Johnson, December 14, 1865, Johnson MSS, LC.

76. Washington Chronicle, February 8, 1866, quoted in McPherson, *The Struggle for Equality*, p. 346; Eric L. McKitrick, *Andrew Johnson and Reconstruction* (Chicago: University of Chicago Press, Phoenix Books, 1960), p. 282; McPherson, *Ordeal by Fire*, p. 498.

77. Stearns, *Life*, pp. 366-368; George L. Stearns to Harry L. Stearns, February 22, 1866, Stearns MSS, MHS.

78. Stearns, *Life*, pp.367-368.

79. Ibid., p. 370.

80. George L. Stearns to Harry Stearns, February 22, 1866, Stearns MSS, MHS; Stearns, *Life*, p. 374.

81. George L. Stearns to J. N. Richards, March 25, 1866, Stearns Collection, HLHU; Stearns, *Life*, p. 373.

82. *The Right Way*, February 12 and 14, 1866; George L. Stearns to Jane Swisshelm, April 6, 1866, quoted in Stearns, *Life*, p. 371; Thayer, "Autobiographical Sketch," p. 25.

83. *The Right Way*, March 17, 1866.

84. George L. Stearns to Charles Sumner, May 1, 1866, Sumner MSS, Houghton; *The Right Way*, May 12 and June 9, 1866; Pearson, John Andrew, 2:264-265; *Boston Commonwealth*, June 2, 1866.

85. *Boston Commonwealth*, May 26, 1866; Stearns, *Life*, pp. 375-376.

86. Stearns, *Life*, pp. 375-376.

87. Stearns, *Life*, p. 376; *Boston Commonwealth*, September 5, 1866; George L. Stearns to Mary E. Stearns, November[?], 1866, quoted in Stearns, *Life*, p. 377.

88. Pearson, John Andrew, 2:313; John Andrew to Montgomery Blair, January 7, 1867, quoted in Pearson, John Andrew, 2:314-315; Stearns, *Life*, p. 378; *The Right Way*, January 12 and 19, 1867.

89. Stearns, *Life*, p. 378; *The Right Way*, January 12 and 19, 1867.

90. *Boston Commonwealth*, January 19, 1867; Stearns, *Life*, pp. 380.

91. Stearns, *Life*, pp. 380-381.

92. *The Right Way*, March 2, 1867.

93. Stearns, *Life*, pp. 381-382.

94. Stearns, *Life*, pp. 382-383; A. Bronson Alcott to Mary E. Stearns, April 13, 1867, and journal entry, April 14, 1867, in Herrenstadt, *Letters of Alcott*, p. 405; A. Bronson Alcott to Mary E. Stearns, October 23, 1867, in Herrenstadt, *Letters of Alcott*, pp. 413, 414.

95. Ralph Waldo Emerson, "Remarks on the Character of George L. Stearns at Medford," April 14, 1867, broadside, Stearns MSS, AAS.

96. John G. Whittier, "G.L.S.," *Atlantic Monthly*, May 1867, quoted in Stearns, *Life*, p. 386.

Selected Bibliography

BOOKS

Abbott, Richard. *Cotton & Capital: Boston Businessmen and Antislavery Reform*

    1854-1868. Amherst, MA: University of Massachusetts Press, 1991.

Abels, Jules. *Man on Fire: John Brown and the Cause of Liberty* .

    New York: Macmillan, 1971.

Baker, George E. *The Life of William H. Seward*. New York: Redfield, 1855.

Basler, Roy P. *The Collected Works of Abraham Lincoln*. 9 vols.

    New Brunswick, NJ: Rutgers University Press, 1955.

Bolles, Albert S. *Industrial History of the United States*. 3d ed., 1881. Reprint.

    New York: Augustus M. Kelly, 1966.

Boston City Council. *Exercises at the Dedication of the Monument to Colonel Robert*

    Gould Shaw and the Fifty-Fourth Regiment of Massachusetts Infantry.

    Boston: Municipal Printing Office, 1897.

Boyer, Richard O . *The Legend of John Brown: A Biography and a History*.

    New York: Alfred A. Knopf, 1973.

Brauer, Kinley J. *Cotton versus Conscience*.

    Lexington: University of Kentucky Press, 1967.

Brooks, Charles, and James M. Usher. *History of Medford, Middlesex County: From*

    Its First Settlement in 1630 to 1855: Revised, Enlarged, and Brought Down

    to 1885. Boston: Rand, Avery, 1886.

Burtis, Mary E. *Moncure Conway*, 1832-1907. New Brunswick, NJ:

    Rutgers University Press, 1952.

Clark, Victor S. *History of Manufactures in the United States, 1607- 1860.*

    Washington, DC: Carnegie Institute, 1929. Reprint. New York: Peter Smith,

    1949.

Commager, Henry S. *Theodore Parker.* Boston: The Beacon Press, 1960.

Conway, Moncure D. *Autobiography, Memories and Experiences of Moncure Daniel*

    Conway. 2 vols. Boston: Houghton Mifflin, 1905.

Cornish, Dudley T. *The Sable Arm: Negro Troops in the Union Army, 1861-1865.*

    New York: W. W. Norton, 1966.

Donald, David. *Charles Sumner and the Coming of the Civil War.*

    New York: Alfred A. Knopf, 1967.

— ."Toward a Reconsideration of Abolitionists." David Donald, ed.

    Lincoln Reconsidered. New York: Alfred A. Knopf Vintage Books, 1956.

Emilio, Luis. *A Brave Black Regiment.* Boston: Boston Book Company, 1894.

Foner, Eric. *Free Soil, Free Labor, Free Man.*

    New York: Oxford University Press, 1970.

Freedley, Edwin T. *Philadelphia and Its Manufacturers.* Philadelphia: Young, 1867.

Furness, J. C. *The Road to Harpers Ferry.*

    New York: William Sloane Associates, 1959.

Garrison, Wendell Phillips, and Francis Jackson Garrison. *William Lloyd Garrison.*

    Vol. 3. Boston: Houghton Mifflin, 1894.

Hall, David Brainard. *Halls of New England, Genealogical and Biographical.*

    Albany, NY: J. Munsell's, 1883.

Herrenstadt, Richard L., ed. *The Letters of A. Bronson Alcott.*

Ames: The Iowa State University Press, 1969.

Higginson, Thomas W. *Cheerful Yesterdays.* Boston: Houghton, Mifflin, 1891.

Hinton, Richard J. *John Brown and His Men.*

New York: Funk and Wagnalls, 1894. Reprint. New York: Arno Press, 1968.

Hughes, Sarah Forbes, ed., *Letters and Recollections of John Murray Forbes.* 2 vols.

Boston: Houghton, Mifflin, 1899.

Jaher, Frederick Cople. "The Boston Brahmans in the Age of Industrial

Capitalism."

Frederick Cople Jaher, ed. *The Age of Industrialism in America.*

New York: The Free Press, 1968.

Johnson, Samuel. *The Battle Cry of Freedom.* Lawrence: University of Kansas

Press, 1954. Reprint. Westport, CT: Greenwood Press, 1977.

Lester, C. Edwards. *The Life and Public Services of Charles Sumner.*

New York: United States Publishing, 1874.

Long, E. B., with Barbara Long. *The Civil War Day by Day.*

Garden City, NY: Doubleday and Co., 1971.

Lowell, Robert. *For the Union Dead.* New York: Farrar, Straus and Giroux, 1966.

McKitrick, Eric L. *Andrew Johnson and Reconstruction.*

Chicago: University of Chicago Press, Phoenix Books, 1960.

McPherson, James M. *The Struggle for Equality.*

Princeton, NJ: Princeton University Press, 1964.

—. *Ordeal by Fire.* New York: Alfred A. Knopf, 1982.

National Encyclopedia of American Biography. 1906 ed. s.v.

"William Penn Tatham."

Nevins, Allan. *A House Dividing, 1852-1857*. Vol. 2 of *Ordeal of the Union*. New York: Charles Scribner's Sons, 1947.

— . *Prologue to Civil War, 1859-1861*. Vol. 2 of *The Emergence of Lincoln*. New York: Charles Scribner's Sons, 1950.

— . *The Organized War, 1863-1864*. Vol. 3 of *The War for the Union*. New York: Charles Scribner's Sons, 1971.

— . *The Organized War to Victory , 1864-1865*. Vol. 4 of *The War for the Union*. New York: Charles Scribner's Sons, 1971.

Nichols, Alice. *Bleeding Kansas*. New York: Oxford University Press, 1954.

Oates, Stephen B. *Our Fiery Trial*. Amherst: University of Massachusetts Press, 1979.

— . *To Purge This Land with Blood*. New York: Harper Torchbooks; 1972.

— · *With Malice toward None*. New York: Harper & Row, 1977.

O'Conner, Thomas H. *Lords of the Loom*. New York: Charles Scribner's Sons, 1968.

Pearson, Henry Greenleaf. *The Life of John A. Andrew: Governor of Massachusetts*. 2 vols. New York: Houghton, Mifflin, 1904.

Rawley, James A. *Race and Politics*. Philadelphia: J. B. Lippincott, 1969.

Rossbach, Jeffrey S. *Ambivalent Conspirators: John Brown, the Secret Six, and a Theory of Slave Violence*. Philadelphia: University of Pennsylvania, 1982.

Rusk, Ralph L., ed. *The Letters of Ralph Waldo Emerson*. Vols. 4-6. New York: Columbia University Press, 1939.

Sanborn, Franklin B., ed. *The Life and Letters of John Brown, Liberator of Kansas and Martyr of Virginia*. Boston: Roberts Brothers, 1891.

— . *Recollections of Seventy Years*. George G. Badger, ed. 2 vols. Boston:

Gorham Press, 1909.

— . *Samuel Gridley Howe, the Philanthropist*.

New York: Funk and Wagnalls, 1891.

Saxton, Martha. *Louisa May Alcott*. Boston: Houghton Mifflin, 1977.

Scheidenhelm, Richard A., ed. *The Response to John Brown*. William R. Taylor

and Arthur Zilversmit, gen. eds. The American History Research Series.

Belmont, CA: Wadsworth Publishing, 1972.

Schwartz, Harold. *Samuel Gridley Howe: Social Reformer*.

Cambridge, MA: Harvard University Press, 1956.

Scott, Otto. *The Secret Six: John Brown and the Abolitionist Movement*.

New York: Times Books, 1979.

Shaw, Robert Gould. *Letters*. Cambridge: University Press, 1864.

Stearns, Frank Preston. *The Life and Public Services of George Luther Stearns*.

Philadelphia: J. B. Lippincott, 1907. Reprint. New York: Kraus Reprinting,

1969.

Stearns, George L. *A Few Facts Pertaining to Currency and Banking; Adapted to the

Present Position of Our Finances*. Washington, D.C.: Gibson Brothers,

1864.

— , ed. *Universal Suffrage and Complete Equality Citizenship*, the Safeguards of

Democratic Institutions. Boston: The Press of George C. Rand and Avery,

May 25, 1865.

Thayer, Eli. *A History of the Kansas Crusade*. New York: Harper & Brothers, 1889.

Tiffany, Nina Moore. *Samuel E. Sewall: A Memoir*.

Boston: Houghton Mifflin., 1898.

Trow's New York City Directory. 1863-1864 ed. s.v. "Benjamin Tatham."

Villard, Oswald Garrison. *John Brown, 1800-1859: A Biography Fifty Years After*.
  Boston: Houghton Mifflin, 1910.

Wendte, Charles W. *Thomas Starr King: Patriot and Preacher*.
  Boston: Beacon Press, 1921.

Whitman, Maxwell. *Gentlemen in Crisis: The First Century of the Union League of
  Philadelphia, 1862-1962*. Philadelphia: The Union League, 1975.

Wilson, Henry. *Rise and Fall of the Slave Power in America*. 3 vols.
  Boston: Houghton Mifflin, 1872.

Wilson, James Grant, and John Fiske, eds. *Appleton's Cyclopedia of American
  Biography*. 6 vols. New York: D. Appleton, 1887-1889.

JOURNAL ARTICLES

Andrews, Horace, Jr. "Kansas Crusade: Eli Thayer and the New England Emigrant
  Aid Company." *New England Quarterly* 2 (Spring 1962).

Cummings, Charles. "Medford in 1847." *Medford Historical Register* 6 (April 1903).

Dame, Lorin L. "The Middlesex Canal." *Medford Historical Register* 1 (April 1898).

De Long, Henry C. "The First Parish in Medford." *Medford Historical Register* 12
  (October 1906).

Gatell, Frank Otto. "Conscience and Judgement, the Bolt of the Massachusetts
  Conscience Whigs." *The Historian* 21 (1958).

Gleason, Hall. "Medford's Part in American Shipbuilding." *Medford Historical
  Register* 38 (March 1934).

Hall, H. D. "Deacon Samuel Train." *Medford Historical Register* 2 (October 1899).

Hallowell, Anna D. "Lydia Maria Child." *Medford Historical Register* 3 (July 1900).

Harlow, Thomas S. "Some Notes of the History of Medford. 1801-1851." *Medford Historical Register* 2 (July 1898).

Hervey, James A. "Shipbuilding in Medford." *Medford Historical Register* 1 (July 1898).

Jepson, Samuel G. "Incidents and Reminiscences of the Fire Department of Medford." *Medford Historical Register* 4 (January 1901).

Johnson, Samuel. "George L. Stearns." *The Radical* (April1867).

"Medford a Century Ago-1819." *Medford Historical Register* 22 (December 1919).

Medford, Massachusetts, Selectman's Records, 4:122, quoted in *Medford Historical Register* 10 (April1907).

Mitchell, Betty L. "Massachusetts Reacts to John Brown's Raid." *Civil War History* (March 1973).

Morse, Sidney H. "An Anti Slavery Hero." *The New England Magazine* (March 1891).

M.W.M. "Medford Turnpike Corporation." *Medford Historical Register* 23 (March 1920).

Preston, Charles Henry. "Descendants of Roger Preston of Ipswich and Salem Village." Essex Institute Historical Collection 65 (1929).

Stearns, George L. Collection. "Equality of all Men Before the Law." Pamphlet dated April17, 1865. Tennessee State Library, Nashville, Tennessee.

Stetson, Thomas M. "An Old Medford School Boy's Reminiscences." *Medford Historical Register* 17 (October 1914).

"The Taverns of Medford." *Medford Historical Register* 8 (April 1905).

"The Tornado of 1851." *Medford Historical Register* 24 (June 1926).

"The Towers of Medford." *Medford Historical Register* 24 (March 1921).

Wilde, Helen Tilden. "Female Union Temperance Society."

Medford Historical Register 12 (October 1906).

NEWSPAPERS AND MAGAZINES

Boston *Commonwealth*.

Boston *Daily Evening Transcript*.

Boston *Express*.

Boston *Post*.

Boston *Whig*.

The Liberator.

Nashville *Daily Express*.

Nashville *Daily Union*.

Nashville *Dispatch*.

The Nation.

National Anti-Slavery Standard.

New York *Daily Tribune*.

New York *Times*.

Philadelphia *North American and United States Gazette*.

The Right Way.

Rochester *Douglass' Monthly*.

Washington *National Intelligencer*.

MANUSCRIPT COLLECTIONS

Abolitionist Collection. Historical Society of Pennsylvania. Philadelphia, Pennsylvania.

Alcott, A. Bronson. Collection. Concord Free Public Library. Concord, Massachusetts.

Andrew, John. Collection. Massachusetts Historical Society. Boston, Massachusetts.

Antislavery Collection. New York Public Library. New York, New York.

Antislavery Manuscripts. Boston Public Library. Boston, Massachusetts.

Armour, Alexander W. Collection. Library of Congress. Washington, D.C.

Brown, John. Collection. Library of Congress. Washington, D.C.

— . Manuscripts. Trevor Arnett Library. Atlanta University. Atlanta, Georgia.

Brown, John, and Thomas Wentworth Higginson. Collection. Boston Public Library. Boston, Massachusetts.

Chase, Salmon P. Collection Library of Congress, Washington, D.C.

Child, Lydia Maria. Manuscripts. University of Massachusetts. Amherst, Massachusetts.

Conway, Moncure D. Papers. Columbia University. New York, New York.

Douglass, Frederick. Papers. Frederick Douglass Memorial Home. National Park Service. Washington, D.C.

Emerson, Ralph Waldo. Collection. Houghton Library. Harvard University. Cambridge, Massachusetts.

Garrison, William Lloyd. Collection. Boston Public Library. Boston, Massachusetts.

Higginson, Thomas W. Manuscripts. Houghton Library. Harvard University. Cambridge, Massachusetts.

Howe, Samuel G. Manuscripts. Massachusetts Historical Society. Boston, Massachusetts.

Johnson, Andrew. Manuscripts. Library of Congress. Washington, D.C.

Lincoln, Robert Todd. Collection. Library of Congress. Washington, D.C.

Massachusetts Kansas Committee. Manuscripts. Massachusetts Historical Society. Boston, Massachusetts.

May, Samuel]. Papers. Boston Public Library, Boston, Massachusetts.

McKim, J. Miller. Collection. Cornell University. Ithaca, New York.

Montgomery, James. Collection. Kansas State Historical Society. Topeka, Kansas.

New England Emigrant Aid Company. Papers. Kansas State Historical Society. Topeka, Kansas.

Norton, Charles Eliot. Collection. Houghton Library. Harvard University. Cambridge, Massachusetts.

Old Military Records Division. Bureau of Colored Troops and Records of the Adjutant General's Officer Commission Board. Record Group 94. National Archives. Washington, D.C.

Robinson, Charles. Collection. Kansas State Historical Society. Topeka, Kansas.

Sanborn, Franklin B. Manuscripts. Concord Free Public Library. Concord Massachusetts.

Slavery Manuscripts. New York Historical Society. New York, New York.

Smith, Gerrit. Collection. Syracuse University Library. Syracuse, New York.

Stearns, George L. Collection. Houghton Library. Harvard University. Cambridge, Massachusetts.

—— . Collection. Kansas State Historical Society. Topeka, Kansas.

—— . Manuscripts. American Antequarian Society. Worcester, Massachusetts.

---. Manuscripts. Massachusetts Historical Society. Boston, Massachusetts.

---. Manuscripts. New York Historical Society. New York, New York.

Stetson, Caleb. Manuscripts. Massachusetts Historical Society, Boston, Massachusetts.

Stutler, Boyd B. Collection. Microfilm. Yale University. New Haven, Connecticut.

Sumner, Charles. Manuscripts. Houghton Library. Harvard University. Cambridge, Massachusetts.

UNPUBLISHED WORKS

By-Laws of the Supervisory Committee for Recruiting Colored Regiments. N.d. Historical Society of Pennsylvania. Philadelphia, Pennsylvania.

Emerson, Ralph Waldo. "Remarks on the Character of George L. Stearns at Medford, April 14, 1867." Broadside. N.d. George L. Stearns. Manuscripts. American Antiquarian Society. Worcester, Massachusetts.

Maslowski, Peter. "Treason Must Be Made Odious" : Military Occupation and Wartime Reconstruction in Nashville, Tennessee, 1862-1865. Ph.D. dissertation. Ohio State University, 1972. University Microfilms. Ann Arbor, Michigan, 1973.

Massachusetts, Commonwealth of. "Voting Records of Massachusetts by Towns." 1840. Microfilm.

Minutes of the New England Emigrant Aid Society. May 29, 1860. Kansas State Historical Society. Topeka, Kansas.

Miscellaneous letters received by the Secretary of the Treasury. National Archives. Washington, D.C.

Stearns, George L. "Last Will and Testament." 1867. Probate File 42218. Middlesex County Court House. Cambridge, Massachusetts.

Stearns, George L., and William A. Rhea. March 13, 1845. File 45846. Middlesex County Registry of Deeds. Middlesex County Court House, Cambridge, Massachusetts.

Stearns, George Lindsey. Letter to author, July 31, 1973.

Stearns, Luther. Last Will and Testament. Probate April1820. File 21287. Middlesex County Court House. Cambridge, Massachusetts.

Stearns, Mary E. "Last Will and Testament." December 1901. Probate File 57312. Middlesex County Court House. Cambridge, Massachusetts.

Subscription paper for the Fifty-Fourth Massachusetts Volunteers. February 13, 1863. Miscellaneous. Massachusetts Historical Society. Boston, Massachusetts. Tablet in the entrance lobby of the Massachusetts State House, Boston, Massachusetts.

Thayer, William Wilde. "Autobiographical Sketch." Unpublished typescript by Laura Conwell Thayer. November 1, 1892. William Wilde Thayer. Manuscripts. Library of Congress. Washington, D.C.

U.S. GOVERNMENT DOCUMENTS

U.S. Congress. House. *Kansas Affairs: Report of the Majority and Minority*. Report 200. 34th Cong., 1st sess., July 1856.

U.S. Congress. Senate. *Reports of the Majority and Minority of the Select Committee on the Harper's Ferry Invasion, with the testimony accompanying, and other Papers*. "Mason Report." Report 278. 36th Cong., 1st sess., 1859-60.

U.S. Government. *War of the Rebellion: Official Records of the Union and Confederate Armies*. 126 vols., Washington, 1890.

U.S. Patent Office. W. P. Tatham. "Making Lead Pipe." September 3, 1850. File 7,624.

Index

Abolitionists, 25, 43, 81, 114, 115, 129, 134, 159, 188, 201; William Lloyd Garrison and followers as, 23-24, 43; G. L. Stearns' views of early abolitionist groups, 23-24; Stearns's relatives' rejection of his interest in, 24, Lydia Maria and David Child as, 41, 142; and exiled Hungarian rebels, 43-44; attacked by Daniel Webster, 49; and John Brown, 79-82, 86-89, 95, 99-104, 109-110; Thomas W. Higginson as, 77; in Emancipation League, 143; and 1864-67 reconstruction policies, 181, 182-83, 186-89 198, 205, 210-211, 213, 214-215; and election of 1864, 185-88, 189-90; and Impartial Suffrage Association, 188-189, 214, 215; stop dissolution of the American Antislavery Society, 193-94; reaction to President Johnson's treatment of Frederick Douglass and Black delegation, 211-213; reaction to proposed Fourteenth Amendment, 216. *See also* Emancipation League; Emancipation of slaves; Free Soil Party; Kansas Free Sailers; *names of individuals including those given above*

Achs, Gideon, 44

Adams, Charles Francis, 34, 36, 97, 115

Adams, Samuel, 3

Advocate (Harvard newspaper), 216

Aetna and Protection Insurance Company, 37

Africa, return of slaves, 19

African-Americans, 1, 43, 48, 61, 99, 141, 144, 146, 147, 149, 156, 157, 158, 159, 160, 162; Fugitive Slave Law and, 48-51; in Boston, 50; John Brown's plans for and use of, 98-99, 112; impressment of, 167; as recruiting agents, 168; camp for those displaced by war, 169; freed, as laborers, 181-182; equality as 1864-65 political issue, 183, 186, 187, 198-99; President Johnson's racial attitude toward, 213; as soldiers: *see* Blacks as soldiers; civil rights for: *see* Civil rights for blacks; suffrage for: *see* Black suffrage. *See also other headings under Black*

Albert Fearing and Company, Boston: G. L. Stearns as partner in, 19 *See also* Fearing, Albert

Alcott, A. Bronson, 143, 146, 202; attends Emancipation League meeting with Freeman, 186, 187-88; and family relations with G. L. Stearns's family, 200-01, 206; and "gift book" for Emerson, 194, 200; supports black suffrage, 201; at Stearns's funeral, 219

Alcott. Louisa May, 145, 199

Alcott, May, 200-206

Allen, Charles, 34

American Antislavery Society, 194-195, 197

American Colonization Society, 19

American House, Boston, Secret Six at, 104

American Land Company, 210-11, 217

American Peace Society, 104

American Revolution. *See* Revolutionary War

American Settlement Company, 77

Ames, Oakes, 147

Andrew, John A., 145, 164, 187; candidacy for Massachusetts governorship, 107; gives G. L. Stearns

245

and Medford fire and tornado, 42; involvement with exiled Hungarian rebels, 43-44; and U.S. political developments of early 1850s, 48-50, 53-54, 59, 60-61; fugitive slave activity, 50-53; friendship and association with Charles Sumner, 36, 52-53, 66-67; passim; speculation in raw lead, 55-56; financial problems, 55-56, 214-217; illnesses, 58, 191-192, 198, 210, 218; physical appearance, 58, 97, 133; reaction to Kansas-Nebraska Act, 59, 101; involvement with Emigrant Aid Company, 71-72, 73, 77, 78-79, 88, 90, 130, 16; relationship with Ralph Waldo Emerson and family, 61-62, 74, 79, 91, 98, 106, 130-131, 145-156, 148, 185, 189-190, 200, 201; and Massachusetts State Kansas Committee work, 72-73, 74-79, 86-87, 93, 106, 115, 116, 117; and vacations, 74, 91, 102, 104, 131-132; first contacts with John Brown, 80-83; and Brown's Sharps rifles, 80, 102-103, 111-112, 115, 116, 117; finding support for Brown, 86-87, 92-93, 989-104, 105-106; annoyed by some of Brown's fund requests, 87, 89, 91; and Brown home in North Elba, New York , 86-87, 102; and revolvers for Brown, 87; and National Kansas Committee, 87; and Kansas political affairs, 88-89, 93-94, 126-130, 134; and Panic of 1857, 93-94, 96-97; helps Peter Butler financially, 97; admires Fanny kemble, 97-98; helps abused boy, 98; as a father, 98, 128, 133, 142, 163, 170; learns John Brown's plans to end slavery, 98-99, 100-101; and Hugh Forbes' revelations about Brown and the

Secret Six, 99-100, 102-103; feelings about Brown's cause, 100-101, 150-151; as member of Secret Six, 101-102, 105-106, 107; and renovation of The Evergreens, 105, 108; and Donate's comet, 106; and the Bird Club, 107-108, 110, 114, 116, 127, 12, 133, 136, 145, 183, 190, 192, 195; and book *The Impending Crisis of the South*, 108; and John Brown, Jr., 108; learns of Harpers Ferry raid, 109; flight to Canada, 110-112; support for Brown family, 113, 142; and last letter from Brown, 112; treatment by associates on return from Canada, 112; appearance before Harpers Ferry Senate Committee, 115-118; opinion of Washington, D.C., and Congress, 115, 118; and 1860 presidential election, 119, 127, 128; travels to Kansas, 129; selects tutor for Frank, 128; attends Republican Party Convention, 129-130; views of Lincoln and his administration, 130, 134, 139, 138-140, 142-14, 170-171, 179, 182; takes Harry and Frank to New York City, 131; as delegate to Massachusetts Republican Convention, 132-133; speaks at election rally, 133-134; visits Washington, D.C. with Governor Andrew, 135-136; views on secession and Civil War, 136-138; trip with Frank to New York City and Washington, D.C., 138-139; and Kansas wartime developments, 138-140, 144-145; advocates emancipation of slaves, 139-142, 145-146, 168, 184, 193-194; and Emancipation League, 141-145, 147-148, 184-185, 197-198; supports use of black soldiers, 143, 147; reestablishes ant-slavery newspaper *The Commonwealth*, 145, 151-153; and emancipation committee with Lincoln, 147-148; suggests war and postwar finance methods, 148-149, 191-192, 213; recruits blacks for 54th and 55th Massachusetts Volunteer Infantry, 2, 149-152, 153; and issues of pay, commissions, unequal treatment, and education of black soldiers, 149, 158, 159, 160, 184-185; gets Frederick Douglass to recruit black soldiers, 150, 152, 160-161; and Secretary of War Stanton, 155, 157, 158, 159, 163, 164, 165, 170; commissioned Union Army major and federal recruiter of black troops, 155-156; and Boston draft riots, 157, 159; Philadelphia headquarters recruitment work, 158-159; and Union League of Philadelphia, 158; establishes Camp William Penn, 158; and defeat of 54th Massachusetts, 159-160; Nashville headquarters recruitment work, 162-170; and General Rosecrans, 163-164; recruiting work and Tennessee's Governor Johnson, 164-166; and conscription, enlistment, and impressment of blacks, 64-165, 167, 168; establishes camp for black refugees and solders' families, 169; resigns his commission, 170-171; and civil rights and suffrage for blacks, 169, 173, 189, 194-199, 207; writes Governor Johnson with advice on recruiting poor whites, 180-181; and 1864-1867 reconstruction policies, 181, 196-197, 201-202, 202-208; buys cotton plantations, 182; meets with General Grant, 182; and

election of 1864, 183, 188-190; criticized by McKim for resigning commission, 183-184; and Emancipation League members' meeting with Fremont, 186; asks Freeman to withdraw his presidential candidacy, 187-188; campaign to found Impartial Suffrage Association, 188-189; sponsors recruiting of Boston Irishman, 190, 1864 financial standing, 190; issues pamphlet *A Few Facts Pertaining to Currency and Banking: Adapted to the Present Position of our Finances*, 190-191; lobbies for cabinet position for John Andrew, 192; fails in request for War Department order authorizing his recruiting blacks, 192-193; helps prevent disbanding of the American Antislavery Society, 192-193; circulates pamphlet supporting black suffrage, 194-195; helps establish *The Nation*, 196-197; writes President Johnson with advice, 191-192, 205-211; issues pamphlet, "Universal Suffrage and Complete Equality in Citizenship," 198; and friendship with Alcott family, 200-201, 206; and reconstruction theories of Theophilus Parsons, 201-202; argument over editorial policies of *The Nation*, 202-204, 213; luncheon meeting with Supreme Court Justice Chase, 204-205; writes Sumner about reconstruction policies, 204-205, 215; interview with President Johnson, 207-208; establishes newspaper *The Right Way*, 209, 214, 217; and the American Land Company, 209-210, 211; trip to Washington, D.C., 212-213; and the Impartial Suffrage Association, 214-215; declines

www.ingramcontent.com/pod-product-compliance
Lightning Source LLC
Chambersburg PA
CBHW021354090426
42742CB00009B/852